D1591166

THE BRITISH ARMY
OF THE
EIGHTEENTH
CENTURY

by the same author

The Pageant of Heraldry
The Mounted Troops of the British Army
Weapons of the British Soldier
Troopships and Their History
Artillery Through the Ages
Tanks in Battle
Battles and Generals of the Civil Wars
Confederates and Federals at War
Napoleon's Army

Chapelon: Genius of French Steam
The Last Steam Locomotive Engineer: R. A. Riddles
G. J. Churchward: A Locomotive Biography

THE BRITISH ARMY
OF THE
EIGHTEENTH
CENTURY

Colonel H. C. B. Rogers
O.B.E.

HIPPOCRENE
BOOKS, INC.
NEW YORK, N.Y.

First published in 1977

ALL RIGHTS RESERVED
HIPPOCRENE BOOKS, INC.
171 Madison Avenue
New York, N.Y. 10016

Library of Congress Cataloging in Publication Data
Rogers, Hugh Cuthbert Basset.
The British army of the eighteenth century.

Includes index
1. Great Britain. army—History. 2. Great Britain
—History, Military—18th century. I. Title.
UA649.R63   355.3'0941   76–16779
ISBN 0–88254–418–7

Printed in Great Britain
in 11pt Baskerville type
by Cox & Wyman Ltd.,
London, Fakenham and Reading

TO MY WIFE
who sees in the British soldier
the salt of the earth

Acknowledgements

In the research undertaken for this book, I owe much to the Society for Army Historical Research and to the London Library, to both of which I am privileged to belong. I am grateful to Messrs John Murray (Publishers) Ltd for their kind permission to quote from the translation by Mr W. C. Horsley of *The Chronicles of an Old Campaigner*. I am indebted to my friend Lieutenant-General Sir Reginald Savory, K.C.I.E., C.B., D.S.O., M.C. for the quotation, translated by him, which appears at the end of Chapter 4. Mr Philip Unwin and Mr John Bright-Holmes of my publishers have contributed a great deal to the final version of the book by their kindly comments and suggestions.

Contents

Illustrations

Introduction

Many of those who have studied the military and political history of the eighteenth century will have encountered criticisms of the officers and men who composed the British Army of the period. The former are often stated to have been ignorant of their job, and the latter represented as the dregs of the nation's manhood, who could only be held to their duty by a harsh and inhuman discipline. To me it seemed that if this assessment were correct, then the achievements of the British Army are incomprehensible. No army can be successful in war against well-trained and well-armed opponents, unless its regimental officers have a sound knowledge of their profession and its rank and file are animated by a high morale, together with confidence in themselves, their leaders, and their weapons. It was such considerations that inspired this book.

Indeed, having regard to its size, it is perhaps fair to claim that never in military history has any other army over a similar period surpassed it in fighting ability. Its many victories (Gibraltar, Blenheim, Ramillies, Oudenarde, Malplaquet, Dettingen, Minden, Emsdorff, Warburg, Wilhelmstahl, Belleisle, Louisbourg, Quebec, Guadeloupe, Martinique, Havannah, St Lucia and many others), emblazoned today on the colours of its regimental descendants read like a roll of drums, and in its few defeats (such as Amanza, Fontenoy and Lauffeld) the glory of its arms often outshone those of the victors. In comparison with the achievements of both enemies and allies, one cannot contemplate the campaigns waged in theatres ranging from India, through Europe and the Mediterranean littoral, to the Americas and the West Indies, without concluding that the British Army of the time was undoubtedly the finest in the world. If this is so, then officers and men must have been of a very high standard indeed, because the best of generals cannot defeat his adversary if his sword is blunt or brittle.

The Army which started its career of conquest under the Duke of Marlborough was a creation of some forty years earlier and had therefore little of tradition behind it. At its start it was a tiny force of only a few regiments. But for no less than fifty-three years of the eighteenth century the Army was fighting in some part of the world, and the succession of wars and the need to provide garrisons for overseas territories acquired as a result of them led to a series of increases in strength; even though Parliament, chronically nervous since the Commonwealth lest a strong standing army should seize power, always endeavoured to cut the Army to the bone after each threat to national security had apparently passed.

Throughout most of the eighteenth century it was the policy of the Government to contain the main military strength of the principal enemy, France, on the continent of Europe, by aiding allies with money and a limited number of troops, whilst pursuing the main aim of colonial conquest. It was an aim that required command of the seas by the Royal Navy and a first class Army to invade and consolidate. The pages that follow examine the nature of that Army and the strategy and tactics by which the Government's aims were pursued.

To show the strategy that was adopted in furtherance of Government policy, the campaigns of the Duke of Marlborough, Sir Jeffery Amherst, and Sir William Howe have been chosen; whilst the tactics by which strategy achieved its ends are the subject of the last three chapters, dealing, respectively, with Marlborough's classic victory at Ramillies, the glorious failure at Fontenoy, and Cornwallis's twin successes at Camden and Guildford Court House.

Table of Principal Military Events
in Europe and America

1702 Start of the War of the Spanish Succession
1704 24 July, capture of Gibraltar by British forces
      12 August, Battle of Blenheim
1706 23 May, Battle of Ramillies
1707 25 April, British defeat at Almanza in Spain
1708 11 July, Battle of Oudenarde
      September, British capture of Minorca
1709 11 September, Battle of Malplaquet
1711 5 August, Marlborough forces the 'Non Plus Ultra' Lines
1713 11 April, Peace of Utrecht
1715 Jacobite Rebellion
      13 November, defeat of Jacobites at the Battle of Sheriffmuir
1742 Start of the War of the Austrian Succession
1743 27 June, Battle of Dettingen
1745 11 May, Battle of Fontenoy
      Start of the Jacobite Rebellion
      30 September, Jacobite victory at the Battle of Prestonpans
1746 28 January, Jacobite victory at the Battle of Falkirk
      27 April, Battle of Culloden; end of the Jacobite Rebellion
1747 2 July, Battle of Lauffeld, British and Allied defeat
1748 Peace of Aix-la-Chapelle and end of the War of the Austrian
      Succession
1756 17 May, Britain declares war against France; start of the
      Seven Years War
      28 May, French capture Minorca
1757 27 July, British capture French fortress of Louisbourg in
      Canada
1759 1 August, Battle of Minden in Germany
      13 September, Battle of Quebec
1760 31 July, Battle of Warburg in Germany
      8 September, Amherst captures Montreal and ends French
      resistance in Canada

1762   Battle of Wilhelmstahl in Germany
1763   Treaty of Paris; end of the Seven Years War
1775   April, affair at Lexington, and start of the American War of
      Independence
      17 June, Battle of Bunker Hill
1776   27 August, Battle of Long Island
1777   11 September, Battle of Brandywine
      17 October, surrender of Burgoyne at Saratoga
1779   Start of the siege of Gibraltar
1780   16 August, Battle of Camden
1781   15 March, Battle of Guildford
      19 October, Cornwallis surrenders at Yorktown
1783   End of the siege of Gibraltar
      Peace of Versailles; end of the War of American Independence
1793   1 February, France declares war on Great Britain
1793–4 Campaign in the Netherlands
1799   Expedition to North Holland under the Duke of York

Chapter 1

STRENGTHS AND ESTABLISHMENTS

After the Restoration of the Monarchy in 1660 both Houses of Parliament were determined that there should never again be a standing army, such as had been organised and maintained by Oliver Cromwell, and that soldiers in permanent employment should be limited to those required to garrison the fixed defences and to provide the regiments of the King's Guard.[1] The acquisition of Tangier in 1660 and the warfare waged in its defence necessitated the raising of other regiments, as did also the military assistance given by Charles II to Louis XIV; but it was never Parliament's intention that these should become a permanent part of the military establishment, which in peacetime was to be limited to the 'guards and garrisons'. Indeed, one could say with fair accuracy that the Regular Army gradually increased in strength, not only because of greater commitments, but also through the omission, for one reason or another, to disband regiments after the services for which they had been raised had terminated.

After the Revolution of 1688, which brought William of Orange to the throne, a standing army was at last, though reluctantly, approved, but only in the form of an increase in the establishment of the guards and garrisons. Parliament, too, insisted on having the right to decide the strength of the Army to be maintained in Great Britain in time of peace, and directed that none but native-born subjects should hold any military command;[2] a proviso that was intended to lessen the danger of a *coup d'état*. In addition, in order that Parliament should retain the right to disband the Army, the 'Declaration of Rights', which William had to accept, contained the words:

'The raising of a standing army within the United Kingdom in time of peace, unless it be with the consent of Parliament, is against the law.' However, Parliament had not a complete say in the matter, because 'the Government, Command, and Disposition of the Army' remained Royal Prerogatives.[3]

Initially the Regular Army (that is, the guards and garrisons) was divided into three separate establishments: those for England (which included Wales), Scotland, and Ireland, each of which was charged to the revenue of the country concerned. When regiments were despatched overseas from Scotland or Ireland they were normally transferred to the English establishment, and the two former countries were permitted to raise new units to replace any thus removed from their strength. After the Act of Union in 1707, however, the English and Scottish establishments were amalgamated into one British establishment, but the Irish establishment remained separate for the remainder of the eighteenth century.

As overseas commitments increased, the guards and garrisons on the English (and later British) establishment came to include, not only the troops serving at home, but also those required to garrison the Channel Islands, the Mediterranean possessions, and the colonial 'Plantations', as well as regiments seconded for 'sea service' with the fleet. They did not include troops engaged in a theatre of war.

The position as regards fortresses in Great Britain was somewhat complicated because they came under the Board of Ordnance, which was not part of the Army. Attached to these fortresses, apart from the infantry garrisons, were small parties of gunners and master-gunners, many of whom were appointed to them for life. In the Establishment Warrant of the Ordnance the master-gunners were listed as part of the civil establishment and neither master-gunners nor gunners were subject to military discipline. The numbers of infantry placed in these fortresses were fixed by an establishment of 1683–84, and at that time, and for many years afterwards, they were organised in unregimented companies, some of which were composed of out-pensioners of Chelsea Hospital, or 'invalids' (that is, men who were not fit for general service).[4]

During the wars waged in Ireland and on the Continent by

William III the Army increased greatly in strength; but when peace was restored in 1697 by the Treaty of Ryswick, it was reduced so quickly and drastically to a 'guards and garrison' status that by 1698 there was only a skeleton force of 7,000 men on the English establishment. Indeed there was a strong movement to abolish the standing army altogether and to reform the Militia so that it could replace it. Before the outbreak of the Civil Wars between King and Parliament, the Militia had been the only substantial military force in the country, and those many politicians to whom a standing army was anathema thought that it would still prove adequate for national defence. In the years after the Restoration it had grown inefficient, as the Duke of Monmouth's rebellion had shown. Anxiety aroused by the mutiny of Dumbarton's Regiment in 1689 resulted in a Bill for its reform being passed by the Commons, but it was held up in the Lords and eventually lost by the dissolution of Parliament in January 1690.[5] A more radical bill to replace the Regular Army by the Militia was introduced in the Commons after the Peace of Ryswick and defeated. The Army was saved from further threats to its existence by Louis XIV. On 6 September 1701 James II died and on 13 September Louis recognised the exiled king's son as James III, King of Great Britain. This was tantamount to a declaration of war, and Parliament found itself with the necessity of raising an army.

The first measures taken were to double the establishments of existing regiments and to raise new ones. This was not too difficult because the old soldiers who had been discharged some four years before could be re-enlisted.[6] The demands made by the War of the Spanish Succession (1702–13), which followed, forced Parliament to vote increasing strengths for the Army, till the forces in the field reached a peak of 75,000 men in 1711. This was the year of the Duke of Marlborough's final feat— piercing Marshal Villars' 'Non Plus Ultra' lines. By the end of the year Marlborough had been dismissed and, as the war drifted to a close, the number of men with the colours dropped rapidly till in 1713 they totalled only some 23,000.[7]

It was not only the war that was drawing to an end, but also the life of Queen Anne, and the final reduction of the Army to its intended peacetime strength was carried out by leading

Jacobite sympathisers in a way that was intended to ensure that Anne should be succeeded by the Jacobite Pretender to the throne. This attempt to use the Regular Army to further a political plot was made by Viscount Bolingbroke, the Secretary of State who had been in charge of the peace negotiations, assisted by the Duke of Ormonde, who had succeeded Marlborough as Commander-in-Chief and Captain-General and who was the leader of the Jacobites in London. Bolingbroke had negotiated privately with the Pretender, 'James III'. In order that there should be no military resistance to his accession, Bolingbroke and Ormonde decided that regiments with a known loyalty to a Protestant succession should be disbanded, irrespective of their seniority. This plan violated the established practice of disbanding the youngest regiments first. It was put into effect, but before it could be completed Queen Anne died and the Elector of Hanover succeeded her peacefully as King George I.[8]

The military situation facing the new King was far from satisfactory. Although the loyalty of the Army was assured, a Jacobite attempt on the throne was to be expected, and the bulk of the troops on the British establishment were in Flanders and the colonial garrisons. In England and Scotland there were only 8,000 men and in Ireland a further 12,000. (The Irish establishment had been fixed at that figure in 1692 and so remained until 1769.) Some of the regiments disbanded by Bolingbroke were reformed immediately, and in July 1715, with a rising in Scotland imminent, the remainder were included in an order for the raising of thirteen regiments of dragoons and eight of foot. Five dragoon and eight infantry regiments were moved to Great Britain from Ireland and, in accordance with their powers, similar regiments were raised by the Government of Ireland to replace them.[9] The reinforced Army proved just sufficient for the task, but defeat was only narrowly averted at the battle of Sheriffmuir. It seemed that the Jacobite threat had disappeared, and there followed the reduction of the Army to a strength which Parliament considered adequate for peacetime.

However, there was one important addition to military strength at this time, for on 26 May 1716, on the advice of the

Duke of Marlborough, now Master-General of the Ordnance, two companies of artillery were formed at Woolwich as permanent units. Previously it had been the practice to form temporary artillery trains as required for particular operations. In 1727 the two companies were increased to four and the new corps was entitled the Royal Regiment of Artillery.[10]

The strength of the Army varied at this period, within narrow limits, according to the political situation. In 1719 there were only 12,000 men on the British establishment. There was a hurried but small increase in that year due to the short Spanish war and the Jacobite landing in Scotland. In 1720 the birth of Prince Charles Edward and the consequent increase in Jacobite activity led to the Government, against bitter opposition, raising the British establishment to 18,000. This was accomplished by increasing the number of men in existing regiments. Sir Robert Walpole, the Prime Minister, announced that this figure of 18,000 would be retained as the standard, but he was bitterly opposed to this and there were strong attempts in both Houses of Parliament to cut it.[11] It still left the Army far too weak to secure national interests at home and overseas.

Any proposed reduction in the Army commanded, as it always has done in peacetime, considerable support; but there was more than the usual hostility to it at this time amongst the civil population. This may have been due to the use of the Army, in the absence of an effective police force, to maintain law and order. Troops had often to suppress riots, but it does not appear that they behaved badly on the whole in the execution of this unpleasant duty. Yet, as Fortescue says, 'In many places the civil population deliberately picked quarrels with the troops in order to swell the clamour against the Army; and officials in high local and municipal station, in their rancour against the red-coats, would stoop to lawlessness as flagrant as that of the mob.'[12] Under such provocation it is remarkable that the discipline of the Army remained as good as it did.

This unhappy state of affairs came to at least a temporary end with the outbreak of the so-called 'War of Jenkins's Ear' against Spain in 1739. But it was typical of the Parliamentary Opposition that, whilst clamouring for war against Spain, they produced a motion for the reduction of the Army! Nevertheless, an increase in the strength of existing regiments was approved, and a remarkable reversal of public opinion was shown by a surge of enthusiasm which resulted in recruits coming forward in numbers far greater than were needed.[13]

Before this war came to an end Great Britain was involved in the much greater struggle of the War of the Austrian Succession. In 1742 Parliament voted to send 16,000 British troops to Flanders, and the British establishment was increased considerably, not only by raising more men in the United Kingdom, but also by incorporating the King's Hanoverian troops, as well as Danish and Hessian mercenaries.[14]

After the victory of Dettingen in 1743, the estimates for 1744 provided for a larger army in Flanders, but as no increase in the total strength had been voted, the additional troops had to be found by depleting the already weak forces in Great Britain. Even then the Army in Flanders was inadequate for the task, and its General of foot, Ligonier, complained to Lord Carteret, the Secretary of State, that, 'Our army is to consist of no more than forty battalions and ninety-two squadrons.' Of that modest total only eighteen battalions and twenty-nine squadrons were British.[15]

Stinginess in voting the necessary military strength in due course exacted its retribution. Taking advantage of his knowledge that Great Britain was almost denuded of trained troops, Prince Charles Edward Stuart landed on the west coast of Scotland on 25 July 1745. To meet a rising of the warlike clans, Sir John Cope, commanding in Scotland, had no more than 3,000 men, mostly half-trained recruits. His almost inevitable defeat was followed by a Government panic, and the Duke of Cumberland, commanding in Flanders, was ordered by the King to send to England the ten best battalions under the command of General Sir John Ligonier. Later he was ordered to return himself with most of the remaining British troops under his command, and an existing treaty was invoked to demand the help of Dutch and Hessian troops. Large bounties were offered to induce men to enlist in the under-strength regiments in England. King and Government only narrowly escaped disaster, and the dangers of a cheese-paring economy in national defence were thus brought forcibly home. Unfortunately the lesson was soon forgotten.

After the defeat of the rebellion, British troops returned to Flanders, and the war ended in 1748 with the Treaty of Aix-la-Chapelle.

The British peace establishment was now fixed at 30,000 men, of whom 20,000 were to serve in Great Britain and 10,000 in garrisons overseas. The Irish establishment remained at 12,000, but this figure embraced thirty-seven regiments of cavalry and infantry, or an average of only 300 per regiment. But by retaining a large number of weak regiments, rather than having fewer at full strength, a nucleus was kept in being on which expansion could take place in war. This policy could not be applied to regiments on the British establishment because they had always to be available for general duties at home or overseas.

Nevertheless regiments were sometimes sent directly overseas from Ireland. An instance occurred in 1754 after Colonel George Washington, at the head of Virginian militia, had been forced to surrender to the French. The Governor of Virginia appealed for two regular battalions. Ligonier, then Lieutenant-General of the Ordnance, expressed the opinion that regular battalions were not likely to be of much value in the forest warfare then being waged on the American frontier, and thought that the provincial militia should be used, with the help of regular officers and supplies of arms. This view was of course quite correct, for it is a lesson that is constantly having to be re-learned that troops should not be used in a type of warfare for which they have not been trained. However, the Duke of Cumberland, then Captain-General, insisted that regular battalions should be sent, but, owing to a reluctance to reduce the forces in Great Britain, two of the weak regiments in Ireland, the 44th and 48th, were increased in strength by drafts from other regiments, and furnished with additional arms to bring themselves up to strength with American recruits. The result was a disaster, for they formed the major component of the force under General Braddock which was defeated on the Monongahela River by French and Indians in July 1755.

Although war had not been declared between Great Britain

and France, the two countries were engaged in full-scale hostilities in America, and the unfortunate affair of the Monongahela created such consternation that small increases in strength already authorised were augmented.

In the early months of 1756 there was a near panic in Great Britain over the possibility of a French invasion, because the measures to increase the Army had hardly begun to take effect and there were all too few troops to meet this danger. The Government asked the King, as Elector of Hanover, for help. This small State had an army of the very respectable size of 29,000 men, and George II agreed to send half its infantry to England. In addition the Government obtained 8,000 infantry from Hesse-Kassel, with which State there was a treaty of subsidy.[16] Apart from these reinforcements, there were renewed efforts to make the Militia into an effective force for home defence.

A bill to reform the Militia laws was passed through the Commons in May 1756, but it was thrown out by the Lords two weeks later. However, the following month Minorca fell to the French, and the fury that this aroused in the nation ensured that supporters of the Militia would get some sort of Act. They were finally successful in May 1757, though the Lords succeeded in making a number of modifications. As passed, the Act authorised a force of 32,000 men, recruited from the larger towns so that it would be easier to concentrate the men for their drills. As far as possible the Militia was to be recruited from volunteers, but if sufficient were not forthcoming the ranks were to be filled by a compulsory ballot amongst the able-bodied men in each parish. So at last the Regular Army was to be supported (not replaced!) by what promised to be an effective auxiliary force to take over some of the responsibilities of home defence. But at this time the Act was limited to a period of five years.[17]

Nevertheless, the new force was brought into being with considerable difficulty; the local gentry proved singularly reluctant to serve as officers, and the preparation of lists for balloting led to widespread rioting. The formation of the Militia units was consequently very slow.

In October 1756 a new administration under William Pitt took office, and at the instance of this dynamic minister estimates were voted for a new British establishment of 49,000, of which 30,000 were to be in Great Britain and 19,000 in the colonies. In addition there were to be 2,000 artillery and engineers; the Royal Artillery being increased to twenty-four companies, grouped into two battalions. An interesting innovation was the formation of two Highland regiments, those of Fraser and Montgomery. The idea, which was remarkably successful, was to give the Highlanders an outlet for their military enthusiasm, other than engaging in Jacobite rebellions.

The Seven Years War, which lasted from 1756 to 1763, was the largest in which Great Britain up till that time had ever been engaged. It entailed a large increase in the strength of the Army, and by 1758 Lord Ligonier, the Commander-in-Chief, had about 90,000 men under his general direction. Of these, some 54,000 were in Great Britain and Ireland; but he could not make use of those in Ireland without the permission of the Lord-Lieutenant—a permission which the latter was always very reluctant to give.[18] The remainder were overseas in North America, Gibraltar, the West Indies, and the East Indies. In July 1758 the troops in Great Britain were depleted by the despatch of the first contingent (a regiment of horse, five regiments of dragoons, and five battalions of infantry) to join the army in Germany under Prince Ferdinand of Brunswick.[19]

The following year resources were so far stretched by commitments overseas, garrison duties at home, and regiments serving with the fleet, that only 8,530 of the troops in England were available to provide a field force, and even these had to provide detachments for various duties. There were neither sufficient regiments to counter a French invasion, nor to mount an expedition overseas. The position was so serious that the possibility of using the new Militia to release Regular troops from static duties was discussed at a Cabinet meeting on 19 February 1759.[20] As a result of this discussion, Lords-Lieutenant were stirred into belated action and by June 1759 there were over 11,000 Militia under arms and about another 7,000 had been raised. On 17 July the King reviewed the Norfolk Militia in London, by which date thirteen Militia battalions had relieved the Regular regiments guarding 25,000 prisoners of war at various places in England. The driving force behind this remarkable achievement had been Ligonier.[21]

The reorganisation of the Militia had only applied to England and Wales, and there was strong pressure on the Government to extend it to Scotland. But the 1745 rebellion was still too recent for the Government to be happy about including Highlanders of the erstwhile hostile clans in the Militia. They were prepared to allow Fencible regiments (Regulars for home service only) and two of these were raised among clans who favoured the Hanoverian regime. Between May and August 1759 the second contingent of British troops arrived in Germany, consisting of seven regiments of dragoons, one regiment of light dragoons, and ten battalions of infantry.[22]

The distribution of the whole Army at this time is of some interest. In round figures there were 30,000 men in Great Britain, 22,000 engaged in operations against the French in North America, 20,000 under Prince Ferdinand's command in Germany, and 13,000 others overseas, located in the West Indies, Gibraltar, West Africa, and the East Indies. In England there were also some 22,000 embodied Militia and in Scotland 2,000 Fencibles. However, the effective Regulars in Great Britain were far less than 30,000, for this figure included recruits under training, old soldiers unfit for general service, and reinforcement drafts under orders for embarkation. The strength available for home defence was indeed dangerously low. Writing to the Marquess of Granby, commanding the British troops in Germany, Ligonier stated the position. There were only two effective regiments of cavalry and these were full of old men who were all right for home service but who would not be able to stand up to a campaign in Germany. The rest of the cavalry were boys 'hardly able to manage their horses'.[23] There were not more than eight regiments of foot and two-thirds of their men were recruits, who would be quite useless if drafted overseas. Of trained men, 2,000 were being embarked for America and another 2,000 were earmarked for despatch to Guadeloupe and Africa. To add to his worries there were indications that the French were contemplating another expedition against Scotland.[24] The load on the shoulders of the Commander-in-Chief is apparent from this letter. With inadequate resources he had to meet the needs of the commanders in the theatres of war, whilst ensuring the security of Great Britain against invasion.

The future of the Militia, too, was cause for some anxiety because the existing Acts were due to expire in 1762. Pitt wanted to bring in a Bill to make the Militia laws perpetual, but George II, who regarded the Militia as a potential threat to the Crown, had exercised his right of veto over money Bills to refuse its introduction. By now, however, the Militia had become an essential part of the forces for home defence, and a compromise Act was at last passed which extended its life for another seven years.[25] This Act was hardly in force before the war came to an end with the Peace of Fontainebleau, which was signed in February 1763. The Militia had been disembodied on 15 December 1762, in anticipation of an end to hostilities, so that it was only saved from disbandment by a very narrow margin.

As soon as the war had ended, Ligonier was ordered to reduce the troops on the British establishment to the 1749 level of 30,000 men. Such a reduction took no account of the increase in territory overseas as a result of the war and the larger forces needed to secure it. To compensate in part for such a small peacetime establishment, Ligonier wanted to retain eighty-five infantry regiments at a low strength in Great Britain and at an even lower strength in Ireland, so as to have cadres on which to expand rapidly in war. The cadre principal was approved, but he could only get authority for seventy regiments.[26]

The rapid disbandment of men and regiments had a bad effect on the quality of the peacetime army, because the expansion in war had diluted the proportion of trained regimental officers and N.C.O.s and there was no time to carry out transfers from the disbanding regiments to ensure that the best were retained.

The foolishness of this drastic and premature cut in the Army's strength was demonstrated by the rebellion in 1763 of American Indians under Pontiac—a rebellion that was only suppressed with considerable difficulty.

In the years after the war, the efficiency of the Militia declined badly. Some counties continued to carry out their training commitments conscientiously, but others lost interest and did very little training at all; so that the potential home defence burden on the Regular Army increased. A few counties had not even started to raise Militia on the excuse that they had not been able to find officers; but as failure to form and train Militia was punishable by fines, most of them had at least skeleton units. However, Derbyshire, Nottinghamshire, Oxfordshire, Staffordshire, Sussex, and Worcestershire continued their refusal to raise any Militia and paid their fines instead.

In 1769 an Act to make the Militia permanent was at last obtained. The following year Worcestershire started to raise its Militia and in 1773 Derbyshire fell into line. The remaining four counties held out until after the rebellion of the American colonies and began reluctantly to form units in 1778. This was of little practical assistance to the country's defence as the Militia was embodied in March of that year following the entry of France into the war.[27]

The size of the county Militia contingents varied according to the population of each county. In the smaller counties the quota might be only one or two companies, but most English counties were able to form a complete regiment, whilst some provided two regiments, and Middlesex and the West Riding of Yorkshire each provided three.[28]

The Militia, though an invaluable second line to the Regular Army for home defence, was much handicapped by politics. On the one hand the King disliked it because it came under the Lords Lieutenant instead of his direct command, and on the other hand many political leaders mistrusted it because republicans saw it as a means of arming the freeholders and abolishing the standing Army. In the end the Militia as organised was a compromise which Parliament on the whole liked because of its dislike and fear of a strong Regular Army. It was safeguarded from a too radical membership because it was under the influence of the English aristocracy, and was composed of men who had means of subsistence other than their pay. Its officers owed their allegiance to the institutions of the country rather than to the King.[29]

The Regular Army had a welcome addition to its paper strength, when in 1769 the Irish establishment was increased from the previous 12,000 to 15,000, as it was decided to raise the strength of regiments stationed in Ireland to that authorised for regiments on the British establishment. However, the increase was rather a hope for the future than of any immediate gain, because the pay was too low to attract sufficient recruits and many regiments were seriously under strength. The shortage was emphasised in 1770 when Spain, encouraged by British weakness, attacked the Falkland Islands and there was imminent danger of war. The Government ordered an increase of 12,000 men on the British establishment, but it proved impossible to obtain them in Great Britain. A recruiting drive was accordingly instituted in Ireland, though it had been against Government policy to enlist Irish Protestants and it was illegal to enlist Roman Catholics.[30]

The war with Spain did not materialise, but owing to the lack of troops in North America it proved impossible to halt the slide of the Colonies into rebellion. Indeed, the totally inadequate strength of the Army both in North America and the British Isles was very soon demonstrated.

On 30 October 1774 General Thomas Gage, Commander-in-Chief in North America, wrote to Lord Dartmouth, Secretary of State for the American Colonies: 'If force is to be used at length, it must be a considerable one; for to begin with small numbers will only encourage resistance and not terrify.' He added that a policy of coercion would entail the reconquest of New England for which a force of 20,000 men would be needed. But Gage was asking for the moon, because it was not possible to provide him with 20,000 men without imperilling home defence. Of cavalry and infantry on the under-strength British establishment, there were 10,612 in England, 1,745 in Scotland, 5,732 distributed between the Channel Islands, the Mediterranean, and Africa, and 1,983 in the West Indies or on passage there. In the whole of the North American Colonies and Canada there were only 6,991. Ireland was even more below establishment than England, for it had only 7,000 infantry out of the authorised 13,500. Dartmouth replied to Gage: 'It is impossible without putting the Army on a war establishment and I am unwilling to think that matters have come to such a pass yet.'[31] Matters in fact had!

On 29 November 1774 the British Parliament voted to

increase the strength of the troops in Boston to 10,000 men. In accordance with this decision, one regiment of light dragoons and seven battalions of infantry were despatched from Great Britain and Ireland. But so weak were these units that large drafts had to be posted to them from other regiments. Of infantry, there remained in Great Britain only the Foot Guards and four battalions of the line.[32]

Not till the summer of 1775 did the British Government awake to the fact that it had a major war on its hands, and only in August did it reluctantly agree to increase the British establishment to 55,000 men. But of course time would be needed to train the recruits and fully trained regiments were wanted quickly. To help out the situation, the King agreed to the transfer of five battalions of the Royal Hanoverian Army (which was not of course under the control of the British Government) to relieve British regiments in Gibraltar and Minorca. Five battalions in Boston had suffered heavy casualties at the battle of Bunker Hill, and to relieve these to come home and recruit, five more battalions were sent from Ireland. The seal on the Government's peacetime ineptitude was marked by the expensive hire in January 1776 of 18,000 mercenary troops from the German states of Hesse-Cassel and Brunswick.

From 1777 onwards, the expansion of the Army was rapid, but when France entered the war after the disaster of Saratoga, a larger proportion had to be allocated to home defence and to theatres outside North America. In fact, out of 120,000 British Regulars, German mercenaries, American Militia, and embodied British Militia in October 1778, only 40,000 could be spared for North America.[33] That invasion of Great Britain was a real possibility was shown in 1779, for in June Spain declared war and a junction was effected at Brest between the French and Spanish fleets, preparatory to transporting an invading army to England. The combined fleets slipped past the watching ships of the Royal Navy, which had been driven off station by the weather, and seized control of the Channel. Some 21,000 Regulars and 30,000 Militia moved to anti-invasion stations; but the enemy dallied, the wind changed, and by the end of August the threat had vanished.[34]

After the end of the war at the beginning of 1783, the inevitable rapid run-down of the Army started again. The new
British establishment was fixed at 36,000, of which 17,500 were
to be in Great Britain, 3,000 in Gibraltar, 9,500 in the 'Plantations', and 6,000 in India. The Irish establishment remained at
15,000, but of these 3,000 were stationed temporarily in the
Plantations. The total establishment of the Army was therefore
little more than it had been after the Seven Years War. Low as
this was, the Government allowed men who had enlisted for
three years to leave the colours whether their time had expired
or not. As a result actual strengths dropped well below establishments because it proved virtually impossible to recruit replacements. During the ten years which remained before the
outbreak of war with Revolutionary France the Army was desper
ately short of men, and in 1790 battalions were cut down to the
ridiculously low establishment of 400 rank and file. It was only
in 1792 that some long overdue improvements in the conditions
of service led to an immediate improvement on recruiting.[35] At
the threat of war with France the establishment of an infantry
battalion was increased in 1793 to the more realistic figure of
850 rank and file,[36] but there remained the problem of getting
the recruits and then training them. General Sir Henry Bunbury,
who was commissioned into the Army in 1795, says of the state
of the Army in 1793: 'The English ministers were trying, with
the miserable means at their command, to afford some assistance
to the House of Orange. About 1,700 of the Foot Guards, with
a few scores of artillerymen, were all that could be mustered for
this service in the first days of the crisis . . . I wish . . . to show
the inefficiency to which our military means had been brought
through the neglect of our Government during ten years of
peace. The results may be painful to contemplate but they
afford a lesson which ought not to be forgotten.'[37] Alas, the
lesson was forgotten, as it had been forgotten after every
previous war, and was to be forgotten again after every subsequent one.

Chapter 2

THE COMMAND
AND ORGANISATION OF
THE ARMY AT HOME

During the whole of the eighteenth century the political control of the Army was both complicated and cumbersome. For practically all of the period there was no such appointment as a secretary of state for war; that is, a minister having a special responsibility for the Army. No less than three ministers were concerned with the Army's affairs, but these affairs were the primary responsibility of none of them.

In respect of British interests, the world, including Great Britain, was divided into two geographical areas, each of which was the responsibility of a secretary of state. The northern part, which included Scotland, came under the northern secretary of state, whereas England and the southern part of the world were the concern of the southern secretary of state. In time of war, all troops in a particular theatre and the operations conducted there were the responsibility of the secretary of state in whose area the fighting was taking place. But if, for example, this was Canada and the troops were to come from England, the southern secretary of state would be responsible for organising the despatch of the force which, when it reached its destination, would come under the political direction of the northern secretary of state for operations and maintenance.

The third minister concerned was, at the start of the eighteenth century, the lord high treasurer, and, towards the end of it, the senior of those into which his office was divided—the first lord of the treasury. As he had to provide the money for any military movement or operation, he could overrule both the secretaries of state.

By the time of the American War of Independence there was a third secretary of state who looked after North America and the West Indies. By this time too the political system had developed to include a Cabinet, presided over by the first lord of the treasury. The Cabinet decided what operations were to take place and what troops were to be sent, and its decisions were to take place and what troops were to be sent, and its decisions were translated into orders by the secretaries of state within their own spheres and sent to the treasury, the admiralty, the ordnance board, and the Army commanders concerned.[1]

There was, however, one civilian official who was concerned solely with the Army—the secretary at war. Originally the holder of this appointment was secretary to the commander-in-chief in the field. Over the years the powers and influence of the secretary at war increased, though they were much greater when there was no commander-in-chief of the Army in Great Britain. Because there was as yet no secretary of state for war, the secretary at war became in fact, though not officially, the representative of Parliamentary control over the Army, and during the long periods when there was no commander-in-chief in Great Britain he assumed many of the attributes of that office. Much of the routine administration and discipline of the Army came under his direction, and he had direct access to the King with regard to commissions, appointments, and courts martial. But when there was a strong commander-in-chief, like Field Marshal Lord Ligonier, in Great Britain, the secretary at war had little say in the formation of military policy; Ligonier, indeed, regarded him as a superior type of clerk![2]

By the time of the American War of Independence, the secretary at war had become a professional politician who sat in the House of Commons and had to introduce the Army estimates, though he was still technically the servant of the commander-in-chief. He had become responsible, as well, for the administration and finance of the Army.[3] The nearest modern equivalent to his eventual position (except that he was a member of Parliament) is the late post of permanent under secretary of state at the war office.

The military command of the Army was almost as complex as its political control. The sovereign always retained the position of commander-in-chief of the Army as a whole, both at home and overseas. Immediately under the sovereign was the somewhat nebulous appointment of captain-general (perhaps best described as deputy commander-in-chief) which might or might not be filled, and which was held, for example, by the Duke of Marlborough under Queen Anne and by the Duke of Cumberland under his father King George II.

There was always a local commander-in-chief in a theatre of war, and he was not subject to the authority of the commander-in-chief in Great Britain, if there was one. In fact, the command functions of the latter were limited to the troops in England and Wales, because Scotland was a separate command within the province of the northern secretary of state. However, an eighteenth century commander-in-chief had additional responsibilities, which were akin to those of the chief of the imperial general staff in later years. Ligonier, appointed commander-in-chief in 1757, and Amherst, who held the office from 1778, had seats in the Cabinet, and so were concerned in the decisions promulgated by the secretaries of state. A suggestion by Pitt that Ligonier should be made captain-general, which would have made him supreme commander under the king of all British military forces, was rejected by the Cabinet; but Ligonier was given the rights of corresponding with commanders abroad on military matters and of inspecting the forces under their command,[4] which gave him most of the powers of the captain-general.

At the start of the period there was no command echelon in Great Britain and Ireland between the top civil and military authorities and the colonels of regiments, but by the time that Ligonier became commander-in-chief England and Wales were divided into a number of military districts, each commanded by a senior general who was directly responsible to the commander-in-chief Great Britain, when there was one, or to the king when there was not. The Scottish command, though not under Ligonier, could in practice be controlled by him through his rights of correspondence and inspection.[5]

By modern ideas the headquarters staff of the Army was

extraordinarily small. There were two principal staff officers to assist the commander-in-chief in Great Britain (or the sovereign when there was no officer holding that appointment), the adjutant-general and the quartermaster-general. They did not necessarily hold high rank, for the Warrant of Queen Anne under which they were appointed gave them only the brevet rank of colonel. When there was no commander-in-chief in England, both officers, though having a direct responsibility to the sovereign, acted under the secretary at war. Of the various functions exercised by the latter, the adjutant-general dealt with all matters relating to discipline, the policy of arming and clothing the troops, and the Regulations and Orders for the Army which were issued from time to time under the king's authority; whilst the quartermaster-general handled movements, operations, quartering, and such defence works which did not come within the province of the master-general of the ordnance. For the construction of defence works the quartermaster-general had at his disposal a small body of engineers known as the 'staff corps'. (The respective responsibilities of the quartermaster-general and the master-general of the ordnance for defence works were not in fact very clearly defined, and there was some resulting interdepartmental jealousy.)

Under Ligonier, both the adjutant-general and quartermaster-general were general officers in rank, and in 1760 the quartermaster-general had six officers on his own staff branch. At the same time Ligonier had a personal staff of four A.D.C.S, a surgeon and his invaluable secretary Richard Cox. After Ligonier's departure the adjutant-general and quartermaster-general were again responsible to the secretary at war, and when Amherst was appointed commander-in-chief in 1778 their offices were much more modestly endowed. The adjutant-general occupied two rooms in Crown Street, Westminster, and the quartermaster-general had one room at the war office, which, as its name implies, was the office of the secretary at war.[6]

The board of ordnance, in spite of its name, was not considered as part of the Army; but as artillery and engineers came under it and as these of course formed part of an army in the field, the board cannot be omitted from a study of the Army's organisation. The chief of this department was the master-general of the ordnance, a post which could be held by a soldier but which was a political appointment, giving its holder (as eighteenth-century government developed) a seat in the Cabinet. The master-general of the ordnance was responsible to the treasury for accounting for, and to the appropriate secretary of state for the issue of, military equipment in accordance with the authorised scales.

The board of ordnance's organisation had been set up by the Duke of York (subsequently King James II) in 1683. Some little time later it fell into disuse, but it was revived again by the Duke of Marlborough when he was appointed Master-General of the Ordnance in 1702. Under the master-general were five principal officers of ordnance; the lieutenant-general, the surveyor-general, the clerk of the ordnance, the keeper of the stores, and the clerk of the deliveries—surely the most magnificent of all the families of official titles! The lieutenant-general was a purely military appointment, and the holder acted as deputy to the master-general. In peacetime, when there was no commander-in-chief, this was the highest professional military post. The lieutenant-general had a particular responsibility for artillery, transport, and contracts. His principal assistant was the master-gunner, who was directly responsible to him for the Royal Artillery. This regiment wore blue coats, instead of red, and differed from the cavalry and infantry in respect of pay and rations. But perhaps the most important difference from these latter arms was that officers of the Royal Artillery did not purchase their commissions or promotion. The surveyor-general, a civilian official, had under him the chief-engineer, who had charge of the fortifications in Great Britain. The Engineer branch was formed in 1717, and by 1754 it consisted of the chief-engineer and thirty-two officers of varying seniority. Commissions were first issued to officers of the Engineers in 1757, and two years later Ligonier reorganised the branch into a separate military Corps of Engineers with similar conditions of service to those of the officers of the Royal Artillery. The rank and file in peacetime were civilians, but companies of miners were raised in war. In 1772, because of the inconvenience of using civilians in the defensive works at Gibraltar, a local company of Military

Artificers, who were soldiers, was formed. In 1788 the Engineers were further reorganised. The military officers of the department were constituted the Corps of Royal Engineers, and a large number of civilian artificers serving in the ordnance department were enlisted as soldiers and formed into a Corps of Royal Military Artificers, which was commanded by 'doing duty' officers of the Royal Engineers.[7] Under the lieutenant-general and the surveyor-general, therefore, were eventually large numbers of soldiers who came under normal Army command for discipline and operations.

Other responsibilities of the board of ordnance included the following: the manufacture, storage, and issue of all pieces of ordnance and of personal weapons to the Army, the Royal Navy, and the Honourable East India Company; the building and maintenance of all fortresses in Great Britain and overseas; barracks; and tentage and camp necessaries in time of war. Its authority did not extend to Ireland which had its own board of ordnance, responsible to the lord-lieutenant for similar matters in that country.

One other body was concerned in the control and administration of the Army—the board of general officers, which was established in 1706. Its original terms of reference were to 'receive, hear, and examine all information and complaints that shall be brought before them of the misbehaviour of any officer or soldier in our service; or any other abuses or irregularities that are or shall be committed as aforesaid.' The first President of the Board was Charles Churchill, brother to the Duke of Marlborough and Lieutenant-General of foot. Three other general officers sufficed to constitute a quorum and the board met as often as required. In 1708 it was made responsible for the inspection of clothing and uniform patterns. By the middle of the century this had become its most important task and the examination of complaints had apparently lapsed. The inspection of clothing and patterns was to ensure that colonels of regiments did not depart from the standards laid down under the sovereign's authority either in design or quality. Patterns were normally produced for the board's inspection by the colonels' agents.[8]

Despite the responsibility of the board of ordnance for barracks, they were in fact practically non-existent. The absence of barracks was indeed a deliberate Government policy dictated by the ever-present fear of a military *coup d'état*. Barracks, it was felt, would increase this danger by withdrawing troops from contact with the civil population, and to ensure that such contact was as close as possible, the Government even encouraged commanding officers to allow soldiers to engage in trade as 'outlyers'. The construction of barracks to accommodate a large number of men was so successfully prevented that in 1697 only about 5,000 infantry could be housed in the few barracks existing in England. Billeting was the only alternative, but a proclamation of January 1689, at the very start of the reign of William III, prohibited the quartering of troops in a private house without the owner's consent; and all houses were considered to be private except victualling houses, houses of public entertainment, and houses in which wine or other liquor was sold by retail, i.e. inns. In these last troops could be quartered on the authority of the chief magistrate and justice of the peace, acting through constables. For troops on the march, the justices had to assess reasonable rates, within the subsistence money paid to the soldier, for all the provisions needed for one or more nights. But in places appointed for their residence the justices were only required to give an assessment covering the night of their arrival. After that, the householders had by law to furnish only lodgings, suitable room for horses, fire, water, and utensils to dress the soldiers' meat. There was no other commitment unless the officers or soldiers made a contract with them for provisions.[9]

General Wade commented on the aversion to barracks when, in 1739–40, difficulties arose over billeting troops in England: 'The people of this Kingdom have been taught to associate the idea of barracks and slavery so closely together that, like darkness and the devil, though there be no connection between them, yet they cannot separate them, nor think of the one without thinking at the same time of the other.'[10]

The political objections to barracks did not apply to Ireland, where their construction was encouraged. In 1707, for instance, additional barracks were being built for two infantry battalions and three troops of cavalry.[11] Having proper barracks was, indeed, one of the advantages of soldiering in Ireland. The country was divided up into regimental areas, and, in the case of cavalry, the barrack accommodation in each of the towns of an area normally sufficed for one or two troops.[12]

In Scotland small barracks had to be built to house internal security garrisons in the Highlands. These were really small forts, and according to the Ordnance vote of 1718, they were for 'preventing the robberies and depredations of the High-landers'. The barrack houses were to be three storeys high, besides garrets, and surrounded by a wall eighteen feet high and two feet six inches thick, with four small towers for defence, 'built of rough stone and good mortar'. The number of rooms depended on the size of the garrison, but each room was to be eighteen feet by seventeen in area and to contain five beds. The five beds were for ten men, as half the garrison would normally be on duty at any one time.[13]

The discipline of the Army at first presented something of a problem. By the 'Declaration of Rights' Parliament had established its control of the existence and strength of the Army, but events soon showed that measures were still needed to assure its allegiance. In March 1689 Dumbarton's Regiment (later the 1st Foot, The Royal Scots) was ordered to proceed to the coast and embark for Holland. When the regiment reached Ipswich it mutinied, declared its allegiance to the exiled King James II, and marched north.

The Government was now in some difficulty because there were no powers under the law for the punishment of military offences in peacetime, other than the civil courts, and these powers were quite inadequate to deal with military mutiny. On active service the position was different because troops were governed by the Articles of War, and punishments were inflicted by courts martial under this military code. A bill was therefore introduced with some haste to legalise the use of military courts in peacetime, and this was passed as the Mutiny Act. Initially it was only for a period of seven months, but thereafter it was passed annually, and is still in existence as the Army and Air Force Annual Act. In the preamble of this Act were inserted the words from the Declaration of Rights. The effect of the Act, which was of paramount importance in the establishment of the standing Army as a national institution, was that such a force could not be maintained unless Parliament approved it, voted money to cover its cost, agreed to its size, and sanctioned the methods for its discipline.[14]

The discipline of the Army was now exercised in peacetime, as well as in war, by the Articles of War under the legal 'umbrella' of the Mutiny Act, and these Articles were brought up to date and issued from time to time by the adjutant-general with the sovereign's authority. Those of 1748 provide a typical example.[15] They are divided into twenty sections, each of which deals with a particular subject and comprises one or more Articles. The sections are concerned, respectively, with Divine worship, mutiny and sedition, enlistment, leave of absence, returns of unit states and garrisons, absence without leave, quarrels and duels, regulations for sutlers, billets, provision of carriages, offences under the civil law, complaints, damage by neglect and losing arms, drunkenness and misbehaviour before the enemy, regulations for courts martial, entry of commissions in official books, officers on half pay, disposal of the effects of the dead, application of the Articles to all ranks of the artillery, and all crimes not mentioned in the Articles.

To ensure the execution of the powers of the Crown under the Mutiny Act there was appointed a judge-advocate-general, under whom were deputy-judge-advocates-general, and these officers acted as legal advisers to military commanders. Ireland had its own judge-advocate-general.

As regards the kinds of punishment for the various offences, the Articles are not very explicit. Apart from death for all ranks (mandatory for mutiny, sedition, and misbehaviour before the enemy), cashiering of officers, reduction in rank for N.C.O.s, and corporal punishment for the rank and file, there is generally only the tantalisingly indefinite alternative of 'or such other punishment'. Courts martial were either 'general' or 'regimental'. The latter could be convened by the commanding officer of a regiment, but it could only deal with minor offences by other ranks and its maximum powers of award were limited to corporal punishment. No sentence of a general court martial could be put into execution until the whole proceedings had been reported to and approved by the sovereign or by the 'general commander-in-chief', or in Ireland by the lord-lieutenant.

It will be apparent that the arrangements for the command and control of the Army were so devised that no one person had the power to organise and move a field force. It was a cumbersome system which hampered operations in war, but Parliament liked it because it made any military revolt the more difficult. Perhaps its most serious defect in peacetime was that it hindered effective inspection of the Army and of defences and thereby promoted laxness, corruption, and inefficiency. An example is provided by the appalling state of the fixed defences at the time of the Jacobite rebellion in 1745. The important harbour of Falmouth was defended by the forty-six guns of Pendennis Castle, but in charge of these was a master-gunner aged ninety, assisted by one gunner. In January 1746 Sir George Oxenden, M.P. for Sandwich, complained to the Government that in a survey of the castles he had found that they contained 'no men and but few gunners, and those ignorant of their business'. Sandown Castle, which commanded the shore near Sandwich Flats, was occupied only by a woman who told him that 'the guns were not loaded and that there was no ammunition'. On 27 September 1745 the officer commanding at Chester Castle reported that he had only two companies of invalids with a total strength of seventy-five men, that the barracks were empty and powder deficient, and, he concluded, 'there is nothing but empty walls, and wants all manner of necessarys'.[16]

Chapter 3

THE REGIMENT

The regiment of cavalry or infantry was the basic unit in the eighteenth century. Much the greater part of the Army was composed of infantry, which consisted of the three regiments of Foot Guards and a large number of regiments of the line. Most of these latter, apart from various garrison units, were the so-called 'Marching Regiments of Foot'; that is, regiments which were mobile and suitable for inclusion in a field force. Some of the line regiments were designated 'Royal', and this was reflected in titles which included 'King's', 'Queen's', or 'Royal' and in the royal blue of their facings and colours.

Whereas some of the line regiments during the eighteenth century had two battalions, the majority had only one, and the term 'regiment' when applied to an infantry unit generally implied a single battalion. In 1756 second battalions were formed for fifteen regiments, the second battalion differing only from the first in that it was usually commanded by a major instead of a lieutenant-colonel and had an extra captain.[1]

The number of companies in a battalion and their establishments varied considerably during the century. A typical strength in other ranks of a company comprised three sergeants, three corporals, and fifty-six privates, but in 1734 regiments on the lower Irish establishment had only thirty-three privates in each company. There could be nine companies in a battalion or as many as thirteen, and of these one was a grenadier company—an elite body of the biggest and best men. During the Seven Years War light infantry companies were formed in some regiments in America, and in 1770, as a result of this successful experiment, it was decided that there should be one light infantry company in each battalion. The grenadiers were assault troops whilst the light infantry were skirmishers.

Bands had been allowed from the earliest days of the Regular Army, but no public money had been provided for their creation or upkeep. In 1757, however, the Duke of Cumberland succeeded in getting money voted for six enlisted musicians in each battalion, with the usual equipment of two hautboys (pronounced 'hoboy' and now usually 'oboe'), two French horns, and two bassoons. Two years later the addition of two fifes, to be borne on the strength of the grenadier company, was approved.[2]

In 1769 each battalion had two guns, which had been included in the establishment for many years and which were manned and served by a sergeant and twelve infantrymen. But from the following year the Royal Artillery were gradually attaching N.C.O.s and gunners to infantry battalions to take over these guns.[3]

The colours, as symbolising its spirit and as forming a rallying point in war, were a very important element in an infantry regiment. At the start of the eighteenth century there were colours for each company of a regiment; those respectively of the colonel, the lieutenant-colonel, the major, and the several captains. During Queen Anne's reign the colours of the line were gradually reduced to three for each regiment; those of the colonel, the lieutenant-colonel, and the major. In the middle of the century a Royal Warrant of 1 July 1751 established the system which was in all its main features the same as that in use today. There were two colours in each battalion of which the first, or King's, was the 'Great Union' (i.e. the Union flag) and the second, or Regimental, was the tincture of the regimental facings (except when the facings were white or red, when the Regimental colour was the red cross on white of St George). Rules governed the devices which were to be borne on each colour. The colours of the regiments of Foot Guards remained unchanged by the Warrant of 1751, but those of the colonel, lieutenant-colonel, and major became the first colours of the 1st, 2nd, and 3rd battalions respectively, and the company colours were taken in turn as the second colours of each of the battalions.

At the beginning of the eighteenth century there were two

types of cavalry, horse and dragoons; the main difference between them being that horse—big men on big horses—were trained primarily for the mounted charge with the sword as their principal weapon; whilst dragoons were expected to be able to fight on foot and therefore to be proficient in musketry. In 1746 some of the more senior regiments of horse were converted into the more generally useful dragoons, but in order that they should not feel they were being down-graded, they were designated 'Dragoon Guards'.[4] In 1756 a troop of light cavalry was added to the establishment of regiments of dragoon guards and dragoons, and as these troops proved very useful in practice, several complete regiments of light dragoons were raised in 1759 and 1760. The light troops in the heavy regiments had all been disbanded by 1763.[5]

There were normally six troops in a cavalry regiment, and these varied as much as, or more than, an infantry company in strength. In the Seven Years War, for instance, a light dragoon regiment was composed of six troops, each of a captain, a lieutenant, a quartermaster (warrant officer), a farrier, two drummers, four sergeants, four corporals, and ninety-eight 'private' dragoons. After the war, in 1764, the number of privates was cut drastically to twenty-six and a trumpeter replaced the drummers.[6] At the outbreak of the American War of Independence the troops strength in the 16th Light Dragoons was approximately the same, with a captain, a lieutenant, a quartermaster, two sergeants, two corporals, a trumpeter, a farrier, and twenty-five dragoons. Before the regiment departed for America, each of the six troops was augmented by a cornet, a sergeant, two corporals, and thirty-eight dragoons, but only nine horses. The troop was then split into two detachments, one mounted and the other dismounted. The six dismounted detachments were grouped into a dismounted division of the regiment, commanded by a captain with a lieutenant as second-in-command.[7]

In order that the trumpeters in a cavalry regiment could form a band when dismounted, the regiment was issued with two French horns, two bassoons, two clarinets, and a fife. One of the trumpeters carried a bugle.

Cavalry regiments carried two types of flag, the standard

which was square and the guidon which was oblong and slit at
the fly. The former was the flag of the horse and the latter the
flag of the dragoons; but dragoon guards, to emphasise that
they had suffered no loss of status, were allowed to retain
the standards which they had carried as horse. Each troop in a
regiment carried either a standard or guidon.

The regiment of either cavalry or infantry was in many
respects the property of its colonel. Authority to raise a new
regiment was generally given to some eminent person, such as a
general, a peer, or a large landowner. In return for the considerable outlay that this entailed, he was entrusted by Parliament with the money voted by it for the regiment (less that
portion allotted to the procurement of arms etc.), and he also
received the sums paid by the regiment's first complement of
officers for their commissions. The money for the regiment's
maintenance in subsequent years was similarly handed over to
him and to his successors in command. Most of the colonel's
income was derived (legitimately) from what he was able to
save in the running of his regiment. This task entailed, of course,
complex commercial and financial transactions in such matters
as the pay and clothing of the men, the purchase of horses, and
the expenses of recruiting. It soon became the practice therefore
for the colonel to be assisted by an agent in the discharge of these
duties. This civilian official was at first known as the 'colonel's
clerk', but by the time of James II the term 'regimental agent'
had become customary. The agency system was officially
established in the reign of William and Mary, and from then
until the passing of an Act of Parliament in 1783, the agent was
paid by the deduction of twopence in the pound from the whole
pay of the regiment. This was a very handsome sum and the
post of agent was in consequence so coveted that the colonel
often sold it to the highest reputable bidder.[8] The appointment
had to be confirmed, however, by the Secretary at War.

The distribution of the Army's pay was the responsibility of
the paymaster-general, who issued it in bulk to regiments,
generally through the regimental agents. The procedures connected with his office varied throughout the period under
review. In 1679 the paymaster-general, in addition to the pay
of his office, was authorised to take one shilling in the pound

from the Army's pay in return for advancing money from his private credit to provide the weekly pay to the regiments. In 1684 he was no longer required to advance funds; nevertheless, the deduction of one shilling in the pound continued, though the paymaster-general now only received fourpence, the remaining eightpence going to the Chelsea Hospital.

For many years the soldier's basic pay was eightpence a day, but of this twopence was subtracted as 'off-reckonings' which, according to the Pay Warrant of 1687, were to be expended by the colonel on the provision of clothing and the payment of 'poundage and other remaining expenses', but excluding the costs of recruiting.[9] For these latter, allowances were made which formed part of a common fund called the 'stock purse' or 'non-effective account' of the regiment until 1783, when the cost of recruiting was transferred to the public.

The unexpended portion of the off-reckonings constituted the profit made by the colonel for his own use. But after a new regiment was raised it was some time before there was any such profit. In 1708 the board of general officers sealed patterns of clothing for horse, foot, and dragoons, and directed that fourteen months off-reckonings should be expended on the first year's clothing of a regiment and ten months for every succeeding year. Thus it was two years before a colonel was all square, and he only made his profit of two months off-reckonings in his third year.[10]

The sixpence paid to the soldier was his 'subsistence', to pay for his food, drink, and minor necessities. When the men were in quarters and messing themselves, they received their subsistence money once or twice a week, 'according to the convenience of the markets', from their troop or company captains. It was then the responsibility of the sergeants and corporals to see that the soldiers bought suitable provisions. Two or three times a week an officer inspected the quality of these provisions, and at dinner time (normally about noon) saw that each mess, of about five to eight men (the normal number in tent or room) 'boiled the pot' properly.[11] When men were fed by the landlord of their quarters, the requisite amount of the subsistence money was paid to him.

Clothing consisted of uniform and necessaries; the colonel

being responsible for providing the former and the man himself the latter. In light dragoon regiments, for instance, the colonel provided coat, waistcoat, and breeches every two years, gloves every year, a helmet every four years, and boots and spurs periodically. Cloaks were provided by him on a regimental basis as required, an average being thirty-six cloaks every fourth year. All the rest of the soldier's clothing were 'necessaries' and were paid for him out of his 'arrears'. These arrears were accounted for to the soldier two months in arrears (hence the name) on the 28th of each alternate month, starting in February. The arrears for two months came to 10s. 2d. (i.e. two pence a day, based on a thirty-one day month), and after the money which the soldier owed for necessaries had been deducted, the balance was paid to him. Cavalrymen had to buy additional articles, but to compensate for this there was 'grass money' at £1 11s. 10d. per man per year. It was the custom in the cavalry to put horses out to grass during the summer for periods of from eight to ten days. This was good for the condition of the horses, but as they could not be worked while at grass, the troops were turned out to grass, one or two at a time, so that the bulk of a regiment was always available for duty. However, the forage ration of twelve pounds of oats and ten pounds of hay was allowed for all horses for each day of the year. The money value of the forage saved whilst the horse was at grass was credited to its rider and paid to him on the pay day of the first of the 'clearance' months after the horse had come from grass. Out of his arrears and grass money a light dragoon had to provide himself with a white stable jacket, leather stable breeches, four shirts, four pairs of stockings, two pairs of shoes, gaiters, cleaning and grooming kit, and other items for his person and his horse.[12]

Saddlery and accoutrements for the men were provided by the Government in the first instance and subsequently by the colonel as they were needed. Muskets, carbines, and pistols were supplied by Ordnance from the Tower of London. Colours, standards, guidons, and horse furniture were supplied by the Government and renewed every fifth clothing.[13]

A Warrant of 19 February 1766 gives the items which could be charged against the stock purse, and which were refunded by the Government. These were: the levy money and expense of each recruit, including his subsistence, until he joined his regiment; the bounty money paid to men on discharge to meet the cost of their journey home; the subsistence of men discharged as invalids and recommended for admission to Chelsea Hospital, from the date of their discharge until their admission or rejection; the expenses of beating orders (under which a regiment carried out its recruiting); expenses relating to deserters; and contingent expenses. These last included the purchase of horses, an allowance to captains for the miscellaneous expenses of their troop or company, and also an allowance to a recruiting officer for each man recruited by him up to a maximum of £3 8s., out of which no more than 'one guinea and one crown' was to be given to the recruit.[14]

When there were heavy casualties from war or sickness the allowances were not sufficient to cover the cost of recruiting, with the result that officers had to pay the extra out of their own pockets. Applications to the Crown for relief on this score were made frequently.[15]

The various moneys to which the regiment was entitled were passed by the agent to the regimental paymaster, who distributed them to the captains of troops or companies. (The regimental paymaster was an officer selected by the colonel to discharge this duty in addition to his normal regimental employment.) The regimental accounts were made up half-yearly on 24 June and 24 December, and submitted to the agent within three months of these dates. They were signed 'upon honour' by the commanding officer, the adjutant, and the regimental paymaster. Annually, within three months after 24 December, the agent had 'to give into the Secretary at War all these accounts with a state of his own disbursements and vouchers for the same.'[16]

The principal events in a regiment's day and also its movements were signalled by drum, bugle, or trumpet. In an infantry regiment the orders for the appropriate action were conveyed by different beats on the drums. The 'General' was an order for the regiment to get ready to march, and the 'March' ordered it to move off. The 'Assembly' was an order to repair to the colours, which were at the regimental alarm post; whilst a 'Beat to Arms' ordered men to stand to arms at local alarm posts. The

'Reveillé' at daybreak directed the soldiers to rise and the sentries to cease challenging. The 'Troop' warned men to parade for roll call and inspection for duty. At sunset when the drums beat the 'Retreat' the roll was called again and the orders of the day were read. 'Tattoo', at 10 p.m. in summer and 9 p.m. in winter, was the signal for men to return to their quarters or barracks, where the N.C.O. of each squad called the roll.[17]

In a cavalry regiment the 'Assembly' was sounded by bugle. If it was intended that the troops should assemble mounted, this bugle call was preceded by the trumpeters sounding 'Boots and Saddles' in all parts of the town. The men were then given sufficient time to dress and saddle their horses before the bugler sounded the 'Assembly'. But if the 'Assembly' was not preceded by 'Boots and Saddles', then the men had to go quickly to the regimental alarm post on foot.[18]

Guards were commonly mounted at 'Troop' beating, which was at 9 a.m. from March to October and at 10 a.m. during the rest of the year. The principal guard in an infantry regiment was the quarter guard; whilst in a cavalry regiment it was the standard guard, so-called because it mounted with the standard or guidon of the troop providing it. A normal strength for both guards was a sergeant, a corporal, and twelve men; but at the 'setting of the watch' in the evening, six additional men were mounted to provide the extra sentries required by night. Cavalry guards were mounted on foot, and the old and new guards were drawn up in line on each side of the two troop standards.[19]

Whenever possible (in default of a barracks) regiments were quartered in a town, of at least moderate size, in order that sufficient billets might be found to keep the men reasonably concentrated. The town would be divided into company or troop areas, in accordance with the billets allotted to the regiment by the chief magistrate. When a troop or company marched into its area, and before moving to the various quarters where the men were to be billeted, the officer commanding divided it into squads, each under an N.C.O., of a size determined by the accommodation in each billet. The squads were then marched off to their billets. On arrival of a cavalry squad at its billet, the men first secured their arms, and then took off bits and bridles and slackened girths. After removing their boots and putting on their stable jackets, they picked the horses' hooves, rubbed hooves and legs dry, gave them a little hay (but no water or corn until an officer had visited the stable), and then tied them up to prevent them lying down. The men then refreshed themselves and waited, without unsaddling the horses, for the trumpet to sound for 'Stables'. This would be within one hour of the troop's arrival at its billets, and an officer, accompanied by the troop quartermaster warrant officer, then examined the backs of the horses.[20]

At 'Troop' beating in an infantry regiment, companies paraded by squads, each under the command of its N.C.O. After roll call the company subaltern of the day inspected all the squads and was handed the sick reports by squad commanders. He then gave out any necessary instructions relating to the day's activities, after which the company marched to the regimental parade ground.[21]

The cavalry day was more complex than that of the infantry because it included stable routine. From Lady Day to Michaelmas there were stables and water at 8 a.m. and 4 p.m., whilst during the remainder of the year they were at 9 a.m. and 3 p.m. Horses were watered twice in the summer but only once in the winter. The horse's feed was always measured out to its rider in the standard measure of the regiment. An officer had to be present in the stables at feeding times at least once a day. This was normally the evening feed, but if it was more convenient for him to miss this on one day, he had to be present at the morning or midday feed on the following day. The troop quartermaster had to be present at all feeds not visited by an officer, and he was also responsible for watering and for supervising the whole stable routine. Horses had to be well groomed at both morning and evening stables, and have their tails and manes combed and their heels rubbed under the close supervision of the squad N.C.O.s. Weather permitting, horses were exercised every day, one man in charge of every two horses. Twice a week they were all saddled and ridden. Squad N.C.O.s were responsible for reporting to the troop quartermaster when a horse needed shoeing, and the latter gave the necessary orders to the farrier.[22]

Because the fitness of its horses was vital to a cavalry regiment and replacements for them were expensive (a maximum of twenty guineas from the stock purse account for the purchase of a horse), penalties for mishandling them were severe. If a farrier, for instance, lamed a horse by paring down the frog, he not only got corporal punishment, but was confined, to stop him drinking anything but water, until the horse was sound; and orders laid down that: 'That cruel and unworkmanlike practice of putting a burning shoe to a horse's foot is to be entirely discouraged and prevented as much as possible under severe penalties.' The farrier had to use shoes which conformed rigidly to the approved regimental pattern.[23]

Much was expected of the junior officer in the daily routine of a good regiment, and the proper preparation of him to undertake his duties was the subject of a Royal Warrant of 11 February 1767. This laid down that every young officer on first joining his regiment (cavalry or infantry) should remain 'in quarters' (i.e. at regimental headquarters) 'until he shall be perfected in all regimental duty'. He was to be instructed by the field officers and the adjutant.[24]

In an infantry regiment a subaltern was detailed every day as officer of the guard. In barracks or camp he did 'rounds' to see that everything was in order; but when the regiment was billeted he remained in the building allotted by the chief magistrate of the area as a guard room, and received the reports of the sergeant of the patrol.[25]

Half an hour after tattoo a patrol went round to every public house, clearing out any soldiers who were still there. After the final roll call the orderly sergeant had to see that all the men's fires and candles had been extinguished, and the officer of the guard was responsible that both the sergeant of the patrol and the orderly sergeants had carried out these duties.[26]

Apart from being officer of the guard, there were plenty of administrative duties for subalterns. The men's quarters were inspected frequently and particular importance was attached to the airing of rooms and freedom from dust. During these inspections all beds had to be 'turned up' and spare clothes tidily arranged. In addition there was a weekly kit inspection at which all items had to be displayed, clearly marked with the owner's number in vermilion and nut oil.[27] Particular attention was paid to personal cleanliness, and an officer had to check that men changed their shirts and washed the whole of their bodies every Sunday and Wednesday.[28] (It is conceivable that some of the men had never done the latter before joining the Army.)

In Hinde's regiment, the Royal Foresters or 21st Light Dragoons, the instructions for officers included the following: 'The humanity of the officers will excite them to make inspection into the care of the sick every day.' 'Inspection into the Men's rooms to be made at least once a week by a commissioned officer, and at hours least expected.' 'It is expected that officers are always the first men upon parades; but it is to be regarded as much a want of punctuality in non-commissioned officers to be too soon, as to be too late in assembling their men.' 'No officer is to leave his troops, or to attend to his own convenience till all his troop is billeted off.'[29]

The records were an important part of the administration of a regiment. Each company maintained a book of standing orders and also a state of the N.C.O.s and men on its strength which gave all their relevant particulars and a brief record of their service. The state was always kept up to date and from it the company commander compiled the weekly and monthly returns that were submitted to the adjutant. These returns were entered in the regimental books. In an infantry regiment the major was responsible for the regimental records but in practice they were usually kept by the adjutant, and from them he compiled the monthly states required by the Secretary at War. The company commander was also responsible for seeing that the paymaster-sergeant and quartermaster-segeant accounted for the company's pay and store returns to the regimental paymaster and the quartermaster respectively.[30]

It will be apparent to officers of the twentieth-century British Army that the foundations of good regimental administration had been well and truly laid two hundred years ago.

Chapter 4

OFFICERS AND MEN

'The danger of intrusting an Armed Host to the will and pleasure of one man in time of Peace has hitherto been recognised by Parliament, and the evil can by no better method be averted than that of having the Officers, subordinate to the Commander-in-Chief, drawn from that social class the members of which are more likely to lose than to gain by Military Aggression. Therefore, as a rule, while the rank and file of the Army have been recruited from the lower stratum of society, the Command of these men has been intrusted to the higher class, and never—save at the time of the Commonwealth—to any other, or even to that class without that substantial guarantee for their good behaviour which the Purchase system gives to the Civil Community.'

Thus wrote Charles Clode in 1869,[1] quoting as his reference Sir Robert Walpole, Lord Holland, Charles J. Fox, Lord Folkestone, and Lord Palmerston. Nearly all the officers of the Army came from the landed and aristocratic classes, or from the minor gentry who had the same social status. Their own interests lay in the stability of the constitution, and their stake in that constitution was enhanced by the system of buying commissions and promotion, which provided an investment for sale when an officer retired. But though Parliament liked the purchase system, the sovereigns, on whole, did not. George I disliked it intensely as detrimental to efficiency, and he tried unsuccessfully to abolish it.

An officer purchased his first commission, and then each step in promotion that an officer senior to him was ready to sell, either because the senior man was retiring or was himself buying promotion, or perhaps the same rank in a more expensive regiment. On the other hand, if a serving officer died or was killed in action, then the next senior to him in the regiment was promoted into the vacancy without purchase; but a step in rank under these circumstances was not usually saleable.

A young man who decided on a career in a marching regiment of foot in the year 1770 would have had to find at least £400, the official price of an ensign's commission, or £450 if the regiment was Royal. The actual cost could well be considerably higher, because the lieutenant who was selling this commission would try and obtain as much as he could to offset the money he had paid for his lieutenancy. The cost of a commission did not end a young officer's expenses, because his uniform, other clothing, and equipment would cost at least another £200. Everything, including his camp equipment of a bed in a waterproof case and a tent, had to conform to the regimental pattern.[2]

Possibilities of purchase beyond the rank of lieutenant-colonel were limited, because appointments to colonelcies of regiments were increasingly made by the king. However, the sale of colonelcies did occur. In 1711, for instance, the Duke of Argyll sold the colonelcy of his regiment, the Buffs, to Colonel John Selwyn for £7,000; and in 1715, when the Jacobite rising was imminent, George I intimated to several generals who were colonels of regiments and who were suspected of Jacobite sympathies, that they must dispose of their colonelcies. General the Right Honourable William Stewart was one of these, and he sold his regiment to Colonel James Cambell.[3] Though the king wished to appoint all colonels of regiments, it was not possible to stop the purchase of regiments immediately, because officers who had spent a lot of money in acquiring command of a regiment had to be allowed to recoup themselves on retirement by its sale. Such regiments, therefore, only became available for command by appointment when their colonels died before retirement.

A general officer in peacetime received no pay for that rank and therefore depended on his income as colonel of a regiment, unless he was given a governorship. In wartime a general in the field had a special establishment voted for him and his staff, including the pay for whatever general's rank he held.

On the whole the purchase system seems to have been popular with officers. The general opinion was probably represented by Lieutenant Delacherois of the 9th Foot, who wrote:[4] 'How inconsistent it is with reason to argue that advancement in the army should not be sought after either by interest or money when in a man's power. The whole argument may be settled in this question: whether it's more the interest of an officer to have his money in stock or higher rank . . . As to the consideration of laying a provision for old age . . . purchased commissions are still allowed to be disposed of and are always worth the same if not more money.' His own promotion to lieutenant from ensign (called in contemporary army slang a 'rag carrier') had not been purchased and was therefore not saleable 'without much favour and interest'.

In March 1770 Delacherois was offered Captain Denshire's company, which was going at a moderate price, because Denshire only received the pay of a lieutenant; but the offer was conditional on Captain-Lieutenant Pompillone waiving his prior right to Denshire's company. However, if Pompillone did buy this company, Delacherois could succeed him in the captain-lieutenancy (that is, the command of the colonel's company of which the colonel was captain) which was going at a very low price. This in fact is what happened and Delacherois became captain-lieutenant. Later another company on lieutenant's pay came on the market. The reason that one or more captains were paid as lieutenants was presumably that the regiment, which was stationed in Ireland, was on a low establishment.

Other examples of the operation of the purchase system are provided by the careers of the Ellison brothers and Richard Davenport. Cuthbert and Robert were two of the sons of Henry Ellison of Hebburn, who owned a fairly considerable property. Their mother, Elizabeth, was the daughter of Sir Henry Liddell, third Baronet of Ravensworth Castle, Co. Durham. It was a family typical of those which provided the eighteenth-century Army with its officers.[5] Cuthbert, the eldest son, decided to enter the Army and was able to find sufficient money (presumably from his father) to purchase in 1723 a commission as captain in the 8th Dragoons, then stationed in Ireland, thereby missing two steps on the promotion ladder. Eight years later he bought his majority in the same regiment, and in 1739 he purchased the lieutenant-colonelcy of the 23rd Foot, also stationed in Ireland, having then sixteen years service. He served on the Continent of Europe from 1742 to 1744 and commanded his regiment at the battle of Dettingen, when it was in the first line of the British infantry. He was obviously well thought of because in 1745 he was occupying a staff appointment as deputy adjutant-general on the headquarters of Field-Marshal the Earl of Stair. In the same year, however, ill health caused him to sell his regimental commission. Nevertheless his staff commission enabled him to continue on the active list. He was promoted colonel on the staff, and, having reached that rank, his further promotion was automatic until he chose to retire. He eventually became a lieutenant-general, but he was not employed again in any higher rank than colonel. He seems to have been a keen and efficient officer, and he had a charm of manner which made him popular in the London society in which he loved to move.

Robert was the youngest son in the family. He was a very different character to Cuthbert—competent and shrewd, and lacking his brother's easy-going ways. His father had intended him to go into the mining profession, but he preferred to study law. He seems to have tired of this, for in 1732 he purchased an ensigncy in the 3rd Buffs. By 1739 he was a captain serving in a regiment of marines, and in 1743 a major in an American regiment of foot. Two years later he was a lieutenant-colonel in another American regiment. Both these regiments were disbanded and he had a period on half pay. In 1755 he was appointed colonel of the 44th Foot in succession to Sir Peter Halkett, who had been killed while commanding the 44th at the disaster to Braddock's force on the Monogahela. Robert may never have seen his new regiment for he died about three months later.

Richard Davenport[6] was commissioned as a sub-brigadier (second-lieutenant) in the 4th Troop of Horse Guards in 1742, having paid about £500 as the purchase price. (The 'private gentlemen', or troopers, of the Horse Guards purchased their 'places' for 100 guineas each.) In 1743 he was hoping to be made adjutant, which would increase his pay by £100 a year. This depended on somebody being found to purchase his rank as sub-brigadier, which was not so easy as in a line regiment because all commissions in the Household Cavalry had to be approved personally by the king. In fact there was no suitable candidate and Davenport decided to pay 1,000 guineas for his commission as adjutant and keep his commission as sub-brigadier as well. He fought at the battle of Dettingen where the Horse Guards delivered a magnificent charge which broke the French *Gardes Suisses* and *Gardes Francaises*, the trumpeter of the 4th Troop sounding 'Britons, strike home!'. In recognition of their gallantry the King gave commissions to two private gentlemen of each troop, but this did not help Davenport as the commissions were a gift and not a purchase.

After the defeat of the Jacobite rebellion in 1746 the 3rd and 4th Troops of Horse Guards were disbanded, and Davenport went on half pay in respect of both his commissions. However, a short time later he returned to the active list by purchasing a commission as sub-brigadier in the 2nd Troop of Horse Guards, so that he now held one commission on full pay and two on half pay. (Redundant officers could not be discharged without the Government paying them the value of their commissions, and they were therefore placed on half pay. This was regarded as a form of retaining fee in case their services should be required in another war. In the case of a keen and wealthy officer like Davenport the idea did not work!)

In 1754 Davenport bought a commission as captain in the 10th Dragoons; thereby gaining two steps in rank, but probably at a moderate cost as he was leaving the Household Cavalry for a regiment of the line. In 1759 he purchased the commission of major in the same regiment. There was only one major in a regiment of dragoons, and as the lieutenant-colonel was often absent Davenport frequently commanded the regiment.

In the class of society from which most of the officers came, men were accustomed to command, and they were in general brought up to a high sense of duty and honour. Coming from such a background, the average officer was conscientious in the performance of his duties, and because of his natural ability as a leader it was easy to train him to fill the place required in his regiment. The purchase system worked much better than might be expected because it was generally the keen and ambitious officers who saved money to enable them to get on in their chosen career. The fighting record of the regiments, indeed, reflected the standard of their officers as leaders and trainers of men. In good regiments pride in and loyalty to the regiment were instilled into the rank and file by officers and senior N.C.O.s, and all ranks regarded and spoke of themselves as belonging to one military family. Officers aimed to give men confidence in themselves and in their ability as soldiers, rather than (as in bad regiments) using brutal methods to try and achieve discipline through fear.[7]

As regards the life of officers in a regiment, Cuthbertson says[8] that it was incumbent on the colonel 'to contrive every method in his power for the establishment of a mess, at which all the officers, without distinction of rank, can be properly and genteely accommodated, and that considerably within the compass of an ensign's pay, which is a circumstance to be principally considered: living always together as one family, must surely strengthen the bonds of friendship between individuals, and unite the whole in that sort of harmony and affection, which in a well regulated corps ought ever to subsist and without which everything goes wrong.' 'Distinctions of rank,' he says, 'should never subsist among gentlemen except on duty.'

In the 1770s, when Cuthbertson was writing, several regiments had started officers' messes, though it was not till the first quarter of the next century that they became compulsory. In most regiments Cuthbertson's injunction about distinctions of rank were observed, and even generals, notably John Burgoyne, waived their rank amongst other officers when off duty.[9] However, uniform was worn by officers in the eighteenth century much more often than it is today. In 1747, in fact, orders were issued that officers were not to wear plain clothes in camp or quarters either on or off duty, and this remained the rule for many years afterwards.[10]

Enlistment of the rank and file of the Army was generally

voluntary, and the period was normally for life; which in practice meant until the soldier was too old or infirm for active service. A colonel carried out the recruiting of his regiment under a 'beating order' which was issued under the Royal Sign Manual and countersigned by the secretary at war. Captain Hinde gives the following example of a beating order:[11]

'GEORGE R.

'These are to authorise you by *Beat of Drum or Otherwise*, to raise so many volunteers in any county or part of Our Kingdom of Great Britain, as are or shall be wanting to recruit and fill up the respective troops of Our 22d regiment of Light Dragoons, under your command, to be the number allowed upon the establishment, and all Magistrates, Justices of the Peace, Constables, and all other Our Civil Officers whom it may concern, are hereby required to be assisting unto you in providing quarters, impressing carriages, and otherwise as there shall be occasion; and for so doing, this Our order shall be and continue in force from the 9th day of May next, being the day on which Our former order will expire, until the 25th day of March following.

'Given at Our Court of St. James's, this 28th day of April 1775 in the fifteenth year of Our Reign.

'*By His Majesty's Command*

'BARRINGTON

'True copy, Ant. Chamier.'

'To Our trusty and well-beloved Colonel Patrick Johnston, of the 22d regiment of Light Dragoons, or to the officer appointed by him to raise men for the said regiment.

'I do appoint Cornet Ogle, Serjeant Foster, Corporal Rockwood, and Trumpeter Green of the above regiment.

'Edward Booth, Major

'Commanding the 22d regiment of Light Dragoons.'

The 21st Light Dragoons, or Royal Regiment of Foresters (Hinde's own regiment which was disbanded in 1763), had their own recruiting instructions, as follows:[12]

'The Officers that Recruit Men for the Royal Regiment of Light Cavalry commanded by Lieutenant-General the Marquis of Granby, and the Right Honourable Lord Robert Sutton, are to Inlist no Man under the size of *Five Feet Five Inches and a Half*, nor above *Five Feet Nine Inches High:* the Officers must be very attentive to the kind of Service these Men are intended for; they must be light and straight, and by no means gummy. The Bounty-Money must not exceed *Three Guineas and a Crown*; but the Officers are to get them as much under as they can. The Officers are impowered to Inlist Men, during the War only, if they seem to like that better than for Life . . .'

The light dragoon regiments were regarded as rather select units and that they could therefore stipulate fairly rigid physical standards for their recruits.

Recruiting, however, was often a very slow and frustrating business. In 1757 the 9th Regiment of Foot was stationed in Ireland, where recruiting was not at that time allowed. In May of that year the 9th (as so often happened to regiments on the Irish establishment) had been 'drafted' to supply reinforcements to other regiments destined for movement overseas, and was now about 200 men below establishment. In November Lieutenant Nicholas Delacherois was sent to Scotland in charge of a recruiting party, with instructions to take no man under five feet six inches in height or aged over twenty-eight.

Delacherois stationed his men at Ayr, Kilmarnock and Glasgow, but found no disposition to enlist among the young ablebodied men in this part of the Scottish Lowlands. In fact, during two months of effort he only enlisted three men, and all of them were Irish!

In 1770, the regiment still being in Ireland, Delacherois was sent to the West Midlands of England on another recruiting mission. He started at Shepton Mallet in Somerset, where he stayed for a week and walked about twenty-four miles a day to the neighbouring towns and villages. But it was harvest time, with plenty of employment available, and all his efforts produced only nine doubtful recruits. Four of them deserted, and of the remaining five only one was found acceptable on arrival at regimental headquarters. Because of the bounty money they had received, and for which Delacherois was responsible, the four deserters represented a loss to him of between £10 and £12.

Later another man whom he sent deserted on landing at Cork, and Delacherois comments sadly, 'so slap went £5'. He continued northwards to Worcester and Kidderminster but had no better success.[13]

In spite of the difficulty of obtaining recruits, any form of compulsion was rarely resorted to. Conscription, or 'impressment', was first used in 1695–96, when imprisoned debtors could be drafted into the Army. In 1702 use was again made of this unfortunate class, though in a more liberal way. An Act authorised their release from prison if they would agree to enlist for the duration of the war, or could obtain someone else to do so on their behalf. The same Act allowed Justices of the Peace to 'raise and levy' able bodied men who were unemployed or without visible means of livelihood. Each such recruit was given £1 levy money, after which the Articles of War were read to him and he was considered enlisted. The constable who produced him was rewarded with 10s. Prisoners convicted of capital offences could also be conscripted;[14] though it seems unlikely that commanding officers of regiments would have been particularly pleased to have them.

After Queen Anne's reign impressment was not enforced again (except for a short period during the 1745 rebellion) until 1756–57. The persons then liable were unemployed or notoriously idle, and they had to serve either for five years or till the end of the war, whichever was the longer. Men under seventeen or over forty-five were exempt, as were also those under the height of five feet four inches and 'known Papists'. To secure these unwilling recruits between the time of their enlistment and joining their regiments, keepers of gaols and houses of correction were bound to receive and subsist them on 'the usual prison allowances'.[15]

Whenever the Army was raised from a peace to a war establishment, short periods of enlistment were introduced. This had a twofold advantage; it encouraged enlistment and it made it easy for Parliament to reduce the Army quickly at the end of a war.[16]

First hand accounts of the life of the rank and file, particularly at the beginning of this period, are rare. One of the few available is the journal of Corporal Matthew Bishop of Webb's Regiment (later the 8th Foot).[17] Bishop was one of those comparatively uncommon men who love active service above any other occupation. He started his Service career by joining the Royal Navy. After considerable war service at sea, he decided that he would like to become a soldier and take part in the campaigns on the Continent of Europe under the Duke of Marlborough. He enlisted by approaching the sergeant of a recruiting party from Webb's Regiment, and then helped the sergeant to persuade young men of the joys of service in the Army. Bishop certainly got his fill of fighting over the next few years, for his regiment was engaged at Oudenarde, Malplaquet, and other actions. Of the battle of Oudenarde in 1708 he writes: 'The Lieutenant, who belonged to the company that I did, was shot through the head. I had reason sufficient to be concerned; for he was a particular friend of mine . . . He seemingly was a man that had a great deal of sagacity, which I thought might have turned out greatly to our advantage; and we could very ill spare such men, especially at that critical juncture.'[18]

Of the Oudenarde campaign in general Bishop has the following comment: 'Give me leave to express my gratitude for the faithfulness of all the commanders in general that campaign . . . I think in my heart, that the Duke of Marlborough ordered his matters so well as to disappoint the French of all their intended encampments . . . though it was the occasion of long marches: but the willingness of our men and their activity withal to guide their actions accomplished our full intent.'[19]

Some time after the battle of Oudenarde, Webb's Regiment was encamped near the site of the action, and Bishop says: 'While we were at that ground I had a great desire to go and have a second view of the ground on which we had engaged the French the last campaign; for being so near Oudenard I was unwilling to miss that opportunity. When I asked my officer, he very readily granted my request. I took along with me several acquaintances that were not there, in order to show them in what manner we were engaged.[20]

Bishop had a great admiration for General Webb, the Colonel of the Regiment. It was General Webb who, in command of a force of twelve battalions of infantry, achieved the brilliant victory at Wynendael in September 1708 over a much stronger

French force. His own regiment fought in the battle, and Bishop is enthusiastic about Webb as a commander in the field. He says: 'He was an old and experienced General, and a man that knew every part of the country, without which he could not have known how to dispose of his men. And this plainly appears from his beautiful disposition of his troops'.[21]

Of a later period than Bishop was William Todd who started his working life on the turnpike between Hull and Hedon. He enlisted in the Associated Companies of Militia of Yorkshire and served during the Jacobite rebellion of 1745–46. From the Militia he enlisted in the 30th Foot, and, when that regiment was at Kilkenny in 1749, Todd started a journal.[22]

Early in 1755, war appearing likely, the 30th and seven other 'Irish' regiments were transferred to England. The following year, Todd being then a corporal, the 30th were in camp at Chatham with four other regiments. There was a tent for every five privates, but each sergeant and corporal had a tent to himself. The major of the regiment issued orders that sergeants were not to drink with corporals, nor corporals with private men. Todd suggested to his fellow corporals that they should establish a corporals' club to meet after roll call in the senior corporal's quarters. This excellent idea was followed by the sergeants, and it is an interesting thought that the establishment of the corporals' room and the sergeants' mess in a regiment may have been due to Todd.

But although there were always a number of men of a higher class who enlisted for the love of soldiering, the bulk of the Regular Army was recruited from the least-educated and least-wanted sections of the community. Indeed, most recruits were illiterate, but they were treated with sympathy and understanding in a good regiment and taught to take a pride in their personal appearance and dress. It was for perhaps the majority of the men a better life than they had ever known before. A good commanding officer tried to keep his men interested in peacetime by running competitions in such subjects as gardening and husbandry, and by introducing orders of merit which were awarded for proficiency in skill at arms, musketry, and field exercises. There was often a regimental school under a sergeant instructor where men who hoped for promotion to corporal could acquire the necessary qualifications of reading, writing, and simple arithmetic. As far as possible defaulters were dealt with by minor punishments, so that instead of being sent before a regimental court martial (with the inevitable sentence of flogging if found guilty) they were given such punishments as twenty-four hours on bread and water, public or private reprimand, and wearing their regimental coat inside out.[23]

Captain Hinde has the following remarks on discipline:[24] 'Discipline cannot be carried out without unanimity in the corps, and without the concurring assistance of the commission, and non-commission, officers . . . It is strongly recommended to the officers, to inspire the sergeants and corporals with a proper sense and spirit of their duty; for on them, in a great measure, the service depends; they on their part, must exact a most strict compliance with their order from their men; and as their authority will be supported, must use it with discretion, and not gratify any personal resentment; on the contrary, must use the men kindly, still avoiding too much familiarity.' Picqueting, the usual punishment in dragoons, was not to be used in light dragoons; but instead double duty, confinement, bread and water, or public rebuke were to be substituted. Courts martial were only to be called on extraordinary occasions and 'whipping' used as seldom as possible. He adds: 'It is recommended to endeavour to pique the men in honour to behave well, and to make them sensible of their faults, without proceeding, if possible, to extremities. Vicious and ungovernable men must be made examples of, and punished with great severity; and turned out with infamy as unworthy of the corps.' A commanding officer of the present day would find it difficult to improve on discipline as taught and practised in the 21st Light Dragoons.

Because practically all the private soldiers enlisted for life, the regiment became for many of them their principal, and sometimes their only, home; so that they not only lived in it during their military service, but turned to it, even after they had been discharged, for help and advice when they were in difficulty or distress. Their parents and relatives, too, often approached the regiment for advice and assistance.[25]

N.C.O.s and men, of course, always wore uniform. In the infantry the most important item was the long red coat, worn over a waistcoat, and which was supposed to be adequate protection for its wearer in all weathers. No great coat was issued to the infrantryman in the eighteenth century. Battalion companies wore a tricorne felt hat which was rather liable to collapse after heavy rain into a shapeless soggy lump. The grenadier wore the tall mitre-shaped cap (the forerunner of the bearskin cap of the Foot Guards) which was originally adopted so that the musket could be easily slung to free the hands for arming and throwing grenades. The disposition of the soldier's equipment and the method of wearing it varied during the eighteenth century, but by 1775 the whole except the knapsack was suspended from two belts slung from each shoulder and crossing the chest. One of these carried the cartridge box which, with its thirty-six rounds of ammunition, rested behind the right buttock, and also the grey canvas haversack which contained the soldier's rations and was behind the cartridge box. From the other belt on the left side hung the bayonet, with above it the white metal water bottle. The knapsack, generally of white goatskin, was carried on the back by leather slings over each shoulder. It contained spare shirts, stockings, and shoes. The soldier might also be required to carry a hatchet and part of a tent, but if so, the number of days rations in the haversack had to be reduced so that the total weight on the man was not much above the generally accepted maximum of sixty pounds.[26]

It was of such troops that a not very friendly foreign critic of the British Army, commented on the British troops in Germany during the Seven Years War:

'The English appeared on the scene at the end of 1748. Their numbers increased from 8,500 to 22,600. These troops had all the good and bad points which they have shown throughout their history. An unquenchable spirit, great stubbornness in defence, bravery amounting often to recklessness in the attack, on the one hand. On the other hand they were difficult to discipline, quarrelsome in quarters, haughty in their attitude to other troops, extravagant with their forage and supplies, and very prone to sickness.'[27]

Chapter 5

REGIMENTAL TRAINING AND TACTICAL ORGANISATION

In 1702 pikemen finally disappeared from the British Army; not only were all regiments now equipped with bayonets but the socket bayonet, which allowed the musket to be fired with the bayonet fixed, was rapidly replacing the old plug bayonet, the handle of which was rammed into the barrel. The last remnant of the pikes was a small body of men, known as the 'piquet', and retained as the immediate guard of the regimental colours. They went; but their designation remained as a permanent part of the British Army's vocabulary to denote a guard of various kinds. By 1702, as well, the matchlock musket had been replaced by the much more efficient and quicker loading flintlock. These changes in weapons resulted (as changes in weapons always do) in new tactical formations; and the consequent battlefield organisation was to endure with comparatively little change until the re-equipment of the infantry with the rifled musket in the mid-nineteenth century.

Because the infantrymen of Marlborough's army all carried the same weapon, they could be formed in one identically armed body, and because the weapon was the quicker loading flintlock musket, they could be formed in fewer ranks. (Infantry armed with the matchlock had to form in a minimum of six ranks because it took such a long time to load. When the front rank had fired the men filed to the rear, forming a new rear rank, and the time spent by the remaining five ranks in firing was needed before they were ready to fire again. With the flintlock the reloading time was cut by half, so that the six ranks could be reduced to three.) In addition, because all the weapons along the front of a regiment were similar, instead of ranks firing in turn, sections of the front could fire in turn; and as the flintlock required less lateral room to reload and men did not need to file to the rear when the firing was no longer by ranks, the files could be closed up and a greater volume of fire delivered on a given frontage.

In the British Army it became the practice to divide a battalion front into tactical sub-units known as 'platoons'. In 1703 a battalion at war strength was marshalled on the battlefield into eighteen platoons (sixteen from the battalion companies and two from the grenadier company). These were organised into three 'firings', each of six platoons and distributed along the battalion front so that every third platoon fired together. Whilst one firing was delivering a volley, the other two firings would be reloading, and by this method each volley came from all parts of the regimental front. Sometimes the fire of the whole front rank was kept as 'fire in reserve' under the control of the colonel or lieutenant-colonel, whichever should be 'fighting the regiment', and who stood in the centre of the line with his drummer beside him. The company officers were allotted to the various firings.[1]

Infantry companies, except when on detached duty, were administrative and not tactical sub-units. This continued the practice which had been necessary when companies were composed of both pikemen and musketeers, because when a regiment formed for battle it was tactically necessary to form all the pikemen in the centre and the musketeers on each wing.

Success in the set-piece battle of continental warfare depended on being able to form and manoeuvre regiments in the rigid close order lines and columns required by the tactics of the times. The continual practice of close order drill was therefore the most important part of training. It trained the officers in the precise execution of the various complicated movements and the control of the firings, and it taught the private soldier to become so accustomed to implicit obedience of orders and to maintaining his place in the ranks, that under fire the instinct to do as he was told was stronger than the instinct to run away. (Modern practice testifies to the value of this eighteenth-century training, for in all regular armies the troops are exercised in close order drill for precisely the same reasons, even though the drill of the parade ground is no longer used in actual combat.)

Most individual training of the eighteenth-century soldier was in the handling of arms: the procedures for loading, presenting, and firing muskets, and the use of the bayonet. In most regiments live firing was carried out only enough to accustom the soldier to the recoil of his musket when the heavy bullet left the barrel and to overcome the natural nervousness of the recruit. Aiming was not considered so important, first because the smooth-bore flintlock was an extremely inaccurate weapon, and secondly because all firing was by volleys and individual shots were not therefore aimed. (Standing up, with the heavy musket levelled, the barrel is inevitably wavering over a considerable portion of the target area. To have any chance of hitting that target, a man must choose his moment to pull the trigger; in volley firing he cannot do so.) Robert Jackson, an army surgeon, wrote:[2] 'The firelock is an instrument of missile force. It is obvious that the force which is missile ought to be directed by aim, otherwise it will strike only by accident. It is evident that a person cannot take aim with any correctness unless he be free, independent, and clear of all encumbrances; and for this reason, there can be little dependence on the effect of fire that is given by platoons or volleys, and by word of command. Such explosions may intimidate by their noise; it is mere chance if they destroy by their impression.'

Marshal Saxe supported this judgement, for in his *Reveries* he wrote:[3] 'The firearm is not so terrible as one thinks; few men are killed in action by fire from the front. I have seen volleys that did not hit four men, and neither I nor anyone else saw an effect sufficient to have prevented us from continuing our advance and revenging ourselves with the bayonets and pursuing fire.' Marshal Saxe, the victor of Fontenoy, certainly did not lack personal experience!

So little importance was attached to target practice that in 1756 the allowance of ball ammunition for a regiment not on active service was limited to four balls annually for each man. In regiments that were keen on shooting, however, it was common to fix the butts against a bank so that the lead could be collected and recast in moulds by the regimental pioneers.[4]

Wolfe, when commanding a battalion under the special conditions imposed by the Scottish Highlands (which were somewhat akin to those encountered by the British-Indian Army on
the North-West Frontier), was very keen on shooting. On 7th
March he wrote:[5]

'We fire bullets continually, and have great need of them . . .
Marksmen are nowhere so necessary as in a mountainous country; besides, firing balls at objects teaches the soldier to level
incomparably, makes the recruit steady, and removes the
foolish apprehension that seizes young soldiers when they first
load their arms with bullets. We fire first singly, then by files,
1, 2, 3, or more, then by ranks, and lastly by platoons; and the
soldiers see the effects of their shot especially at a mark, or upon
water. We shoot obliquely, and in different situations of ground,
from heights downwards and contrarywise.'

In 1728, at the direction of George II, a drill book was pub-
ished entitled *The Exercise of the Horse, Dragoon, and Foot Forces.*
As far as the infantry were concerned, it established the company as a tactical sub-unit. This important reform allowed
decentralisation of command inside the regiment, which was
particularly needed in the British Army to meet the demands of
colonial and maritime warfare. In the much admired army of
Frederick the Great, which had no such commitments, the
platoon and company remained the tactical and administrative
sub-units respectively. During the Seven Years War the five
musketeer companies in a Prussian battalion were divided tactically into four divisions each of two platoons. The battalion
included a grenadier company as well, but this was always
taken away in war and grouped with other grenadier companies
to form grenadier battalions.[6]

Frederick the Great's organisation and methods exercised,
indeed, a profound influence on the British Army from the War
of the Austrian Succession up till the end of the century. Trans-
lations of the Prussian infantry regulations were published in
England in 1754 and both infantry and cavalry regulations in
1757. In 1756 the 1st Foot Guards were exercised for the first
time in the Prussian drill.[7] In 1785 there occurred the last

manoeuvres of the Prussian Army under the eye of Frederick the Great. They were viewed with astonishment by Lord Cornwallis, fresh from the loose formations and light infantry tactics of the American War of Independence. He wrote:[8] 'Their manoeuvres were such as the worst General in England would be hooted at for practising—two long lines coming up within six yards of one another and firing until they had no ammunition left; nothing could be more ridiculous.' Cornwallis's comment was to be justified when, twenty-one years later, Napoleon destroyed the Prussian Army at Jena and Auerstaedt. But another visitor to this review was much more impressed. Colonel David Dundas had not served in the American war and viewed with considerable disapproval the drill and tactics which had arisen from its lessons. Dundas went home from these manoeuvres and wrote a drill book based on what he had seen. In fact, a drill book was badly needed because there were wide differences between regiments in the drills and organisations that they had adopted to meet conditions in America. Dundas's book was accepted officially and issued under the authority of the Adjutant-General at the War Office on 1 June 1792 as *Rules and Regulations for the Formations, Field Exercise, and Movement of His Majesty's Forces*. This book, in spite of its unpromising origin, was in fact of great benefit to the Army, because the old drill books had been clearly outdated by the war in America and there was nothing to take their place. Although Dundas's drill, inspired as it was by the Prussians, was too rigid and formal, he laid down a thoroughly sound system of training and tactical formations that could be modified as circumstances showed necessary. Furthermore, although he had objected strongly to what he considered was the over emphasis on light infantry, there was a place for it in *Rules and Regulations*.

There was nothing new in the concept of mobile infantry operating largely as skirmishers, but the necessity of having such troops was brought heavily home to some British officers through the disaster suffered by the force under General Braddock at the Monongahela River on 9 June 1755 at the hands of an inferior force of French and Indians. Braddock's troops fought gallantly enough, but the stiff parade ground lines of Frederician tactics were mown down by Indians sheltering behind trees, whom the British soldiers never saw. As General Fuller says: 'If Frederick the Great himself had been in command of this British column, he could not have done more than Braddock did, and he would have suffered a similar fate.'[9]

Six months after the Monongahela, the 60th Royal Americans were raised under their famous leader, the Swiss Colonel Henry Bouquet, with the object of forming a regiment of regular troops capable of 'combining the qualities of the scout with the discipline of the trained soldier'. Bouquet's training instructions to achieve this object were a complete departure from those suited to the conventional warfare of the time. The soldiers were to be taught first to keep themselves clean and to dress in a soldier-like manner in order that they should be healthy and have pride in their personal appearance. They were then to be taught to walk well and afterwards to run, and were to be awarded small prizes for competition. The next stage was to train them to run in ranks in extended order, and to wheel in that formation so that they could fall unexpectedly on the flank of an enemy. They were to disperse and rally on given signals and be able to leap logs and ditches. Only when perfect in these exercises were young soldiers to be given their arms, and then they were to be taken through the various exercises again on all sorts of ground. They were to be taught to load and fire very quickly, standing, kneeling, or lying, and were to fire at a mark without a rest and were not to be allowed long in taking aim. Hunting and small prizes would soon make them expert marksmen. They were to learn to swim, pushing before them a small raft carrying their clothes and equipment. They were to be instructed in the use of snow-shoes and on how to entrench, make fascines, fell trees, saw planks, and build canoes, carts, ploughs, barrows, bridges, ovens, log-houses, etc. The men should take turns to go on hunting expeditions with their officers and remain out of camp some weeks, relying, except for a little flour, entirely on the game and fish which they shot and caught. Finally, great care was to be taken over purity, manners, order, and decency among the men.[10]

As can be seen from these instructions, Bouquet aimed at producing a keen, self-reliant, and individual fighter; a man trained to think and act on his own rather than fitting into the shoulder to shoulder movement of line and column. Robert Jackson quotes the case for the use of light troops as follows:[11] 'If an army is furnished with light troops, the General can oppose them to the enemy's; if the enemy is destitute of them, his cavalry and infantry will be continually harassed and fatigued in such a manner as to be very little able to act offensively.' Jackson was no doubt remembering how the infantry lines of the Allies were harassed by the skirmishers who preceded the columns of the French Revolutionary Armies during the Duke of York's campaign in Flanders.

In 1757 Lord Howe arrived in America with his Regiment, the 55th Foot. He set to work to learn forest warfare under Robert Rogers, the famous commander of the Rangers, an American Provincial irregular unit. He then turned the 55th into light infantry, making officers and men cut off the skirts of their long coats, cut their hair short, brown the barrels of their muskets, wear short leggings, and replace the useless hair dressings etc. in their kit by thirty pounds of meal.[12]

In 1758 the 80th Regiment was raised as 'Light Armed Foot', and was known, after the Colonel of the Regiment, as 'Gage's Light Infantry'. The 80th had only five companies, but these were on an especially high establishment. All ranks were clad in dark brown skirtless coats without lace. The officers were expected to wash their own clothes and carry knives and forks.[13] The men carried a lighter equipment and the barrels of their muskets were cut to carbine length and browned. (This 80th Foot was disbanded in 1764, and was not the 80th which became the South Staffordshire Regiment.)[14]

In 1759 the 90th Regiment was raised in Ireland as light infantry and despatched to America. In 1761 it fought at Belle Isle, off the French coast, and in 1762 at the siege of Havana. Also in 1759, the 85th Light Infantry was formed at Shrewsbury. It too fought at Belle Isle. Neither of these regiments had any connection with later ones of the same number.[15]

The culmination of this revolution in infantry tactics lay in Lord Amherst's battle drill and organisation of 1760. In 1758 at the siege of Louisburg, there being no light infantry regiments or companies present, Amherst withdrew 550 marksmen from the various regiments and formed them into a corps of light infantry. He raised further light infantry from the marksmen of battalions in 1759, directing that they should be formed in two ranks in place of three. Following the success of these troops, Amherst, in the following year, ordered the formation of special corps of light troops, modified the drill of the whole Army to suit the conditions of warfare in America, and instructed all regiments to fight in two ranks instead of three.[16]

Captain Nicholas Delacherois had a spell of light infantry service during the Havana campaign of 1762, and wrote: 'I engaged myself into a service called the Light Infantry, a company of 'em having been formed out of each regiment and the whole joined together. We are a corps of reserves and are employed upon all material services and are exposed to more fatigue than all the army.'[17]

At the peace of 1763 all the light infantry disappeared and the Army reverted to pure Frederician tactics. War lessons were derived from the fighting in Germany, whilst the campaigns in America were forgotten. However, in 1770 a company of light infantry was added to each battalion of the line; but it was too late. By this time commanding officers were so indoctrinated by Prussian tactical principles, that the light companies were used as a home for the worst characters in the regiment. There was so little training in light infantry functions that in 1774 General Howe (brother of Lord Howe, who was killed in America in 1758) was directed by George III to form a camp at Salisbury to instruct light infantry companies in a tactical drill that he had devised.[18]

In spite of Howe's efforts, the light infantry companies at the start of the American War of Independence were generally so in name only; hence the near disaster during the retreat from Lexington, through harassment of the column by a swarm of irregular skirmishers, who could easily have been kept out of range and dispersed by flanking parties of properly trained light infantry.

As in the Seven Years War, so in the War of American Independence, action took place largely in heavily wooded country, and this inevitably influenced tactical formations and methods. Ranks were again reduced from three to two, and sub-units, and even individuals, moved and fought with an independence which was quite foreign to the parade ground drill and close formations of European warfare. A contributory factor was the small part played by cavalry in America, so that many of their functions, including reconnaissance and protection, had to be undertaken by infantry. British officers returned to England convinced that the bayonet was of little use and the intelligent application of firepower of paramount importance. They believed that a third rank in the infantry line of battle was not needed because its fire was ineffective, and that the extra men made available by its abolition should be used to develop a greater frontage of fire.[19] Sir Eyre Coote had come to this same conclusion in India, for in December 1780 he directed that all units should in future parade in two ranks unless ordered otherwise.[20]

It was the very looseness of formation and the absence of any standard doctrine for infantry regiments that offended Dundas's tidy mind. His original book, which was the basis for *Rules and Regulations*, was published in 1788 under the title *The Principles of Military Movements*. In it he referred to this loose order as being largely due to the importance that light infantry had acquired, and continued:

'During the late war, their service was conspicuous, and their gallantry and exertions have met with universal applause. But instead of being considered as an accessory to the battalion, they have become the principal feature of our army, and have almost put grenadiers out of fashion. The showy exercise, the airy dress, the independent modes which they have adopted, have caught the minds of young officers, and made them imagine that these ought to be general and exclusive. The battalions, constantly drained of their best men, have been taught to undervalue themselves, almost to forget that on their steadiness and efforts the decision of events depends, and that light infantry, Jägers, marksmen, riflemen, etc. etc., vanish before the solid movements of the line.'[21]

So speaks Dundas, and one can almost visualise Frederick the Great breathing approval over his shoulder.

The *Rules and Regulations* laid down the formation of the company and the battalion as follows:

'The company is formed three deep . . . Each company is a platoon . . . Each company forms two subdivisions, and also four sections. But as sections should never be less than five files, it will happen, when the companies are weak, that they can only (for the purpose of march) form three sections . . .

'The battalion is in ten companies 1 Grenadier

8 Battalion

1 Light

Each company consists at present of 3 officers, 2 sergeants, 3 corporals, 1 drummer, 30 privates.' [Since five files in three ranks amounts to 15 men, it is apparent that in a company at such a low peacetime establishment could only provide three sections by forming in two ranks; and this is probably what happened.]

'The eight battalion companies will compose four grand divisions; eight companies or platoons; sixteen subdivisions; thirty-two sections, when sufficiently strong to be so subdivided, otherwise twenty-four for the purposes of march. The battalion is also divided into right and left wings. — When the battalion is on a war establishment, each company will be divided into two platoons.—When the ten companies are with the battalion, they may then, for the purposes of firing or deploying, be divided into five grand divisions.'

This reference to the occasional presence of all ten companies is interesting, because it implies that the two flank companies (the grenadier and light infantry companies) were normally removed in a theatre of war to form separate grenadier and light infantry battalions. In Frederick the Great's Prussian Army, grenadier companies were always removed from their regiments in wartime to form grenadier battalions, and this practice had been copied in other European armies, including the British. The idea was to use these elite companies of each regiment to form battalions of shock troops. In practice it was not always successful because such provisional units often lacked the *esprit de corps* of their parent regiments.

The *Rules and Regulations* are particularly interesting on the rates of marching, because they codify what were probably the normal marching paces throughout the eighteenth century. In the training of the recruit in these, Dundas writes that the instructor 'must allow for the weak capacity of the recruit; be patient, not vigorous, where endeavour and good-will are evidently not wanting . . . Recruits should not be kept too long at any particular part of their exercise, so as to fatigue or make them uneasy.' His description of the various steps in marching is as follows:

'*Ordinary Step*. The length of each pace is 30 inches, and the recruit must be taught to take 75 of these steps in a minute . . . The recruit must be carefully trained . . . to maintain it for a long period of time together, both in line and in column, and in rough as well as smooth ground . . . This is the slowest step which a recruit is taught, and is also applied to all movement on parade.' [This is the time of the present slow march in the British Army.]

'*The Quick Step*. . . . Quick time, which is 108 steps in a minute, each of 30 inches . . . This is the pace to be used in all filings or divisions from line into column, or from column into line; and by battalion columns of manoeuvre when independently changing position.—It may occasionally be used in the column of march of small bodies, when the route is smooth and no obstacles occur; but in the march in line of a considerable body it is not to be required, and very seldom in a column of manoeuvre; otherwise fatigue must arise to the soldier and more time will be lost in hurry and inaccuracy, than is attempted to be gained by quickness.' [In more recent days this has been the normal marching pace of the Regiment of Foot Guards.]

'*The Quickest Step*. The quickest time, or wheeling march, is 120 steps of 30 inches each . . . This is applied chiefly to the purpose of wheeling . . . In this time also should divisions double, and move up, when passing obstacles in line, or when in the column of march the front of divisions is increased or diminished.'

This is the normal marching pace today of British infantry, though it has been superseded as the 'quickest step' by the

140 paces in the minute of the Rifle and Light Infantry regiments.]

It will be observed that the 'Ordinary Step' was the normal pace of the infantry. This gives a marching rate of 2 m.p.h. without any halts, or, say, $1\frac{3}{4}$ m.p.h. with a ten-minute halt every hour, as compared with the standard speed of today, which is reckoned as $2\frac{1}{2}$ m.p.h. with a halt of ten minutes in each hour.

In the cavalry, as the century advanced, the dragoons increased in favour as compared with the horse. Then the light dragoons were formed to meet the same need in the cavalry for light troops, as there had been in the infantry.

The Duke of Cumberland, in about 1755 when he was Captain-General, produced some standing orders for heavy dragoons which throw some light on how that branch of the cavalry was used in action.[22] First of all, dragoon officers were to remember that they were dragoons and not horse, which meant that they must be prepared to march and attack on foot. Men's boots, therefore, were not to be encumbered with great spur leathers and chains which would impede their movement over obstacles. The Duke insisted on nimble and active horses, instead of the hairy-legged cart horses which were all too often bought. At dismounted reviews regiments of dragoons were to go through the Manual Exercise and Firings, taking the drill of the First Regiment of Guards as their model.

The Duke's instructions on the mounted attack are of particular interest, because they mark the end of an era during which cavalry charges were carefully controlled and carried out at a trot.[23]

A regiment advanced in column of squadrons with each squadron in line, in two ranks, and in close order. The object of the squadron formation was to give weight to the charge, because the rear rank pushed the front rank on when the enemy was encountered. However, the rear rank was not to be too close or it would be checked at the same time as the front rank and the impetus would be lost.

Officers commanding squadrons, in preparing for the charge, first ordered the men to draw swords, then to shorten their bridles, and finally to bring their swords to their thighs.

The initial advance was at a walk or slow trot, but the leading squadron commander was to select a point sixty yards from the enemy where he would order the squadron to break into a fast trot, or trot out. If he could manage it (though it was a difficult thing to do in action) he was to try to move his squadron obliquely to the right, so as to hit the left of the opposing squadron in superior force. If the enemy squadron was driven back, the squadron was to halt at a point previously selected by the squadron commander, and reform to await the counter-attack by the enemy's second line or the arrival of its own supporting squadron or squadrons. If the attack failed, the men were to break to the right and left to clear the front of the supporting squadrons.

In each squadron, some of the officers and the troop quarter-masters were left behind out of action in order to rally men driven back and bring them forward again to sustain the second line.

This is probably the way that cavalry attacks were carried out during the first half of the eighteenth century.

By the time of the Seven Years War the tactics of the cavalry charge had changed. At the battle of Warburg on 31 July 1760, for instance, 'The British cavalry, which had been approaching the French horse . . . at a sharp trot, now received successively the orders to gallop and charge.'[24] The change was probably due to Frederick the Great. The cavalry that his father left him, he says, was poor—heavy troopers on large horses which were far too slow. Frederick got rid of these and insisted on horses no larger than $15\frac{3}{4}$ hands for the horse and $15\frac{1}{2}$ for the dragoons. 'No Frisians,' he directed, 'which are too heavy, but rather horses from Holstein and also New Mark and East Prussia.' He reduced, too, the height required of the troopers, saying that a dragoon should be from 5 ft 5 in. to 5 ft 7 in. and a hussar between 5 ft 2 in., and 5 ft 5 in. As regards the cavalry attack he wrote:

'All movements of cavalry are swift. It can decide the fate of a battle in one instant. It must be used only at the right time . . . Cavalry cannot act on rocky ground or steep slopes. It attacks at the gallop; therefore the terrain must be smooth . . . When the general orders the attack, the line advances at a walk, quickens to a trot, and when two hundred paces from the enemy, the cavalry gives the horses free rein and gallops at full speed.'

Having driven the enemy cavalry from the field, part of the cavalry was detailed to prevent it from returning, whilst the remainder attacked the enemy infantry in the rear.[25] Here we see a transformation from the slow and carefully controlled mounted attack described by Cumberland to the torrent of men and horses in the charge advocated by Frederick.

Frederick's doctrine was embraced enthusiastically by the British cavalry, who put it into famous effect at the Battle of Warburg in the great charge led by the Marquis of Granby. (Granby lost his wig, and his bald head shining in the sun was the origin of the phrase 'going for it bald-headed'.)

It is conceivable that the British cavalry went from one extreme to another; for in 1779 Lord Amherst issued a general order forbidding 'the continued vehemence of the charge which served only to break up the squadrons', and he directed that cavalry should advance to the attack at the trot and only break into a gallop when they were within fifty yards of the enemy.[26]

Relations between man and horse received especial emphasis in the training of the cavalry soldier. Recruits were taught: 'to saddle, unsaddle, bridle and unbridle, and to put on their baggage with all the care and attention necessary to prevent sore backs. Love of the horses should be strongly inculcated from the beginning; and to keep it up, as few changes ought to be made as possible; which are easily prevented by well sizing men to their horses, when fit for the ranks, and not taking them from them afterwards, on account of either growing a little.' A few days would suffice for this instruction, during which the men were also to learn foot drill. They then went to the riding school, where the riding master was enjoined to, 'speak mildly to the recruits' in his instruction. 'The service of light dragoons requiring personal activity and address', the collective training of recruits was directed towards this end.[27]

Amongst the fighting arms, however, the greatest development during the century took place in the Artillery. It seems to have started with the foundation of the Royal Military Academy and the appointment of John Muller as headmaster. Such was his ability that when it was reorganised he was appointed Professor of Fortifications and Artillery, retaining this post until his retirement in 1766. In 1741 the artillery possessed only three marching companies, but from then on it was rapidly increased till there were twenty-four companies organised in two battalions at about the start of the Seven Years War, and by 1751 the number of companies had grown to thirty-one in three battalions. This reflected the increasing importance of artillery in mobile operations and the provision of ordnance light enough for the role.[28]

Muller, who exercised a great influence on the development of ordnance, wrote the first edition of his *Treatise of Artillery* in 1757, and the third and final edition appeared in 1780, four years before his death at the age of eighty-five. Muller believed that powder charges were too great and pieces too heavy, and he was a strong advocate of light field pieces in the British Army. In the 1747 campaign on the Continent, the British field artillery train consisted of six 12-pounder guns, six 9-pounder guns, fourteen 6-pounder guns, twenty-six 3-pounder guns, and two 8-inch howitzers. The wretched Flanders roads necessitated very large teams of horses—a 12-pounder had fifteen horses to pull it, a 9-pounder had eleven, a 6-pounder seven, a 3-pounder four, and an 8-inch howitzer five. From the 3-pounder were provided the two guns which accompanied each infantry battalion.

By the time of the Seven Years War, due to the efforts of Major-General William Belford (Commander Woolwich District in 1758) the Army had a light field piece in the short 6-pounder gun. It was this equipment that was used so effectively by the British light artillery brigades at Minden and when they charged with Granby's cavalry at Warburg. The short 6-pounder was known as 'General Belford's' gun. The gun limber at this period consisted only of an axletree, wheels and shafts, with a pintle (vertical spike) which went through the pintle hole in the trail transom of the gun carriage.[29]

The efficiency of the light artillery brigades on the Continent during the Seven Years War (where they seem to have performed very much like horse artillery) is the more remarkable in that the guns were drawn by horses with civilian drivers, generally hired for the campaign. The morale and *esprit de corps* amongst these drivers must have been excellent.

Although the artillery was organised in companies, these were administrative and not tactical units. Men and equipment were formed into an artillery train, which also included all the supporting vehicles. Guns and howitzers were grouped according to calibre and the tactical requirements into 'brigades', and officers and gunners were allotted accordingly. The two light brigades in the British Army in Germany during the Seven Years War each consisted of nine short 6-pounders. The gunners normally marched, but to make these brigades as mobile as they were, the gunners were probably mounted on spare horses from the artillery train. The site occupied by one or more brigades, or by a portion of a brigade, in action was termed a 'battery'.

The vehicles included in the artillery train are discussed in the next chapter.

Chapter 6

ADMINISTRATION IN THE FIELD

Compared with the present day, the needs in the field of an eighteenth-century army were simple. The staple food (and only official ration) was bread, usually supplemented by such meat, plodding along 'on the hoof', and other delicacies that the regimental sutler could provide; whilst corn, hay, and straw were required for that universal means of transport, whether in saddle or draught, the horse. Ammunition supply for the slow-firing ordnance and muskets of the period did not normally present much of a problem. But though wants were indeed simple, agriculture was still comparatively backward, and poor communications as well as shortage of transport made it difficult to transfer the agricultural products of one district to an army operating in another. Both the size of an army in the field and its movements depended, therefore, on the capacity of the region in which it was located to provide the food and forage necessary to sustain it.

It was normal to cease operations in the winter and go into quarters because the mainly unmetalled roads of the period were frequently in too poor a state during this season to permit movement of either supply vehicles or those of the artillery train. When spring arrived the start of operations might have to wait until there was sufficient green forage available to feed the horses, and the length of time during which an offensive could be conducted against the enemy often depended on how long the local resources of provisions and forage would last.[1]

The maximum use was made of navigable rivers because they did enable supplies and stores to be moved in bulk over long distances; but in winter the tow paths could be submerged by floods and ice could block all movement.

The chief administrative officer in a theatre of war was the commissary-general, a civilian appointed by and responsible to the Treasury. Over the years of the century there were many changes in the chain of responsibility and command, but the general principles remained the same.

During Marlborough's campaigns the commissioners of victualling in the United Kingdom were responsible for the supply of such food and forage as the Home Government provided and the commissaries-general were responsible for its distribution.[2] The main commodity was flour, which was drawn from the victualling board of the Navy, made up into bread at the field bakeries, paid for by the soldier out of his subsistence. The ration of bread was 1½ lb per man per day and a soldier paid 5d. for a 6-lb loaf. The bread was usually baked in towns at some distance from the camps and escorted to the front. During the siege of Tournai in 1709, for instance, bread was baked at Menin, and, when the enemy was besieging Mons after the battle of Malplaquet later in the same year, the bread was brought from Brussels as far as Enghien, where it was handed over to regimental transport. (The empty bread wagons were then used to carry back those wounded who were fit enough to stand the rough journey.)[3] The issue bread was known to the soldiers as 'ammunition bread'[4]—a term which has lasted in reference to Government issues up to our own time.

Later in the century large field bakeries were organised on the system inaugurated in the army of Frederick the Great. A field bakery was a very considerable and important affair. In 1762 a French column threatened the field bakery of Prince Ferdinand of Brunswick, commanding the army in Germany in British pay. The field bakery was on the move with an escort of only 400 infantry. Its loss would have resulted in very great administrative difficulties, and Ferdinand, learning of the threat, despatched a strong force with instructions to engage the enemy and protect the field bakery 'cost what it may'. This bakery had twenty-nine ovens, each of which could probably bake up to 1,000 6-lb loaves every twenty-four hours, or four days' rations for 1,000 men. The bakery was installed in its new site on 23 September 1762, well dug in and surrounded by field works for defence. It was divided into two sections, one for the British troops and the other for the German.[5]

Most other food was purchased out of the soldier's subsistence from the sutlers who accompanied the regiments in the field. Each regiment generally had one grand sutler with, under him, a petty sutler for each company of infantry or troop of cavalry. Sutlers were civilian contractors and it was the responsibility of the major of the regiment to ensure that their stocks were of good quality and that accurate weights and measures were used in their sale. By the campaigns of 1744–8 all sutlers were licensed. They were allowed forage for their horses, which were limited to fourteen in an infantry battalion, twelve in a dragoon regiment, and fifteen in a horse regiment. Vegetables were always an important item of the soldier's diet, to prevent scurvy, and if these were available in the local fields, parties of soldiers were sent out to gather them.[6] In 1781 there were no facilities for growing vegetables in Fort St Philip, Minorca. Scurvy struck the garrison, which eventually had to surrender because there were no men left fit to fight. The garrison of Gibraltar also suffered from the disease for the same reason, but they were saved by the arrival of a cargo of lemons from Algiers.[7]

Up till the end of the seventeenth century cheese had been an official issue, as well as bread, but it was removed from the ration in 1702.[8] However it appeared occasionally on special operations, apparently, because on the St Malo expedition in the Seven Years War the soldiers landed carrying 3 lb of biscuit and 1½ lb of cheese. After this had been consumed they were expected to live on the country.[9] As regards this latter, Todd describes a practice of allowing owners of large properties to escape being plundered or foraged by the payment of a considerable sum as ransom. The premises were then protected from foragers by a party of British troops assigned as a 'safe-guard'. The safe-guards were in their turn respected by French troops, who allowed them to re-embark under a flag of truce, so that it would appear that the practice was well-known and followed by other armies.[10]

Vegetables, of course, were not the only items of food which soldiers gathered. On 12 November 1761 the 12th Foot, Todd's regiment, were ordered into cantonments at Halfroth and Eimbeck—a miserable area with barely adequate accommodation for the three regiments sent there, the 12th, the 24th, and the 37th. Daily outposts and picquets were still required and a corporal was detailed to take a party of two pioneers from each regiment and go out with the picquets to cut wood and any other necessary work. When Todd was the pioneer corporal for this duty, it gave him and his men a chance to acquire a goose, three ducks, and two hens, which they presented to the officers of Todd's company. They were amply rewarded by these officers and some of their friends![11]

Fear of scurvy was probably the reason for a letter which, towards the end of 1760, Ferdinand wrote to the Marquess of Granby, in his capacity as representative of the Treasury, instructing him to provide money for an extra allowance for each man of lard, beans, groats, peas, and rice.[12] A perhaps more welcome addition is described by Todd. In 1761 units had to move often because they had consumed all the local supplies, and the sutlers were failing to keep up with the troops. In about September the Marquess of Granby recommended that commanding officers should take on a 'Geneva cart' which should keep constantly with each regiment and supply the men at a moderate price; the contractor being provided with rations and forage. Todd commended this as a 'reasonable relief'.[13] (Perhaps in this vehicle lies the origin of the modern military slang term of 'gin palace'!)

The commissary-general in the field was also responsible for transport, which included not only the vehicles but also horses and drivers. Most of these were obtained by local requisitioning or hiring. Once hired, however, they came under the jurisdiction of the wagon-master-general, who was an army officer responsible to the commander-in-chief and not to the commissary-general.[14] The type of transport varied, of course, considerably because it was made up mostly from the carts and wagons used by the farmers and traders in the theatre of operations. Much use, too, was made of pack animals, particularly in Flanders where most of the few roads were exceptionally bad.[15]

Transport for baggage was a regimental responsibility, and

each regiment had its own wagon-master who might be an officer or a N.C.O. These wagon-masters received their orders daily from the wagon-master-general.[16] The regimental baggage moved in the army baggage column, but in Marlborough's campaigns a commanding officer was allowed to retain two of his wagons to move with the regiment. The baggage column escort was under the command of the wagon-master-general and was usually composed of a corporal and one man from each troop of cavalry in the force. On the march the sutlers followed the baggage column which in turn followed the train.[17] In the operations leading up to the battle of Minden in the Seven Years War a regiment was allowed two wagons for its captains, one for its subalterns, two for regimental headquarters, and two for each squadron or company. These wagons were generally used for tents and blankets. Every squadron had a forage cart and there are references to farriers' carts, which were presumably the travelling forges. Generals had their 'chaises' or coaches and other officers had their bat horses (referred to at the time as 'bass' horses—a peculiar anglicism for the French *cheval de bât*, or pack-horse). It was forbidden to employ soldiers to lead these horses.[18] Todd records that at one time much baggage was lost owing to 'the excessive bad roads'; the wagon-drivers abandoning their wagons and going off on their horses when the enemy drew near.

Provision of the train for the Army was the responsibility of the board of ordnance. The train was composed of artillery equipments, spare gun carriages, ammunition carts and wagons, pontoons and their carriages, wagons for artillery and engineer stores, and specialist vehicles. It was under the command of a controller, who had under him wagon-masters, commissaries of draught horses, and conductors. The wagon-master-general was responsible to the lieutenant-general of the ordnance for the movement of the train.[19] The specialist vehicles included a 'tumbril', a two-wheeled cart used to carry the tools of the pioneers and miners, and also the money for the Army; a two-wheeled powder cart with shot lockers and an oilcloth roof to stop damp reaching the powder, of which each cart could stow four barrels; an ammunition wagon which had four wheels and was lined round the inside with basket work, so that it could be used also to carry bread; a travelling forge which had two wheels (though later models were being made with four wheels), fitted with a fireplace, iron hearth, trough for water, bellows, and tool boxes; and a four-wheeled block carriage, used to transport guns which were too heavy to be moved on the march on their own carriages.[20]

Of artillery vehicles, Muller writes:

'All carriages made use of in the artillery have shafts; and to prevent the great length of those that require a great number of horses, the rule is to draw by pairs abreast, which is an absurdity nowhere else to be met with; for when the road is frequented by carriages drawn by two horses abreast, there is always a ridge in the middle, which the shaft-horse, endeavouring to avoid, treads on one side, whereby the wheels catch against the ruts and stop the carriage; and when the fore-horses bring them back, he treads on the other side, where the same happens again; so that the shaft-horse, instead of being useful any other ways than to support the shafts, becomes a hindrance to the rest . . .

'The *Span*, or interval between the wheels, varies in different countries; even every county in England observes a different width, which is very inconvenient for those who travel in carriages. The artillery carriages are made like those in *Flanders*, which is four feet eight inches.'[21]

On the mainly unmetalled roads of the period the distance apart of the ruts made by the wheels would affect considerably the convenience and comfort of travelling. As every English county had its own standard width between the wheels of carts and carriages (i.e., track gauge) there would probably be some reluctance to drive beyond the county boundary. The Army could not, of course, be restricted in its movements by any such inconvenience; but there would be advantages in being able to use the 'rut gauge' of the country in which it did most of its fighting. It is likely that English makers of road wagons and carriages became impressed with the advantages of a common gauge, and so the distance between the wheels of the Flanders wagons became, through this eighteenth-century decision of the board of ordnance, the gauge of railways, first in England and then in most countries of the world.

Muller gives the composition and order of march of the artillery train during the short campaign in Flanders of April and May 1748.[22] The train was preceded by a strong body of infantry provided by the Army as 'guard'. The first element of the train was a company of miners 'with their tumbrel of tools drawn by 2 horses', and they were followed by the forward part of the train's own escort, the 'regiments of artillery front guard'. Next came the carriage in which were mounted the Artillery's kettle drums, drawn by four horses and accompanied by two mounted trumpeters. Then came the flag gun, a 15-pounder on which was displayed the Union flag of the artillery headquarters. Five more 15-pounders followed each drawn by fifteen horses, though the flag gun was allotted seventeen. Behind these guns came their eleven store wagons, each pulled by three horses. Then came in order, each followed by varying numbers of store wagons, six 9-pounders each drawn by eleven horses, fourteen long 6-pounders each with seven horses, two howitzers each with five horses, and six short 6-pounders with only two horses each. Six small mortars came next, carried in four wagons with their stores. The tail of these ordnance equipments was brought up by spare gun carriages for each type of piece. After the ordnance there followed twenty ammunition carts, nineteen wagons with small arms cartridges, thirty wagons with powder, thirty wagons with small arms shot, twenty-five wagons with entrenching tools, six wagons for artificers, and thirty-two baggage wagons. Each wagon was pulled by three horses except nine of the baggage wagons which had four horses and were therefore probably pole and not shaft draught. All the above groups, except the baggage, included spare wagons, in addition to the numbers given, because casualties on the Flanders roads were heavy. The last vehicles were thirty pontoons in their carriages, followed by three spare, and each pulled by seven horses. Behind these came the artillery rear guard and then the rear guard of infantry provided by the Army. Muller adds:

'It must be observed that there are parties of gunners and matrosses marching with the guns; there are likewise some parties of pioneers interspersed here and there to mend the roads when they are spoiled by the fore carriages. There was then 1,415 horses employed in this campaign, 32 guns, 2 howitzes, 6 small mortars, 244 wagons and carts, and lastly 30 pontoons; 20 of these last are esteemed sufficient for any part of Flanders, because there is no river in this country that requires more to make a bridge over it.'

The army of the eighteenth century depended as much on the horse for its mobile arm and its transport as does that of today on the armoured fighting vehicle and motor truck respectively; and the acquisition, care and feeding of the horses were not the least of its problems. The average farm horse of any country was suitable for draught, but not all horses were suitable for the saddle, and the type preferred varied during the century.

During the reign of William III many Dutchmen settled in the Fens of East Anglia, which were so much like their own country, and they imported the heavy black horses bred in Flanders and the Netherlands for the work of draining them. The native English 'Great Horse', the ancestor of the Shire, was also predominantly black and was in later times called the 'Black Horse'. In this same period a considerable number of the black Oldenburg coach horses and mares were also imported. Breeders, therefore, had a large number of black stallions to breed from and black became the colour considered correct for the horses of the British cavalry. There were, of course, exceptions such as the Queen's Bays and the Royal Scots Greys.

During the reigns of George I and George II most regiments of horse and dragoons were mounted on black horses; the latter on horses not over 15 hands and the former on horses of 15 hands 1 inch and over. In 1745 the first Light Horse, Kingston's, were raised and they departed from the established custom by riding much lighter horses of various colours. The following year the regiment was disbanded, but was immediately reformed as one of heavy dragoons. As perhaps a reminder of its former state, however, it was mounted on chestnut, instead of black, horses which were probably lighter than the normal dragoon type.

In 1753 there was a report on 'the 1st or Royal Dragoons who are well mounted on black horses . . . The horses are of a lower size and lighter sort than other Dragoons with a good deal of saddle horse in them; quarters not so heavy as the common run of black horses.' This implies that the usual cavalry mounts of the time were of the heavy carriage-horse type, rather than the contemporary civilian saddle-horse. They may well have been a mixture of Shires, Flemish, and Oldenburgs. Weight-carrying horses were indeed needed in the cavalry. From about 1758 troopers had valises to carry their kit and part of their equipment, and these were fastened behind the saddle. As forage was also carried here, a horse could be heavily loaded.[23]

The warrant authorising the raising of light troops for regiments of dragoon guards and dragoons directed that the horses were to be '14 hands 3 inches and not under. They are to be well-turned nimble road horses as nigh to the colour of the horses of the Regiment as can be got.'[24] This was a type of horse new to the cavalry—the short-backed cob which was in widespread use by business men and others for general road travel. There would be plenty of them available for purchase by the Army.[25]

It was on this same type of horse that the first regiments of light dragoons were mounted when they were raised in 1759 and 1760. They were not black, nor were they of any one colour throughout a regiment. From about 1760, indeed, the black horse gradually ceased to be the only mount in regiments of dragoon guards and dragoons. Eventually only the Household Cavalry were mounted exclusively on black horses. As this is still the rule in those regiments today, and as the other cavalry regiments have lost their horses, one could perhaps say that once again the black horse is the only British cavalry mount!

The black horse was replaced in dragoon guards and dragoons by the Hackney, which in the mid-eighteenth century was being developed as a road saddle horse and was the sort of weight-carrier that the heavy cavalry needed. Light cavalry continued to ride the smaller horses.[26] Some regiments had the horses in each troop of the same colour. In 1779, for instance, the 15th Light Dragoons had one troop mounted on chestnut horses, one on brown, one on bay, and two on horses that were mostly bay. The record of the remaining troops is missing. There was a grey horse in the chestnut troop and also in one of the bay troops, whilst the black troop had one brown horse.[27]

The horses furnished by contractors for the artillery and those hired or requisitioned for the transport of the Army were generally of the farm horse type, which has changed little through the ages. It was used both in draught and as a pack or 'bat' horse. Pack animals were common in many countries, where routes between smaller towns and villages were tracks, unusable by wheeled vehicles. They were often ponies, rather than horses, but quite suitable for army use.

Horses presented a particular difficulty in the American War of Independence. They were none too plentiful in the thinly populated colonies and there were difficulties in keeping them healthy, or even alive, during the long transatlantic voyage. This was the main reason why so few cavalry were sent from Great Britain. After the battle of Long Island, Howe managed to buy 100 horses from loyalist farmers for the artillery train, and he hired eighty two-horse wagons with their teams and drivers for general transport;[28] but these were all too few in relation to his needs, and lack of transport was a continual handicap during the operations in North America.

It was often more difficult to provide forage for horses than it was to supply food to the men. Forage was even more dependent on local procurement because the chronic shortage of transport for the troops' bread resulted in few or no vehicles being available for the carriage of oats and hay.

During the campaign in Germany during the Seven Years War, Prince Ferdinand, on 29 September 1760, wrote to Frederick the Great saying that the country in which he was operating had become a veritable desert as far as forage was concerned, and that there were no straw, hay, corn, or carts. He added that his greatest obstacle was always the lack of forage, and that as he lived only from day to day he would not be able to procure enough supplies for an operation.[29] Ferdinand's position was in fact very similar to that of Rommel, handicapped during the Alamein operations by acute shortage of that modern forage, petrol.[30]

Shortage of transport affected seriously the distribution of rations to the troops. In March 1761 carts and wagons were unobtainable from local resources, and those which the Army already had were so badly delayed in movement by the appalling condition of the roads, that the turn-round of supply columns after discharging their loads was held up, making the shortage of vehicles worse. In addition, flooding had made the River Weser unnavigable, so throwing a further burden on to the roads. Almost inevitably keen regimental wagon-masters made matters still worse by retaining the wagons that brought their supplies and refusing to give them up. The depot at Carlshafen had plenty of supplies, stores and ammunition, but no vehicles to transport them.[31]

The commissariat arrangements in Ferdinand's army were predominantly British, and under a British commissary-general, because his troops from Hesse, Brunswick, Bückeburg, and Saxe-Gotha were maintained at British expense, and his Hanoverian soldiers were, of course, subjects of the King of Great Britain in his capacity of Elector of Hanover. Ferdinand therefore stated his requirements to the commissary-general, who was responsible for meeting them within the financial limits allowed him by the British Treasury. Unfortunately these limits were often too low to cover the costs of Ferdinand's needs, and the commissary-general had to apply for supplementary grants which inevitably entailed delays.[32]

These were not the only troubles. The commissariat was grossly under-staffed, and the commissaries were consequently too overworked to do their job efficiently. Frederick Halsey, who went to Germany in June 1760 as commissary of accounts under the Commissary-General Michael Hatton, found his official life governed by three great wants: want of bread, want of forage, and want of wagons.[33]

A typical instance shows how little Ferdinand understood the difficulties of the commissariat. He wrote to Halsey about the victualling of the strategically important depot at Munster. The bourgeois inhabitants were, he said, to be ordered to provide themselves with food for four months. Those not able to do so were to leave the town. By this means, he explained, there would be a good stock of provisions on which the garrison of Munster would be able to depend if the town was besieged. The commissariat was to supply the flour and the Chancellery of Hanover was to provide whatever stores were necessary for the ten battalions he proposed to quarter there. The commissariat was also to supply salt and arrange for the surrounding countryside to provide 250 cattle for salt beef and the salt in which to preserve it. All other provisions for the garrison were to be taken from the countryside. In return for these contributions, Ferdinand ordered the relaxation of an inquiry into sums paid for winter quarters in 1760–61. Whatever the countryside could not provide was to be made good by the commissariat. In addition a note was to be taken of all provisions in the hands of the merchants of Munster so that they could be requisitioned in the event of a siege in return for receipts.

This was an almost impossible order for Halsey to comply with. If he arranged for inventories of tradesmens' stocks, the purpose would be obvious and the tradesmen would promptly sell as much as they could and as quickly as possible. And how was he going to be able to persuade people to spend money on large stocks of food which could be taken from them to feed the soldiers? Further, if the countryside could not provide their quota of provisions, Halsey had no other source on which he could draw. Ferdinand, however, thought that he had, as the following letter from him to Halsey shows: 'I have learned with great displeasure that the greater part of the salt meat has been spoiled ... we must therefore have recourse to the Commissariat, and I request you, Monsieur, to obtain for us, for the needs of the Munster garrison, 200 more cattle than were already commanded.'[34]

Ferdinand's worries over forage were expressed in two letters from Hatton to Halsey, in which he said: ''Tis not possible to describe to you how uneasy the Duke is at the Hay and Straw coming in so slow', and 'I can't think how to get more, for the country is absolutely eat up.'[35]

In May 1760, in an attempt to cut down the inevitable delays in obtaining supplementary grants, the Marquess of Granby, as commander of the British troops, was authorised to approve such grants, and a British colonel was appointed to his staff to deal with these matters and to coordinate arrangements with the commissariat. But the colonel had not the knowledge for the job and there was little improvement.[36]

Apart from their troubles over food and forage, the British troops often suffered considerable discomfort in their winter accommodation. Todd says[37] that their tents were thin and cold and let the rain in. Accordingly, when they were under canvas in cold and wet weather they 'hutted' and 'hurdled' them. Good shelter for cooking places was provided by small trees 'set up over end with their tops fastened together and the thick ends well out at root'; and trenches were dug to 'keep the men's backs warm when cooking'. Todd, as pioneer corporal, fell foul of the quartermaster of the 12th Foot, Lieutenant Barlow, who was dissatisfied with him for not 'bowing' (i.e. screening with boughs) the officers' 'necessary' adequately, and placed him under arrest. Todd insisted on being brought before the major. He then asked to be relieved of his duties as pioneer corporal and be allowed to return to his company. The major would not hear of it, whilst other officers declared that the 'necessary' had been 'bowed' more than adequately.

What it was like to march through rain and mud on the unmetalled roads is described by Matthew Bishop of Marlborough's army. He writes:[38]

'I always thought myself indefatigable till Swiney's Day in March, and then, I must needs own, I began to be leg weary. But there was cause enough to complain. I remember the greatest part of the Welch Fusiliers marched without shoes. The excessive rain that accompanied us that day, had put all the infantry into so great disorder, that it rendered them unfit for marching for a considerable time after. It had no less effect upon the cavalry; for many were obliged to dismount and lead their horses in their hands. Then I began to think our station was preferable to theirs; though our Regiment had orders to march a league beyond the rest of the Army, in order to cover the General's quarters. After we had received these orders, there were not above a hundred men to bring up the Colours of our Regiment and necessity obliged me to mount the quarter guard. But you must needs think it was very uncomfortable after I had borne the severity of the weather, to stand with not so much as one dry thread upon my back, and wet garments that struck excessively cold. But I nourished the inward man by drinking brandy.'

One can well imagine the toil and discomfort of trudging wearily along through deep mud in heavy rain—mud which so dragged at the men's shoes that the Welch Fusiliers preferred to march without them and which so hampered the horses that the cavalrymen had to dismount and, in their long boots, lead them through it.

The peculiar conditions of warfare in India presented administrative difficulties that were perhaps even greater than those experienced in Europe, but in almost laughable contrast. John Shipp, who served under Sir Eyre Coote as a baggage master, describes the vast number of non-combatants and animals which followed Coote's army in the field. He cites a force of 8,000 men which was accompanied by approximately 80,000 men, women, and children, consisting of the families and relations of the sepoys, animal drivers, traders, dancing girls, prostitutes, and servants and attendants of various kinds. The British officers of the Company's Army had, from the latest joined subaltern upwards, expected in the field the luxuries that were part of the compensation for the all too short expectation of life which service in the employment of the Honourable East India Company afforded. So that every officer had up to twenty servants to deal with his tent, baggage, and provisions, as well as a groom and a grass cutter for his horse; and there might be another 100 servants for the regimental mess. The animals for this force included 50 elephants, 600 camels, 11,000 bullocks, horses, and ponies, and 500 goats, sheep, and dogs.[39] Practically all draught was by slow plodding oxen, of which in 1780 there were twelve pairs to a 24-pounder gun, nine to a 18-pounder, six to a 12-pounder, seven to a wagon, and five to a tumbrel.[40]

At the same time that Coote was fighting in India, yet another type of administrative problem was being posed by the war in America against the rebellious colonies. At the start of the War of American Independence it was anticipated that, as in Europe, most provisions could be obtained in the theatre of war. It was soon found, however, that the colonies were too sparsely populated for adequate supplies to be gathered from the country in

the immediate neighbourhood of the Army, and there was too
much hostility or indifference amongst the inhabitants to have
provisions, as in the Seven Years War, transported from farther
afield. The bulk of the Army's supplies, therefore, had to be
shipped from the British Isles. Cork in southern Ireland was the
main base and food depot, and to this town provisions
were transported from all parts of the British Isles. At Cork
the provisions were inspected and then loaded on to the
transports, which sailed with their cargoes to sub-depots
at Montreal, Quebec, Halifax, New York, Philadelphia,
Charleston, and Savannah, as well as to St Lucia for the West
Indies.[41]

Flour was the main food item, and from this bread was baked
either at the sub-depots or by the troops on the march. Apart
from flour, the principal commodities were beef, pork, pease,
rice, butter, and salt. As a prevention against scurvy there were
issues of sauerkraut, spruce beer, and vinegar. Rum was a
regular issue and the soldier in the field received the very hand-
some ration of $1\frac{1}{3}$ to $1\frac{1}{2}$ gills a day, with an additional gill during
inclement weather or on especially hard duty. The food supplied
to the soldier was often, however, of extremely poor quality, and
was the subject of continual complaints by commissaries-general
to the Treasury. Some of the responsibility for this was apparently attributable to unscrupulous contractors together with
lax, or perhaps corrupt, inspection; but careless stowage and the
lengthy Atlantic passage probably spoilt many provisions which
were perfectly satisfactory when shipped. Owing to its bulk,
forage was mostly obtained in America, but the difficulty of
gathering it frequently hampered operations and influenced the
disposition of the troops.[42]

In addition to his other commitments, all medicines and
medical stores were consigned to the commissary-general and
issued by him to the hospitals and the regimental surgeons.
Until 1747 medical supplies came from the Apothecaries' Hall;
but in that year George II granted to a private individual the
monopoly of the supply of medicines to the Army, with the right
to pass on this monopoly to his heirs.[43] The medical staff of the
Army consisted of surgeons, hospital mates, and apothecaries.
Some of these were good, but as qualifications were not regularly

tested, some of them were very inefficient indeed.[44] The soldiers, however, suffered far more from the shortage of medical officers rather than from their deficiencies.

After the battle of Wandewash in 1760 Coote was distressed at the condition of the wounded, both of his own army and that of his opponent, Lally. He wrote to Madras:

'Really the scene is now dreadful to see. Such a multitude of poor objects, and not in my power to give them the least assistance for want of every one necessary requisite for an hospital. I make no doubt upon the representation you will do everything humanity can direct. If it is possible to send surgeons and proper people from Madras to attend the wounded here who are very numerous, you may by that means save the lives of many gallant men, several of whom have not been dressed since the day of the action. As I shall be obliged to carry away some surgeons out of the few, numbers must lose their lives.'

However, in response to a request from Coote to Lally for medical aid, the Irish commander of the French forces sent two surgeons to the British camp. At about the same time a Mr Briggs was appointed surgeon-general and placed in charge of the medical departments of both the King's and the Company's troops.[45]

By modern standards medical knowledge was very limited. There were, of course, no anaesthetics, so that amputations and other major surgical operations could only be eased for the unfortunate patients by giving them plenty of brandy to drink. Orderlies then held them steady until the surgeon had completed his task. But losses from sickness were far greater than those from enemy action. In Prince Ferdinand's army winter privations and insufficient food led to the hospitals being filled with the sick, and the medical staff were too few to look after them properly.[46] The West Indies posed the greatest problem in health, because the appalling sickness and death rate from yellow fever often reduced regiments stationed there to mere skeletons of their establishments. Nevertheless, medical science, towards the latter part of the century, had discovered a relationship between the lush vegetation of the lowlands with the disease and had also discovered the beneficial effects of quinine. At St Lucia in 1779 General Grant was relying absolutely on quinine to combat the fever amongst his troops. On 4 April he wrote to Lord George Germaine: 'Without bark we should not have a man fit for duty in three months; but the hospital at New York would not give so much as I looked for.' The following year a hurricane levelled the tropical forest in St Lucia and converted it from a deadly station into one that was comparatively healthy.[47]

There was no organisation to look after the health of the horses. Treatment of their ailments was entrusted to the farriers, who had acquired and passed on to each other various remedies from practical experience.

The treatment of prisoners of war in the eighteenth century was far in advance of any period before or since, including our own day. During the Seven Years War an agreement was signed between the British and French Governments in 1759 which provided for the exchange or ransom of all prisoners of war within fifteen days of capture. Exchanges were to be in equal numbers, rank for rank; but if this was not possible different ranks and numbers could be handed over provided that ransoms were paid for the differences. A scale of ransoms was arranged which ran from £2,500 for a field marshal to 8 shillings for a dragoon or private of the infantry of the line. Certain categories were exempt from being made prisoners at all, including chaplains, surgeons, civil officials, provost staff, and personal servants. Every prisoner was to be given a ration of bread and a cash payment of about 6d. a day and was to have fresh straw for bedding every eighth day. An officer or commissary with a passport was to be allowed to stay with prisoners and look after their interests, and each prisoner was to be allowed to send an open letter giving news of his capture. Sick and wounded prisoners were to be allowed the attention of doctors and surgeons of their own army, who, with the necessary passports, could stay with them. On the whole these very humane arrangements were observed.[48]

The Army was generally accompanied in the field by some of the wives of the rank and file. The number permitted was strictly limited. During the campaigns in America of 1776 and

1777, General Sir William Howe allowed a maximum of six wives for each infantry company. These, as well as their children, were fed and clothed out of the public stores. Nurses were sometimes recruited from them to look after the sick and wounded of the regiment.[49]

Chapter 7

COMMAND AND STAFF
IN THE FIELD

During Marlborough's campaigns the infantry were grouped more or less permanently into brigades of generally four or more battalions. Cavalry regiments remained independent, but were brigaded as required. There was no permanent higher headquarters between the brigade and the commander-in-chief in the field, but a number of brigades might be, and generally were, placed under the command of a general officer for a particular operation. There were normally several generals available who were not assigned to any regular command or duty. In the Blenheim campaign, for instance, Marlborough had at his disposal in the British contingent his younger brother Charles Churchill as 'general of foot', Lieutenant-General Lord Cutts, Lieutenant-General Richard Ingoldsby, Lieutenant-General Henry Lumley, Lieutenant-General Lord Orkney, Major-General the Honourable Charles Ross, and two other major-generals. Brigadier-General Lord Cadogan was his quartermaster-general and Brigadier-General Thomas Meredith his adjutant-general.

The army under Marlborough's command at Blenheim consisted of ninety squadrons of cavalry and fifty-one battalions of infantry, made up of British, Hanoverian, Hessian, Danish, and Dutch units. Of these, nineteen squadrons and fourteen battalions were British. There were seven British cavalry regiments, five of horse and two of dragoons; Lumley commanded the horse and Ross the two regiments of dragoons. The British infantry were in three brigades commanded, respectively, by Brigadier-General Archibald Row, Brigadier-

General Frederick Hamilton, and Brigadier-General James Ferguson.

At the Battle of Blenheim, Cutts was placed in command of the force to assault the village of that name, and he had for the task two brigades of British infantry, one Hessian infantry brigade, and one Hanoverian infantry brigade. In his centre Marlborough had a line of infantry, behind which were two lines of cavalry, and in rear of the cavalry a second line of infantry in support. Churchill commanded the first line of infantry and Orkney the support line, which included the remaining British infantry brigade. Ingoldsby and the other major-generals were probably used on such tasks as representing the commander-in-chief for orders and liaison in different parts of the widespread battlefield, and also for bringing information to him on the progress of events.[1]

The brigade remained the highest permanent formation in the field until the end of the century, but whenever an army was large the grouping of brigades into formations of all arms for any operation gradually became the normal practice; a practice which foreshadowed the creation of the permanent divisions which fought under Wellington in the Peninsula. Rather strangely, there was no such grouping of brigades in the army of Frederick the Great. The King himself always exercised a strong central control over the main body of his army in the field. He imposed a rigidity, indeed, which needed genius to direct it; and when that genius was removed the stiff inflexible Prussian Army was defeated by the very flexible corps and divisions of the Army of Napoleon. In the British-paid army in Germany commanded by Prince Ferdinand of Brunswick matters were quite differently arranged. The grouping of brigades into larger subordinate formations was normal; perhaps due originally to the different national contingents which composed the force, and the resulting number of senior commanders. National contingents did not, however, necessarily remain under their own national command, for the higher formations were often composed of brigades and regiments from different states or nations. At the battle of Vellinghausen on 15/16 July 1761, for instance, Prince Ferdinand's army consisted of formations commanded and composed as follows:

1. The Erbrinz of Brunswick—four large 'brigade groups' of Hanoverian infantry, cavalry, and artillery.
2. Lieutenant-General Conway—two British infantry brigades and one British cavalry brigade.
3. Lieutenant-General Howard—an infantry brigade and a cavalry brigade, both British, and a 'brigade group' of two German infantry battalions and British and Hanoverian artillery.
4. Lieutenant-General Prinz von Anhalt—three infantry brigades (Hessian, Brunswick, and Hanoverian) and a British cavalry brigade.
5. Lieutenant-General von Watgineau—two infantry brigades of Hessian, Brunswick, and Hanoverian troops, and a Hanoverian and Brunswick cavalry brigade.
6. Lieutenant-General the Marquis of Granby—a number of infantry and cavalry brigades and some artillery composed of British, Brunswick, Hanoverian, Prussian, Hessian, and British 'foreign legion' troops.

These major subordinate commands were not permanently organised as such, but indeed altered at every operation. They do not seem to have had any definite collective name, but were sometimes referred to as 'columns' and sometimes as 'corps'.[2]

This practice of grouping brigades as required was resumed in the American War of Independence. General Sir William Howe, when his army landed on Staten Island (opposite Long Island), organised it into seven brigades, a reserve of eight battalions, and a 'light force' of three battalions of light companies and two regiments of light dragoons. For the attack on the American forces on Long Island these troops were grouped into three divisions of varying strengths and one independent brigade. At the battle of Brandywine in 1777, Howe's army consisted of two columns—Cornwallis's and Knyphausen's—each composed of two infantry brigades and 'divisional troops' of infantry, light cavalry, and artillery.

Marlborough's quartermaster-general and adjutant-general have been mentioned, and these, with varying numbers of subordinates, were the principal staff officers throughout the eighteenth century. The commander-in-chief in the field did his own operational planning and issued his orders either verbally to his major subordinate commanders, or in writing through his A.D.C.s, or both. His secretary, a civilian, was responsible for committing these orders to writing. However, the quartermaster-general was responsible for the detailed arrangements of all the operational moves necessary to implement the commander-in-chief's plan. He was also responsible for supply, transport, and other logistical planning, though the commissariat-general had to find the food, forage, and vehicles to meet the 'Q' plans. All matters concerning personnel, including discipline, came within the province of the adjutant-general, and to assist him in this latter function he had under him the provost-marshal and, for legal matters, the judge advocate-general.

At brigade headquarters the quartermaster-general and adjutant-general duties were combined in the brigade major. On the regimental or battalion headquarters the adjutant dealt with adjutant-general matters and those quartermaster-general matters which affected operations. Other 'Q' business was the responsibility of the quartermaster.

Marlborough, unlike most generals of the eighteenth century, used his quartermaster-general in many ways as a chief of staff. The Earl of Cadogan, the Quartermaster-General, was, however, a very remarkable man. He could see into his Commander-in-Chief's mind and knew in any circumstance the action which should be taken to further the latter's intentions, and the type of information which Marlborough would need in order to plan. Because of his ability in both these directions, Marlborough often placed him actually in command of the advanced guard of the army. He was so placed at Ramillies in order that he could reconnoitre and report back to Marlborough the position of the French and the nature and possibilities of the terrain. After battle had been joined he conveyed the Commander-in-Chief's instructions and intentions to the major subordinate commanders. At Oudenarde he commanded the advanced guard again and conducted the encounter battle which enabled Marlborough to develop his plan.[3] In all Marlborough's battles he was well forward during the approach to contact, sometimes accompanying the cavalry screen which was probing the enemy's positions; searching for information as to their extent and nature, and scanning the ground for suitable areas for deployment and likely lines of attack.[4]

Adam de Cardonnel, Marlborough's Secretary, was another unusual and invaluable member of his staff. He dealt with all Marlborough's correspondence on both military and political affairs. This included letters to political chiefs and foreign heads of states, and instructions, information, and orders to allied and subordinate foreign commanders. He took a vast load off his chief's shoulders by drafting many of these letters himself for Marlborough's signature and by putting Marlborough's own hurried efforts into clear and grammatical English.[5]

In the army of Frederick the Great the quartermaster-general and the King's first cabinet secretary functioned in very much the same way as Cadogan and Cardonnell, except that the quartermaster-general was never employed as a commander. Prince Ferdinand of Brunswick had a staff organised on the Prussian model when he commanded the British-paid army in Germany during the Seven Years War. His Quartermaster-General, Colonel Friedrick Wilhelm von Bauer, was very much the chief of staff. He was not only responsible for getting out the detailed orders required to put Ferdinand's plans into effect, but was also frequently entrusted with coordinating the actions of the commanders concerned.[6] The staff work on Ferdinand's headquarters was remarkably efficient, and written orders for the most complex moves were worked out in the greatest detail.

The British element of this army became well accustomed, of course, to the Prussian staff system, and though it was never imitated in full by the British Army, it undoubtedly had its influence on the development of staff work in the field.

The rank of brigadier-general poses something of a problem. During the whole of the eighteenth century the terms 'brigadier' and 'brigadier-general' seem to have been used indiscriminately to denote the same rank, and records show colonels as promoted to either. The Army List of 1740, for instance, includes 'Brigadier Cornwallis's Regiment of Foot' and 'Brigadier-General Pagett's Regiment of Foot'.[7] One could perhaps be justified in assuming that, whilst the full title of the rank was 'brigadier-general', it was customary to address such officers as 'brigadier', whilst a major-general was addressed as 'general'. Although apparently a substantive rank up till about the middle of the century, after that it seems to have been confined to local rank given for particular appointments overseas, either in command or on the staff.[8] In 1757 Wolfe, then a brevet-colonel, was appointed a brigadier for service in America. This was a local appointment and he reverted to colonel on return to England. It was as such that he was promoted major-general (missing out brigadier) to command the Quebec expedition.

Whatever the organisation of the army in the field and its staff, success in war depends very largely on the ability of its commander. This seems an obvious fact; and yet even today it is rarely, if ever, taken into account by pundits who assess the chances in battle of rival forces. Military history, however, shows many occasions when a general of genius has gained victory despite inferiority in both numbers and material. The strategic and tactical ability displayed by British commanders of the eighteenth century is the principal theme of the remaining chapters in this book. Before proceeding to this study, however, it might be appropriate to describe in his own words the qualities which Marshal Maurice de Saxe, himself one of the greatest of eighteenth-century commanders, considered to be the mark of the great general. In his *Rêveries*,[9] Saxe writes as follows:

'The first of all the qualities of a general is valour, without which I would place little value on the others, because they would be useless. The second quality is inspiration; he should be bold and ingenious in his plans and actions. The third quality is good health.

'A general should be calm and never ill-tempered. He should not know what it is to hate. He should punish without favour, above all those who are his favourites, but he should never get angry. He should regard himself as bound to comply strictly with the military regulations . . . and must rid himself of any thought that he himself punishes, but understand, and make others understand, that he only administers the military law. With these qualities he will be loved, he will be feared, and, without doubt, he will be obeyed.

'The skills required of a general are infinite: the art of knowing how to subsist an army and to be sparing of it; the ability to so dispose it that he is not obliged to fight unless he wishes; knowing how to choose positions and the best of a number of different ways of drawing up his army; and the genius to seize those favourable opportunities which occur in battle and which open the way to victory. All these subjects are immense, and they are as varied as the places and chances which produce them.

'A general must not be concerned with day-to-day affairs. His examination of the ground and his disposition of the troops should be as expeditious as the flight of an eagle. This done, his plan should be short and simple ... His subordinate generals will then have to be singularly stupid if they do not understand his orders, or the movements they are to execute with their own commands. The commander-in-chief himself should not be occupied or embarrassed with these details ... Indeed, I urge that he should not concern himself with the direct conduct of an action. He will then be able to observe events better, will retain a sounder judgement, and will be better able to profit by openings presented by the enemy in the battle. When at last he sees his fair lady of opportunity, he should kiss her hand and go at once to the critical spot, striking hard with the first troops on which he can lay hands. It is thus that decisive victory is gained. I do not suggest how or when this should be done because it will depend on a variety of situations and positions which can arise in battle and indicate the opportunity. The art is to see it and to know how to profit by it ...

'If a man is not born with the talent for war he will never be other than a mediocre general. It is the same with all the talents: it is necessary to be born with that for painting to be a first class artist; with that of music to be an outstanding composer; with that of poetry to write good verse; etc. All those things that aim at the sublime are the same; which is why so few men excel at any art—centuries pass without producing them. Study corrects thought, but it never produces genius—this is the work of nature ...

'A general must concern himself with watching the demeanour of the enemy and the manoeuvres he is attempting when he moves his troops. He must try and make the enemy uneasy about some locality so that he makes a false move. He must disconcert him, profit by opportunities; and know how to deliver the fatal blow as soon as he makes a mistake. But to be able to do all this he must keep his judgement unfettered by preoccupation with minor matters.

'I am not, however, at all in favour of battles, particularly at the start of a war, and I believe that an able general can, throughout his life, manage affairs without being forced to engage in one. Nothing puts the enemy in such a difficult position as this method of waging war, and nothing advances ones affairs better. It is necessary to harry the enemy frequently and, so to speak, melt his strength away until he is forced to take cover.

'I do not mean by this that, if an opportunity arose of crushing the enemy, one would not attack, or that one would not profit by any mistakes he might make; but I do say that one can make war without taking chances, and this is the height of ability in a general. But when one does give battle it is necessary to know how to profit from victory and, above all, not to remain content with having gained control of the battlefield, as is the general custom.

'There is a proverb, followed religiously, which says: "It is necessary to make a golden bridge for one's enemy.". [i.e. to leave the enemy an escape route.] This is wrong: on the contrary, it is necessary to push him and to pursue him to the utmost; until an apparently orderly retreat, once he becomes alarmed, is soon converted into a rout.'

Saxe's description of the character and the qualities required of an ideal general could hardly be bettered—not only in the eighteenth century, but even at the present day; and he shows the importance of a competent staff by the need for the general to be free from the worry over minor details during the conduct of a battle. Saxe's views on battles have been widely misunderstood because his statement that an able general could do without them has been taken out of context. What Saxe, in fact, says is that battles are not necessary for successful war and that an able general may be able to wear down and exhaust his adversary without risking the hazard of a battle. On the other hand, if an opportunity should arise of crushing his enemy he should seize it. The following chapters will show how British commanders of the eighteenth century measured up to Saxe's standards in character, powers of command, strategic ability and tactical skill.

Chapter 8

THE DUKE OF MARLBOROUGH'S STRATEGY

===

Before starting a chapter on strategy, it would be well to consider the respective spheres of strategy and tactics. There is much confusion and some difference of opinion as to the dividing line between them. In fact the only writer known to the author who has stated precisely the province of each is General von Clausewitz, in his monumental work *On War*. He writes:[1]

'The conduct of War is, therefore, the formation and conduct of the fighting. If this fighting was a single act, there would be no necessity for any further subdivision, but the fight is composed of a greater or less number of single acts, complete in themselves, which we call combats ... From this arises the totally different activities, that of the *formation* and *conduct* of these single combats in themselves, and the *combination* of them with one another, with a view to the ultimate object of the War. The first is called *tactics*, the other *strategy* ... According to our classification, therefore, tactics *is the theory of the use of military forces in combat*. Strategy *is the theory of the use of combats for the object of the War* ... The former occupies itself with the form of the separate combat, the latter with its use.'

Clausewitz's definition is open to the criticism of being too narrow and rigid, but it is doubtful whether it has ever been bettered in neatness and clarity. In normal usage strategy is divided again into 'grand strategy' which is concerned with the conduct of a war as a whole, and the strategy pursued in a particular theatre or campaign. In this connection, the Duke of Marlborough is unique amongst British military commanders, because he was almost entirely responsible for British grand strategy during the War of the Spanish Succession, as well as for the strategy of the Allied forces which he commanded personally in the field.

The difficulty in writing about strategy is that the most brilliant operations often appear so obvious and simple that the genius of the commander who devised them and conducted them is not readily apparent. Clausewitz deals with this point too. He says:[2]

'As long as we have no personal knowledge of War, we cannot conceive where those difficulties lie of which so much is said, and what that genius and those extraordinary mental powers required in a General have really to do. All appears so simple, all the requisite branches of knowledge appear so plain, all the combinations so unimportant, that in comparison with them the easiest problem in higher mathematics impresses us with a certain scientific dignity. But if we have seen War, all becomes intelligible ... Everything is very simple in War, but the simplest thing is difficult. These difficulties accumulate and produce a friction which no man can imagine exactly who has not seen War.'

Marlborough had more than his share of these difficulties.

As the situation in Europe drew towards open war, the 'Grand Alliance' of England, Holland, and the Empire was ranged against France and Spain. Later, Prussia and Denmark joined the Grand Alliance, whilst Bavaria broke with the Empire and joined with France and Spain. Subsequent adherents to the Grand Alliance were Portugal and Savoy. France, by far the strongest military power in Europe, had gained an important strategic advantage by occupying the Spanish Netherlands before the outbreak of war, and at the same time seizing the 'Barrier' fortresses in that area which had been assigned to the Dutch at the Treaty of Ryswick. These included all the fortresses on the Upper and Middle Meuse, with the exception of Maastricht. The French had also occupied the

Electorate of Cologne, thus threatening to cut the communications between Holland and the Imperial capital of Vienna. In addition, as soon as they had marched into Flanders, the French had improved their position by constructing a chain of fortifications from Antwerp to Namur which they called the Lines of Brabant. To make the strategical situation even worse, the Emperor had an insurrection in Hungary to deal with, which seriously weakened the forces that he could put in the field in support of the Grand Alliance.[3]

It was apparent to Marlborough that the Allies were faced with a long and difficult contest, and with the military balance so weighted against them that it would be essential to concentrate the major part of England's sea and land forces in Europe, whilst any distant operations overseas must take second place, however much they might serve England's interests. Marlborough was indeed well aware of those interests, for he told the Imperial Ambassador to Holland that England meant to take all she could of the West Indies.[4]

As compared with the Grand Alliance, France, with its ally Spain, occupied a central position and hence they had the advantage conferred by interior lines of being able to concentrate their forces for any planned operation more rapidly than their opponents. The Grand Allies, particularly the Empire, were therefore faced with the threat of defeat in detail. Marlborough saw that the only strategical counter to this was the complete encirclement by land and sea of the hostile powers. The English fleet already dominated the seas washing the west European coast, but the Mediterranean had yet to be gained. English squadrons could, and did, operate in the Mediterranean, but they lacked a first-class harbour where ships could shelter and refit, and without which they could not stay in and command that sea. Since all the good harbours in the Mediterranean and at its approaches were in the possession of France or Spain, there was a prime strategical need to wrest one of these from the enemy.

An attempt in 1702 to seize Cadiz as a naval base failed. In 1703, after Portugal had joined the Grand Alliance, Lisbon was used for a short time, but proved unsatisfactory for the purpose. In 1704 the capture of Gibraltar met the need in part; but only in part because it was not at that time suitable for refitting ships. Nevertheless, when Marlborough was asked for his views as to its value he replied that it would be 'of vast use to our trade and navigation, and therefore that no cost ought to be spared to maintain it'.[5] This advice was accepted and troops were despatched at once to provide a garrison.

In 1707 Marlborough arranged for an attack on Toulon by an Austrian army under the command of Prince Eugene, supported by a British fleet under Sir Cloudesley Shovell. The operation so nearly succeeded that the French, not venturing to risk action against Shovell's superior force, used their sailors to man the guns ashore and turned some ships into floating batteries to keep the British bomb vessels out of range. However, the British bombardment, apart from the loss inflicted on French warships, did so much damage to the arsenal that Toulon was out of use as a naval base for some time afterwards.[6]

A first-class naval base was eventually gained when in 1708 Minorca was captured by a joint army and navy expedition, which was despatched for the purpose on Marlborough's advice. Port Mahon in Minorca was, indeed, the best harbour in the Mediterranean, and the military garrison established in the island gave the fleet a secure station from which they were enabled to harry so continuously the Mediterranean coasts of France and Spain, that both countries were forced to detach troops from their field armies to safeguard their maritime towns.

Portugal's agreement to join the Grand Alliance had been conditional on the despatch of an Anglo-Dutch force to operate with the Portuguese in the Iberian Peninsula. The decision to agree to this was largely the responsibility of Marlborough, on the grounds that such operations would create another diversion to draw troops from the enemy field armies on the decisive fronts.

It is now time to turn to Marlborough's strategy as a commander in the field. In May 1702, as captain-general of the English forces at home and abroad, he arrived at the Hague, and the following month the Dutch somewhat reluctantly agreed to his appointment to the supreme command of their own army. They insisted, however, in hanging a strategical

1. Officer and Private of the 4th (King's Own) Regiment of Foot, 1680 (later the King's Own Royal Regiment). *Reproduced with permission of the National Army Museum.*

Private of Fox's Marines (later 32nd and subsequently 1st Battalion The of Cornwall's Light Infantry) by Charles en. *Reproduced with permission of the Royal es Museum.*

3. A Gunner of the Royal Artillery, 1722 by Charles Stadden. *Reproduced with permission of Stamp Publicity (Worthing) Ltd.*

4. A British Grenadier of 1
Reproduced with permission of
National Army Museum.

5. Officer and Other Rank
the First Guards, 1745. *R*
duced with permission of the Nat
Army Museum.

millstone round his neck in the shape of two Dutch civilian deputies on his headquarters with the power of veto over his employment of Dutch troops.

The military situation of Holland at this time was extremely critical. The French army in the Spanish Netherlands consisted of some 90,000 men under the command of Marshal Boufflers. The main part of this force, under Boufflers himself, was at Xanten on the Rhine, about forty miles downstream from Düsseldorf, threatening to strike down the Rhine and the Waal into the heart of the territory of the Dutch States General. Behind him, Boufflers had occupied and garrisoned the important fortress of Kaiserwerth on the Rhine, about five miles north of Düsseldorf and in the Electorate of Cologne, and this gave him complete control of that river for the movement of troops and supplies. The main Anglo-Dutch force facing Boufflers was under command of the Earl of Athlone (the Dutchman, Ginkel) and was in the neighbourhood of Cranenburg, between Nimwegen and Cleves. For the Grand Allies, the capture of Kaiserwerth and the blocking of the Rhine was a pressing need, and at the end of April the Prince of Nassau-Saarbrücken had been despatched down the right bank of the Rhine with 25,000 men to besiege it. Boufflers sent Tallard with 13,000 men to hamper the siege, though he was unable to cross to the right bank on which were both the fortress and the besiegers.

Early in June Boufflers advanced quickly in two columns through Cleves and Gennep to try and surround Athlone's force. The Dutchman, outnumbered by nearly two to one, saved himself by a rapid retreat to the shelter of the guns of the fortress of Nimwegen. Boufflers then withdrew to Gennep, where he took up a position with his left flank covered by the Meuse. In the meantime Kaiserwerth had fallen, depriving Boufflers of his control of the Rhine. Athlone was reinforced by 8,000 men of the besieging force, whilst the remainder moved up the Rhine to reduce the remaining French garrisons in the Electorate of Cologne and restore direct communication with the Imperial forces.

Nevertheless, Nimwegen, the sole fortress denying access to the Rhine delta, was still in danger. By July Marlborough had

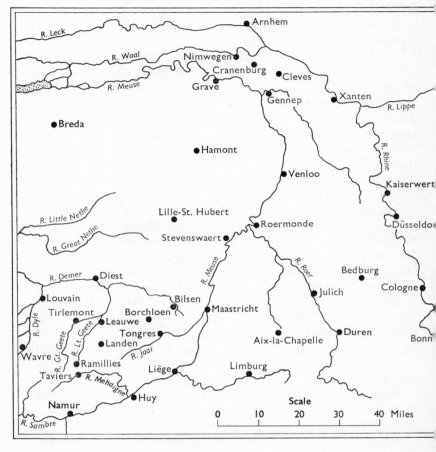

1. The campaigns of Lille-St Hubert and Ramillies.

some 60,000 men under his command, a strength somewhat outnumbered by Boufflers' army at Gennep. The Dutch viewed
Marlborough's position about Nimwegen as the only obstacle
to a French invasion. When, therefore, he proposed to take the
offensive by moving his army away from that area, thus apparently leaving Holland wide open to attack, they objected
strongly. Marlborough, perhaps the earliest exponent of the

strategy of 'indirect approach', saw that if he moved against Boufflers' communications, the latter would have to conform. An advance towards Maastricht on the Meuse, well garrisoned and stocked with supplies for the replenishment of Marlborough's troops, would so threaten Boufflers' lines of communication with his own bases behind the Lines of Brabant, that he would have to retire rapidly, leaving uncovered the Meuse fortresses of Venloo, Roermonde, and Stevenswaert, which the French had seized.

After ten days of argument Marlborough eventually won Dutch agreement to his crossing the Meuse at Grave, but only on condition that he left twenty squadrons of cavalry and eighteen battalions of infantry in front of Nimwegen. This was such a large proportion of his force as to prejudice severely his chance of success in battle. At last, on 26 July, he crossed the Meuse at Grave with 50,000 men, including all the British troops, and marched south. On 30 July he was at Hamont and the next day halted at Lille-Saint Hubert, forty miles from Grave.

As soon as Boufflers learned of Marlborough's move, he appreciated that his own position was no longer tenable, and, striking his camps at Gennep, he marched rapidly down the right bank of the Meuse to Roermonde, directing Tallard, who was near Düsseldorf, to join him. The Dutch saw the menace suddenly disappear, and realised that their insistence on retaining troops at Nimwegen had been quite unwarranted.

Marlborough had not yet finished with Boufflers. He was some twenty miles due west of Roermonde, and Boufflers would have to march across his front to reach his bases. Indeed, if he did not do so, Marlborough would be able to demolish the Lines of Brabant, for they had no permanent garrison. Boufflers saw this too, and started his march westward that night, without any certainty that he would reach his destination. At dawn, his army, badly strung out, was moving towards a heath close to Marlborough's camp and was about to present its flank to the Allied army drawn up in order of battle. However, although they had previously agreed to a battle, the Dutch Deputies implored Marlborough not to attack, and Boufflers escaped certain defeat.[7]

It had been, nevertheless, a remarkable campaign. With hardly a shot being fired, the threat to Holland had been removed and the French-garrisoned fortresses on the Meuse abandoned to their fate. It was a campaign which Saxe might well have held up as a model. It would also have been approved of by Clausewitz, for he held that 'Possible combats are on account of their results to be looked upon as real ones', and adds, 'The overthrow of the enemy's power is only to be done through the effect of a battle, whether it be that it actually takes place, or that it is merely offered, and not accepted.'[8] Marlborough had certainly offered battle and Boufflers had declined it. It is true of course that if it had not been for the Dutch Deputies, Boufflers' army would have been completely destroyed.

Marlborough's strategic genius was never better displayed than in his march to the Danube and subsequent operations in 1704. The military situation at the end of the campaigning season of 1703 was disappointing, and indeed dangerous. There had been no appreciable gains in the Netherlands; the Imperial army had been defeated at Hochstadt in September by Marshal Villars; Marshal Tallard, on the Rhine, had retaken the important fortress of Landau, fifty miles north of Strasburg, and so secured French communications with Bavaria; and in Italy Marshal Vendôme was threatening the Imperial left flank. There was the obvious possibility that, while the Anglo-Dutch armies were held in play in Flanders, the Empire might be knocked out of the war. The decisive theatre for the campaign of 1704 was therefore the Danube, and Marlborough appreciated the importance of transferring a considerable force to that area under his own command. But if the action required was simple, the way to do it was not. The Dutch would never agree to an operation which would apparently leave them uncovered to enemy invasion, and if he surmounted this difficulty, he was still faced with a march of some 250 miles across the front of numerous enemy forces which were well placed to strike at the flank of his army, as he had threatened the flank of Boufflers' army in 1702. He knew, too, that such a march could not be concealed because there was no means of preventing the large numbers of French agents who operated between the armies from reporting it. If he was to undertake this march, therefore, he would have to deceive both the French and the Dutch as to his intentions, and also any other allies who might unintentionally give his purpose away.

In spite of these problems, Marlborough decided that the march was essential to the successful prosecution of the war, and he planned, therefore, to take the British troops with him, together with the various German contingents in British pay and, if possible, the Danish troops in Dutch pay. The bulk of the Dutch troops he would leave to defend the Flanders fortresses. To deceive the French he would tie their available forces down by threatening successively lines of attack against objectives vital to their interests.

Ranged from Flanders to Italy were four French armies and the Bavarian army. In the French plan of campaign for 1704 Villeroy, based on the Lines of Brabant, was to remain on the defensive in Flanders, whilst Tallard on the Upper Rhine and Marsin and the Elector of Bavaria on the Danube were to attack the Empire. In Italy Vendôme was directed against Savoy. The strategic position of the French was strong. The River Moselle, which offered a gateway into France, was held by the fortresses of Treves and Trarbach on that river. Farther south, the strong fortress of Landau, which the French had captured, controlled the Upper Rhine and secured the routes leading into France between the Hunsrück and the Vosges Mountains towards the fortresses of Metz, Thionville, and Saarlouis. Farther up the Rhine the French held the bridgehead fortresses of Kehl (opposite Strasburg) and Old Brisach, west of Freiburg, so controlling the Rhine crossings for any move into Germany.

Before the start of operations on the Danube, Marsin's army needed to be brought up to strength, and for this purpose 10,000 reinforcements had been assembled at Strasburg. Tallard, with 18,000 men of his own army, was to convey these reinforcements as far as Villingen on the Danube where Marsin would meet him with supplies and would take over his reinforcements.

The Imperial forces, distributed along the Rhine, were commanded by Prince Louis, the Margrave of Baden. He had built

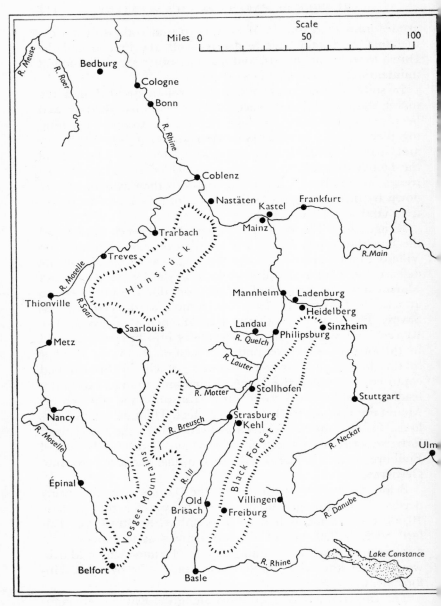

2. Marlborough's March to the Danube.

the strong Lines of Stollhofen, nine miles in length, between the Rhine and the Black Forest and some fifteen miles downstream from Strasburg, to stop any advance by the French down the right bank of the Rhine. He had detached a corps of about 10,000 men under his second-in-command, Count Styrum, to watch the Bavarian army which was in the neighbourhood of Ulm. Styrum was in very inferior strength as Marsin and the Elector had about 50,000 men between them. In addition, his troops were not very efficient and he was not himself a very bright commander.

During the winter of 1703/4 Marlborough paid a visit to Holland and suggested to the Dutch that the Moselle valley presented the most promising theatre for the Anglo-Dutch campaign of 1704. The suggestion was ill received, for the removal of their main army from the close defence of their territory and barrier fortresses would be followed immediately, they believed, by a French assault on them. The lesson of 1702 had not been learned. After unavailing argument, Marlborough declared that he intended to march to Coblenz in any case, taking with him the whole of the British troops and those in English pay, and he displayed Queen Anne's authority for him to do so. The Dutch then gave way and agreed to support him.

To support this cover plan of a campaign in the Moselle valley, Marlborough ordered the commanders of the Hanoverian troops and the German troops in English pay, which were about Nuremberg, to march to Coblenz, and in February he had written to the King of Prussia telling him that the Moselle was the most effective area of operations, with the result that the Prussian contingent was also directed to Coblenz. It does not appear that any particular attempt was made to keep these moves secret, so that Villeroy was soon alerted to the likelihood of an Allied attack up the Moselle.

Meanwhile Marlborough had arranged for a detailed reconnaissance of the route to the Danube, and had contracts placed for supplies and shoes at Frankfurt and other towns of the Middle Rhine which, whilst they were intended to serve his march to the Danube, were also quite consistent with a Moselle campaign. In addition, the various troops converging on Coblenz would be as well sited for the Danube as for the Moselle.

In March the British troops assembled at Maastricht and set out on the forty-mile march to the rendezvous at Bedburg, twenty miles north-west of Cologne. They consisted of nineteen squadrons of cavalry, fourteen battalions of infantry, and thirty-eight guns, with a total strength of about 14,000 men. On 10 May Marlborough arrived at Maastricht, and on 16 May he followed after his troops, reviewing them at Bedburg on 18 May.

On 13 May Tallard crossed the Rhine at the start of his march with Marsin's reinforcements, and on 4 May the Elector and Marsin marched with 30,000 men to meet him, leaving 14,000 to cover Ulm. Styrum was aware of this latter move and proposed to strike at the flank of the long vulnerable column with its mass of supply vehicles, but Prince Louis ordered him to wait until he joined him with the major part of his troops from the Rhine. The junction took place on 19 May, but it was then too late as Marsin and Tallard had already met at Villingen. Louis then planned to strike the Franco-Bavarian force on its return march as it passed the defile of Stockach north of Lake Constance, but he was again too late. He then settled down with his main body to confront the forces of Marsin and the Elector in the neighbourhood of Ulm, while Tallard returned to Strasburg.

Marlborough had hardly left Maastricht before an agitated message reached him from Overkirk, who had been left in command of the Dutch troops around Maastricht, saying that Villeroy had crossed the Meuse and was threatening an attack on the fortress of Huy on that river. Marlborough, knowing that Villeroy's intention was merely to make him retrace his steps, told Overkirk to draw troops from the garrisons and drive him off.

On 19 May the British troops marched out of Bedburg on the way to the Rhine. Villeroy could wait no longer: leaving Bedmar with 25,000 men to hold Overkirk in check, he marched in the direction of the Moselle, and by 27 May he had reached Arlon, eighty miles from Huy and forty miles due west of Treves. On the same day the British infantry marched into Coblenz, seventy miles from Bedburg, though Marlborough with the cavalry had passed through the town two days earlier and crossed to the right bank of the Rhine. The artillery and heavy baggage were being lifted up the Rhine in barges, keeping pace with the infantry column. In Coblenz Hanoverian, Prussian, and other German infantry joined the British battalions, whilst Hessians were assembling to join farther south.

At this time Tallard was just entering Strasburg on his return from Villingen. He was about 100 miles from the Moselle, or, say, eight days march, so that both he and Villeroy were well placed to concentrate in the Moselle valley before Marlborough could hope to cover the sixty miles from Coblenz to Treves, having taken Trarbach on the way. But Tallard dared not leave the Rhine until Marlborough was committed to the Moselle. Equally, Villeroy dared not venture too far, because he was uneasily aware that Marlborough had assembled so many boats on the Rhine that he could move his whole force downstream at a very much faster pace than Villeroy could march, and that if he moved well into the Moselle valley Marlborough could be back on the Meuse before he could, with time to make things very unpleasant for Bedmar. Had the two Marshals known that Marlborough's destination was the Danube, it would have been easy to stop him. Tallard could have attacked him in the flank and Villeroy could probably have reached Mannheim in time to attack Marlborough's rear. Not only were Tallard and Villeroy uneasy, Marsin and the Elector halted their operations whilst awaiting news of Marlborough's objective.

On 22 May Prince Louis of Baden sent a message to Marlborough, saying that he thought that Tallard was moving to attack the Lines of Stollhofen which were thinly held and asking for his assistance. Marlborough promptly ordered contingents of Prussian and Hanoverian troops to march to the Lines. This suited him well because it assisted his next diversionary threat. On 29 May Marlborough and the cavalry were at Kastel, on the right bank of the Rhine opposite Mainz, and the infantry had left Coblenz and, crossing the Rhine, had arrived at Nastäten, some fifteen miles farther on, and on the Mainz road. It was now obvious that the Moselle was not the target.

Marlborough was now directing the attention of the French to his next threat. He had asked permission from the Landgrave

of Hesse to have the latter's artillery contingent sent to Mannheim, and he had requested the Governor of Philipsburg to
construct a bridge of boats across the Rhine. By the time Marlborough reached Mainz the Prussian and Hanoverian reinforcements had reached the Lines of Stollhofen, the construction of
the bridge at Philipsburg had started, and the Hessian artillery
had reached Mannheim. Tallard and Villeroy came to the conclusion that Marlborough intended to attack in Alsace, and
that the bridge at Philipsburg indicated the Fortress of Landau
as his first objective. They were not displeased as they could
concentrate fairly quickly to meet such an attack. Tallard
marched north to take up a position on the River Lauter to
cover Landau, whilst Villeroy marched to join him and sent a
message to Bedmar directing him to send reinforcements. (At
the same time the Dutch States General, in great alarm for the
safety of their fortresses, were appealing to Marlborough to send
back to them the German mercenary troops.)

On 31 May Marlborough crossed the Main with the cavalry
and three days later was throwing a bridge across the Neckar
near Ladenburg. On 2 June the infantry reached Kastel. The
guns had now left the Rhine barges and rain on the unmetaled
roads was making the going wretchedly slow. Marlborough
therefore halted to rest the horses and give the infantry and
guns a chance to catch up. He now had a considerable force of
cavalry, for the contingents of the various German States that
had joined during the march had brought the strength up to
eighty squadrons. At this point Marlborough broke the news to
the Dutch States General that the Queen had ordered him to go
to the assistance of the Empire and that he was accordingly
marching to the Danube.

On 6 June Marlborough continued his march with the cavalry
as far as Wiesloh, fifteen miles south of Ladenburg and ten miles
north-east of Philipsburg. The infantry were now approaching
Heidelberg, where Marlborough had arranged for a supply of
shoes for them to replace those worn out on the march, and
here they rested for four days.

The flotilla of boats was still on the Rhine and within one
day's march of the columns. Both Villeroy and Tallard still
thought that Marlborough was making for Landau, but the

former remained hesitant and unhappy because he knew that, if by any chance the march had been a feint to draw him away from Flanders, Marlborough's troops, with the current to aid them, could be disembarking at Cologne within two days of embarking at Mannheim. Then on 7 June Marlborough's cavalry turned east for Sinzheim, and at last the French knew that he was on the way to the Danube—but it was far too late to intervene.[9] There followed two months later the crushing defeat of the united armies of Tallard, Marsin, and the Elector at the battle of Blenheim.

The only historical parallel with this remarkable march that comes to mind is that of Sherman through Georgia and the Carolinas. There is the same paralysis of the enemy by diversionary threats, but with the important difference that Sherman was not opposed by enemy forces as strong as, or stronger than, his own, whilst Marlborough was. The administrative arrangements were excellent by the standards of any period in military history. Men and horses reached the Danube well fed, well shod, and in excellent physical condition.

It will suffice to discuss one more example of Marlborough's strategy: his famous forcing of the 'Non Plus Ultra' Lines, which was, apart from the siege and capture of the fortress of Bouchain which followed it, the last major operation which he commanded in the field.

In June 1710 the important fortress of Douai had fallen to Marlborough, and to repair this and other breaches in his fortress barrier, Marshal Villars started the construction of a new defensive line, based on fortifications and inundations. Two of his original fortress bastions remained. On the west Dunkirk, Ypres, and St Omer denied access to the ports of Calais and Boulogne, whilst on the east Valenciennes, Maubeuge, and Le Quesnoy barred an advance up the Sambre. But between these there remained only the thinnest of defences to cover the heart of France. Here, Arras, Bouchain, and Cambrai were fortresses vital to the defence, but they were all too vulnerable without additional support.

From the autumn of 1710 Villars put all his resources into the construction of an eighteenth-century equivalent of the Maginot line, stretching from the Channel coast to the River Sambre.

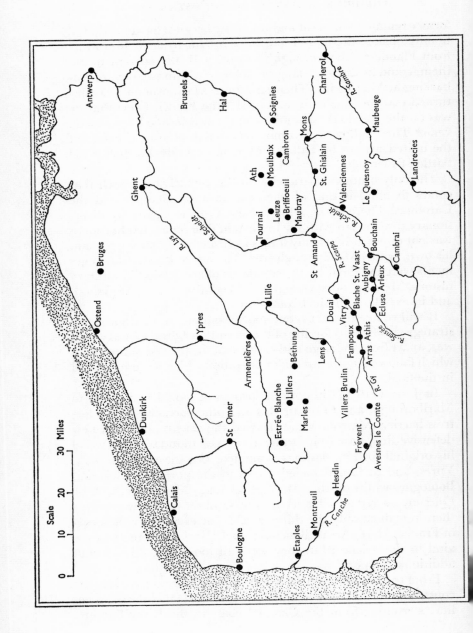

From the west the line followed the River Canche, with its minor fortresses of Montreuil, Hesdin, and Frévent. Thence strong field works ran to the River Gy. Three miles west of Arras the Gy joined the River Scarpe, and both these rivers were dammed so as to flood the country bordering them as far as Biache Saint-Vaast, ten miles east of Arras. From here a canal had been built to the River Sensée at Ecluse through marshes and flooded fields, the canal being fed mainly from the Sensée by the partial damming of that river. Between Ecluse and Bouchain, where the Sensée joined the Scheldt, the former river remained a considerable barrier. Bouchain was a powerful fortress and was connected with Valenciennes by the Scheldt. From the latter town entrenchments, supported by the fortresses of Le Quesnoy and Landrecies, ran to the Sambre, which was secured by Maubeuge and Charleroi. For offensive sallies by his troops, and also for the use of the local inhabitants, Villars had built passages over the inundations, at Athis, Fampoux, Biache Saint-Vaast, Arleux, and Aubigny.

Villars was very proud of his lines, which he regarded as impregnable. At about that time there was a joke circulating in both armies that Marlborough had purchased a new scarlet coat, and the tailor who had cut it was so pleased that he described it as 'non plus ultra'. Villars thought that this so characterised his new lines that he adopted it as their name.[10]

At the end of April 1711 Marlborough's field army was concentrating between Lille and Douai, whilst Villars' army was deployed behind his lines from just west of Bouchain to Monchy le Preux, five miles east of Arras. The respective strengths were: Marlborough, 145 squadrons and 94 battalions; Villars, 185 squadrons and 110 battalions.[11] After its concentration had been completed, the Allied army deployed south of Douai.

Marlborough was faced with the problem of penetrating these formidable lines, defended by an army rather stronger than his own, as a necessary preliminary to the capture of Bouchain or, alternatively, Arras, which lay on the south side of the Scheldt and Scarpe respectively. A crossing between these two places over the inundations was necessary, and Marlborough settled on Arleux, which was near to the junction of the Scarpe–Sensée canal and on the latter river. It would not be difficult to capture it, because Villars could not defend the whole of his long line in strength, but he would have time to concentrate in strength in front of Arleux before Marlborough had time to push sufficient troops over the causeway to make good an adequate bridgehead. He could doubtless destroy the fortifications at Arleux before he withdrew, with the idea of making a second crossing there a quicker operation; but Villars would immediately reconstruct them.

His knowledge of Villars' character helped Marlborough to a solution.[12] Marlborough came to the conclusion that if he captured Arleux, strengthened its defences, broke the dam which diverted part of the water of the Sensée into the Scarpe to form the canal, and withdrew, leaving it with a small garrison, then Villars would destroy the Arleux fortifications himself. He would assume that Marlborough wished to hold Arleux to stop the dam being repaired and so creating a gap in the Lines. It would be necessary to draw the main French army westwards by threatening an attack on the Lines west of Arras, so that as soon as the French had destroyed the Arleux fortifications, the Allied army would march swiftly back to cross the undefended causeway. This would entail very careful timing, because owing to the shape of the Lines and to the roads he had constructed parallel to them, Villars would be closer to Arleux both in distance and time than Marlborough, whose army would have to march partly across country.

On 13 June Marlborough moved the bulk of his field army westwards, crossing the Scarpe above Douai and halting near the Vimy Ridge, south of Lens. On 6 July Arleux was captured in a night attack by an Allied infantry battalion. The dam was then broken and the defences strengthened, the work being covered by a strong force under the Dutch General Hompesch, posted at Goeulzin three miles north of Arleux. Three days later Villars reacted as expected with a dawn attack. He was repulsed at Arleux, but French troops crossed the inundations three miles farther east at Aubigny and surprised Hompesch who lost about 1,000 of his troops.

On 20 July Marlborough marched farther westwards, concentrating his army north-west of Arras in the area Estrée Blanche–Lillers–Marles. At the same time he reinforced the garrisons of Douai, Lille and Tournai, and he left his pontoon train at Douai. On 23 July Villars followed him, marching behind his lines to take up a position facing Marlborough; but he detached Montesquieu with a strong force to capture Arleux and level its defences. In due course Marlborough received an urgent message from Arleux saying that it was under attack by the French in considerable strength and asking for help. He sent Cadogan off with a relieving force, but it was noted by some that Cadogan did not hurry unduly and that troops were not sent from the very much nearer Douai. Indeed, before Cadogan had covered half the distance news was received that Arleux had been captured. Montesquieu destroyed its fortifications and restored the flow of water to the canal. Feeling this sector of his defences to be now secure, Villars sent Montesquieu to reinforce Maubeuge and threaten Brabant. This move became known to Marlborough who, in apparent reply, sent Lord Albemarle to Béthune with 24 squadrons and 12 battalions on 28 July. Interspersed in Albemarle's column, and unnoticed by the French, were the heavy artillery and heavy baggage with orders to continue to Douai.

Two days earlier Marlborough had reconnoitred the French lines about Avesnes-le-Comte, accompanied by many generals and staff officers and a large escort of cavalry, so that the French would be bound to notice him. His escort in fact had a slight encounter with French light cavalry.

Marlborough now arranged some verbal indiscretions by himself and others in such a manner that they were bound to reach the French, to the effect that he intended to attack the lines in two or three days' time.

From 30 July a large body of pioneers were employed in preparing the roads by which the Allied army would advance to contact, and the cavalry were directed to make thousands of fascines to hurl into the trenches in front of the French lines to enable the attacking infantry to cross.

During 1 and 2 August the Allied columns marched slowly southwards to an area about Villers Brulin about four miles north of the Lines. On 4 August Marlborough carried out another reconnaissance with the same numerous staff and escort. All the Allied commanders were now given their orders for the attack; but while friend and foe were watching these activities with intense interest, the field artillery stole quietly away and marched east. Villars, convinced that an attack was pending, concentrated his army on the threatened sector and kept his troops perpetually under arms.

Cadogan, now, with a small cavalry escort rode rapidly to Douai, and into this place under cover of dark marched detachments from Tournai, Lille and Saint-Amand, bringing the garrison strength up to 17 squadrons and 23 battalions.

On the main front the last movement the French saw of the Allied troops was a strong body of light cavalry moving towards their left. But after dark in the Allied camp the whole picture changed dramatically. By 9 p.m. the army was drawn up in four columns each with a staff officer to guide it, and soon all the columns were marching east under a bright moon (without which the movement would hardly have been possible). As dawn broke the leading troops were crossing the Scarpe at Vitry, where pontoon bridges had already been laid for them, and where they caught up with the field artillery. At about this time Marlborough received information from Cadogan that he had occupied Arleux at 3 a.m. with the troops assembled at Douai and had established a bridgehead inside the enemy's lines.

Meanwhile Villars had received unconfirmed information of Marlborough's march about two hours after he had started; but he had also learned of an apparent Allied move against his left, headed by the body of light cavalry that had been seen at dusk. It was 2 a.m. before he got confirmation of what had really happened, and, with a ten miles shorter march over a much better route, he started immediately. Marlborough had sent A.D.C.s down the columns to impress on the troops the need to hurry, and it was not long before the leading infantry could see the head of Villars' cavalry level with them on the other side of the French defences. But by 8 a.m. Marlborough was already over the Sensée, and long lines of Allied cavalry were forming up to bar the French advance.

Marlborough was through the Non Plus Ultra Lines without a battle. The siege and fall of Bouchain followed. France now lay open to invasion, but the Governments were already negotiating.[13]

Officer of the 61st Regiment, 1759
2nd Battalion The Gloucestershire
ment). *Reproduced with permission of the
nal Army Museum.*

7. A Grenadier of the 53rd Foot, 1768 (later
1st Battalion The King's Shropshire Light
Infantry. *Reproduced with permission of the
National Army Museum.*

8. The 25th Regiment in Minorca, c. 1770 (later The King's Own Scottish
Borderers). *Reproduced with permission of the National Army Museum.*

9. Cornet Thomas Boothby-Parkyn, 15th Light Dragoons, 1780 (later 15th Hussars). *Reproduced with permission of the National Army Museum.*

10. 16th Light Dragoons, c. 1795; 'A Glimpse of the Enemy' (later 16th Lancers). *Reproduced with permission of the National Army Museum.*

Chapter 9

MAJOR-GENERAL SIR JEFFERY AMHERST IN THE SEVEN YEARS WAR

═══════════

The military direction of the Seven Years War has a special importance in the history of British warfare, because it was the precursor of that which proved so successful in the Second World War—joint chiefs of staff under a prime minister of drive and inspiration.[1] Not that one could quite equate the temperamental and rather unbalanced William Pitt with Sir Winston Churchill, but Lord Ligonier and Lord Anson were not unworthy predecessors of Lord Alanbrooke and Sir Dudley Pound. This command system was not in being at the start of the Seven Years War, which, like the Second World War, began with a disaster. But as Winston Churchill came to power after the defeat of the Allied armies in the West in 1940, so did Pitt after the loss of Minorca in 1756.

It is difficult to assess now the respective responsibilities for grand strategy in the Seven Years War, but it would seem that Pitt expressed the desirable aims of the war, that Ligonier advised him as to the military forces which would be necessary to achieve these aims and how they should be used, and that Anson commented on the practicability of carrying them out with the naval forces and merchant shipping available. Pitt gave the principal aim as the conquest of French territory overseas in North America, India and the West Indies, with priority allotted to Canada. Ligonier would have pointed out that in order to do this France must be prevented from sending strong reinforcements from her large army at home to her

colonial territories. This would entail threatening France herself
by an army based on the Continent, supplemented by expeditions against the French coasts.[2]

This strategy would have been approved by Clausewitz, for,
writing some seventy years later, he pointed out that, 'The
centre of gravity of French power lies in its military force and
in Paris.'[3] And as regards attacks on the French coasts, he wrote:

'As England has the upper hand at sea, it follows that France
must, on that account, be very susceptible with regard to the
whole of her Atlantic coast; and consequently, must protect it
with garrisons of greater or lesser strength. Now, however weak
this coast defence may be, still the French frontiers are tripled
by it; and large drafts, on that account, cannot fail to be withdrawn from the French Army on the theatre of War.'[4]

Such, in brief, was the brilliant maritime strategy of the indirect approach which was the basis of the most successful war
in British history, and which was summarised by Pitt as that of
winning Canada in Germany.

Ligonier developed the military aspect of the grand strategy
as follows. In Germany a strong army consisting of British,
Hanoverian and German troops in British pay, all under the
command of Prince Ferdinand of Brunswick, operated against
the main French armies, in loose conjunction with Frederick
the Great whose army was fighting against the Austrians and
Russians. The object of this British-paid army was well put in
the following contemporary verse:

> 'Our troops they now can plainly see
> May Britain guard in Germany;
> Hanoverians, Hessians, Prussians,
> Are paid t'oppose the French and Russians:
> Nor scruple they with truth to say
> They're fighting for America.'[5]

The forces necessarily retained in England as a defence
against invasion were concentrated in the Isle of Wight, with
troopships standing by ready to carry them to any part in the
United Kingdom much more quickly than they could march.

But instead of being held solely for this purpose, soldiers and ships were employed on diversionary raids on the French coast which, without compromising their primary role, ensured the retention in France of troops which would otherwise have been free to reinforce those engaged with Ferdinand.

Whilst the primary theatre overseas was North America, operations against the valuable 'sugar islands' of the West Indies were of very great importance to British trade. The elimination of the French and their allies in India was also a major objective, but operations in this theatre could be entrusted mainly to the army of the Honourable East India Company.

To North America Ligonier allotted some 24,000 men, of which 14,000 were to capture and destroy the French fortress of Louisburg on Cape Breton Island, as a preliminary step to an advance up the St Lawrence against Quebec, and 10,000, supported by 20,000 American Provincial troops, were to capture Fort Ticonderoga, the key to the southern approaches to Montreal, and seize the French positions on the headwaters of the Ohio and at the south of Lake Ontario.[6]

So much for the grand strategy. The very able general who was destined to implement Ligonier's strategy in America and to conquer Canada was Jeffery Amherst. In 1757 Amherst was a colonel in Germany on commissariat duties. Ligonier had known him for years and had a great opinion of his ability. In January 1758 he summoned him to England and placed him in command of the force to attack Louisburg, with the local rank in America of major-general.

The British troops effected a landing on Cape Breton Island on 8 June 1758. Amherst's very able conduct of the operations and the excellent co-operation between him and the naval commander, Vice-Admiral the Hon. Edward Boscawen, resulted in the capitulation of this very strong fortress on 27 July, the key to the entrance into the St Lawrence River. But four days after this success, news was received by Amherst of the defeat of Major-General James Abercromby at Fort Ticonderoga. Abercomby, a singularly inept commander, had tried to carry the fort by a direct assault instead of using his artillery to destroy the wooden defences, and in spite of the gallantry of his troops he had failed with heavy casualties. This defeat stopped any plans for an immediate advance up the St Lawrence to Quebec. Abercromby was Amherst's senior and commander-in-chief in North America. After sending expeditions to capture Isle St Jean (now Prince Edward Island) and destroy French settlements on the coast of the Gulf of St Lawrence, Amherst departed for Boston on 30 August, taking part of his troops to reinforce Abercromby.

Abercromby was recalled early in November and Amherst was appointed commander-in-chief in his place. At about the same time Brigadier-General John Forbes marched into Fort Duquesne, which the French had evacuated in face of his advance, and renamed it Fort Pitt (now Pittsburgh) in honour of the Prime Minister.

Ligonier's instructions for the campaign of 1759 were that Wolfe, under Amherst's overall command, was to advance up the St Lawrence and capture Quebec, while Amherst was to send a column into Canada by way of Ticonderoga and Crown Point, with the object of either effecting a junction with Wolfe or creating a diversion in his favour. In addition, Amherst was to initiate any other enterprise which he thought would weaken the enemy.[7]

At this time the French military posts stretched from Quebec, up the St Lawrence through Montreal to Lake Ontario, then Fort Niagara between Lakes Ontario and Erie, Fort Presquille on the south of Lake Erie, and, south of this, Fort Le Boeuf and Fort Venango on French Creek and the River Alleghany. Between Lakes Erie and Huron was the important post of Detroit, and to the east, in the northern part of the colony of New York, the French held Fort Ticonderoga at the south of Lake Champlain and controlling the approach to Montreal. The following distances give some indication of the size of the theatre: Quebec–Detroit 600 miles, Quebec–Montreal 160 miles, Montreal–Fort Ticonderoga 100 miles, Fort Ticonderoga –Albany (British concentration area) 100 miles, Albany– Oswego (British post on the south shore of Lake Ontario) 170 miles, and Montreal–Lake Ontario 160 miles. All these distances are approximate and in a straight line. Roads were few and practically all communication was by water, through the lakes and rivers; and over watersheds and past some falls there were 'carrying places' where boats and their contents had to be lifted overland. For the carriage of the troops, provisions, artillery, ammunition, and stores, large quantities of boats of various kinds had to be assembled and even constructed. On the lakes warships had to be built in order to wrest command of them from the French before the flotillas of boats carrying an expedition could proceed. As a column advanced, forts had to be built and garrisoned to protect the lines of communications from the numerous Indians in French pay, so that the farther a column advanced the smaller became the striking force at its head. Much of the area was forest where the rigid infantry lines of European warfare were quite inappropriate, and the troops had to be taught new tactics. Communication between widely separated columns through such country was at best slow and sometimes impossible.

Ligonier wrote to Amherst: 'I hope the operations of the future campaign in your part of the world will be so concerted as to take place at the same time as near the nature of the thing will permit, which cannot fail of creating a diversion equally advantageous to both [i.e. the Quebec and Ticonderoga columns].—I wish you all the success imaginable and sincerely hope you will have the honour and happiness of finishing the war in North America this ensuing campaign.'[8] Amherst must have reflected that the 'nature of the thing' was unlikely to 'permit' any such happy result!

Clausewitz's theory of the strategical centre of gravity has been mentioned briefly above. He writes: 'A certain centre of gravity, a centre of power and movement, will form itself, on which everything depends; and against this centre of gravity of the enemy, the concentrated blow of all the forces must be directed.'[9]

It was clear to Amherst, from his study of the situation, that the French strategical centre of gravity in Canada was their regular army. The capture of Quebec, and even Montreal as well, would not necessarily lead to the end of hostilities, because the French army could fall back on to Detroit, or some other centre, and carry on the war indefinitely. On the other hand, if he could crush the French regular regiments, Canada would be his, because the French Canadian militia felt a greater allegiance to their homesteads and farms than they did to Imperial France. It was essential, therefore, to so conduct operations that the French army was cut off from all avenues of escape. This, however, would entail a strategical envelopment, which is always a risky operation because the separate converging forces incur the hazard of defeat in detail. It would be even more hazardous because the difficulty of intercommunication would make co-ordination, after the initial orders, impossible.

The expedition against Quebec under Wolfe was to be supported by a squadron under the command of Vice-Admiral Sir Charles Saunders. Owing to the absence of communication the force was completely outside Amherst's control until it had either succeeded or failed in attaining its objective. Amherst decided to command the Ticonderoga column himself. In accordance with his instruction to initiate any other enterprise which would weaken the enemy, Amherst selected the reduction of Fort Niagara and the three forts of Presquille, Le Boeuf, and Venango, as a preliminary to seizing command of Lake Ontario and advancing down the St Lawrence towards Montreal.

It is most unlikely that Amherst thought he could complete this ambitious programme in one campaign. First, the administrative difficulties were immense; secondly, storms on the lakes and freezing of rivers made major operations in winter impracticable; and thirdly, more than half the troops consisted of the provincial regiments—the colonial militia raised by each colony—which were generally poorly trained and disciplined, and which would need further training before they could take the field.

Amherst ordered the troops to start concentrating at Albany on 1 May, and arrived there himself on 3 May. Some of the British regiments were already there and within three weeks there were ten battalions. The provincial regiments came in much more slowly, and by the end of the month the regiments which had reached Albany had as yet only 2,550 of their men out of an establishment of 4,575, whilst some regiments had not arrived at all. Some of the difficulties in collecting these troops are apparent from a letter to Amherst from the Governor of New Hampshire, saying that their provincials had decided to move by land, and that Amherst would 'think it very odd after their desiring I should order them to go by water which I had done, but that when I was as well acquainted with them as he is, nothing of this sort would surprise me'.[10]

The troops collecting at Albany consisted of units for the Ticonderoga expedition, the Fort Niagara expedition, and for garrison duties on the long lines of communication. On 15 May Brigadier-General Prideaux, who was to command the Fort Niagara force, arrived at Albany. After the capture of Fort Niagara, Prideaux was to return to Oswego and then move down Lake Ontario to capture Fort La Galette on the south bank of the St Lawrence. Brigadier-General Stanwix, who was already in Pennsylvania, was to relieve Fort Pitt, which was under French pressure, and then move north to capture Forts Venango, Le Boeuf, and Presquille. To support Prideaux's operation, Amherst put in hand the movements necessary to secure the line of communications along the Mohawk River and thence to Fort Oswego on Lake Ontario, and directed that Fort Stanwix, near the end of the navigable part of the Mohawk, should be stocked with provisions. At Prideaux's disposal he placed three battalions of British infantry and two battalions of New York provincials.

On 22 and 23 May the 17th and 27th Foot and part of the 42nd Highlanders of the Triconderoga force started on their way north, and on 24 May Amherst ordered Gage's 80th Light Infantry to move to Fort Edward, some sixty miles up the Hudson from Albany, to reinforce the troops there who were threatened with attack by French employed Indians. From then on the troops of the Ticonderoga column were steadily moving north, but trouble had already broken with some of the provincials. On 27 May Amherst noted in his journal: 'The Provincial Troops deserted most shamefully'.[11] On 4 June Amherst overtook the Connecticut troops going up the river in their 'batteaus', which was 'very heavy wet work'.[12] On 6 June he went along 'the worst communication I ever saw', and, after inspecting a fortified post, he arrived at Fort Edward, the most northerly post on the Hudson River. The next day he saw the 42nd arrive 'half drowned', and on 9 June the

77th rowed in, 'the men greatly fatigued'. Amherst commented: 'I wish the Regts. were up. Tis time I should get forward.'[13]

On 11 June Amherst ordered 600 men to be put on to repairing the roads over the fifteen-mile stretch between Fort Edward and the southern end of Lake George to take artillery and vehicles. He sent a subaltern and one scout to Crown Point, over fifty miles away, to reconnoitre and report, and followed them up with two more scouts the next day. On 13 June he received a letter from Brigadier-General Gage saying that two prisoners captured at Crown Point (presumably by Indians) on 29 May reported that the Regiments of La Reine, Languedoc, Berry (two battalions), and 500 Canadians had passed through Crown Point on their way to Fort Ticonderoga. Some time before this 300 of the French employed Indians had passed. This was quite a strong force for a defensive operation. Amherst had eight regular battalions, eight provincial battalions, and the New England Rangers, but these included the troops required to man posts on the line of communications.[14]

On 13 June he ordered Lieutenant-Colonel Grant, commanding the 42nd Highlanders, to take his regiment, two 6-pounders, and other detachments to erect a post at Half-way Brook on the road to Lake George. During the next few days he was busy moving vehicles and stores forward and also arranging for the repair of the roads, which were still very bad and causing considerable damage to wagons and gun carriages. On 21 June the main body of the army marched to Lake George, leaving the 77th Highlanders and two provincial battalions behind to await their men who were still coming up. At the Half-way Brook post Amherst left three provincial battalions as a guard for the stores. At a new post three miles south of the lake he stationed the 1st Battalion 1st Foot, the 55th Foot and one provincial battalion, and marched into camp at the lakeside with 6,236 men.[15] From here Lake George, four miles wide at its greatest width, stretched northwards for thirty-three miles to the falls of Ticonderoga, whence its waters flowed into Lake Champlain.

On 25 June Amherst received a letter from Lieutenant Coventry at Albany giving news of an Indian scalping raid on the Mohawk River line of communications and of a mutiny by

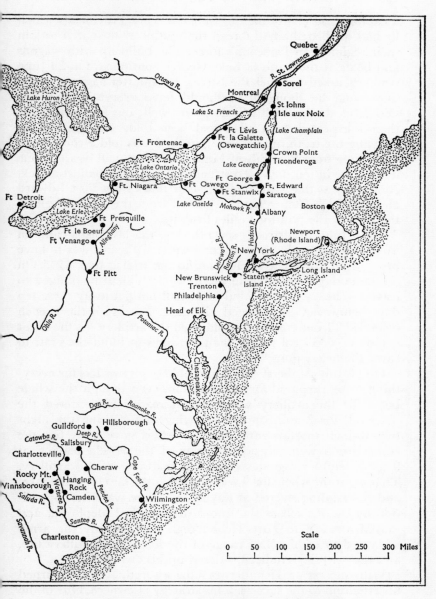

4. **The Campaigns of Amherst, Howe, and Cornwallis.**

a captain and eighty men of the New York Provincials which he had quelled; he had forced the mutineers to march to join their regiment in Prideaux's force. The build up with wagons and boats at the south of Lake George continued. On 29 June Amherst asked Colonel Bradstreet, his quartermaster-general, 'how soon he thought we should have everything up. He said seven days, which will do pretty well; but is much longer than I expected from all I had been told, and there is no knowing the truth but by seeing it, for I was told I could have everything from Fort Edward in a day, which will be well done if 'tis done in ten days.' To strengthen his posts against attack, Amherst sent the 55th to a post four miles from Fort Edward and Whiting's Connecticut Regiment from the lake to replace the 55th at the post four miles from it.

On 5 July, Bradstreet's seventh day, the last loads came in from Fort Edward. Amherst comments: '19 teams was to have brought all off but when it came to the trial it took 114.' On the same day he entered in his Journal: 'I shall be obliged to leave the heavy guns behind or I shall not get away these ten days.' However, he changed his mind, because if the French defended Ticonderoga he would need the artillery. In the event it took a good deal longer than ten days to build the craft to carry the heavy guns.[16]

On 20 July Amherst was at last able to give orders for everything to be prepared for embarkation, even though the whale boats for the artillery were not all ready. He ordered the 'General' for 2 a.m. on the following day. During the night two 10-inch mortars sank and the wharf gave way, but the embarkation went ahead, the rear of the flotilla leaving at 9 a.m., whilst Gage stayed behind to bring on the artillery. That night the whole force was massed at the far end of the lake, and the landing started at daybreak. There was some opposition by the French as the troops disembarked, deployed, and moved forward to Fort Ticonderoga. On 23 July the army advanced to within close range of the fort under artillery fire, and the next day Amherst ordered up his own artillery.

With success at Ticonderoga now assured, Amherst turned his attention to the success of his strategy elsewhere. One of the provincial regiments, the New Hampshire, was sent back to the new Fort George at the south end of the lake, under the guidance of a staff officer, who was instructed to conduct the regiment as quickly as he could to Oswego, so that Prideaux, on his return from Niagara, would have sufficient force for his operation against La Galette. Work before Ticonderoga now went ahead in getting the batteries into position; but on the night of 26 July a deserter arrived and reported that the garrison were evacuating the fort and were about to blow it up. An explosion soon followed and the fort was seen to be on fire. The next day Ticonderoga was occupied and the troops set about bringing the fire under control.

On 28 July Amherst learned of the accidental death of Prideaux, a most able officer, and despatched Gage to Oswego to take over command.

Scouts reported that the French had concentrated at Crown Point, ten miles north of Ticonderoga, at the south end of Lake Champlain. Amherst was now exerting every effort to push ahead, but getting the necessary boats ready imposed delay, and friction amongst his own staff did not help matters. He says: 'It is a little unlucky that three principal People in their Departments, viz., Bradstreet [quartermaster-general], Loring [captain, Royal Navy], and Ord [artillery] are always pulling different ways. I try to keep them as good Friends as I can and to convince them that their duty is to forward everything for the good of the Service and to assist one another.' The principal difficulty over the boats was that they could not be rowed from Lake George along the river connecting it with Lake Champlain because of the falls two miles upstream from Ticonderoga and had therefore to be moved by road. On 1 August Amherst entered in his journal: 'I can go the instant I can get the batteaus.' But the next day he wrote: 'A Rain coming on this morning made the Roads so slippery that Col Bradstreet wrote me word it had totally put a stop to carriages passing.' However a scouting party came in with the news that the French had abandoned Crown Point. Amherst's immediate reaction to this was to despatch the 2nd Battalion 42nd Highlanders to Oswego as reinforcements for Gage. By 4 August there were enough boats ready to move the regular infantry and part of the artillery, and Crown Point was reached and occupied that evening. Amherst wrote: 'This is a great post gained, secures entirely all the country behind it, and the situation and country about is better than anything I have seen.' That night he received information that the French post at Niagara had surrendered.[17]

There now followed a period of consolidation and preparations to secure the naval command of Lake Champlain, without which no further advance could be made. Amherst was also extremely anxious to receive news of Wolfe. He had no idea where his subordinate was. If he had been defeated the major part of the French army would be free to concentrate against Amherst, so that Crown Point and Ticonderoga, together with their communications, must be made as secure as possible. Amherst has been criticised for not going to Wolfe's assistance; but the critics have omitted to explain how he was to assist a force, the location or fate of which he did not know, but which at its possible nearest was separated from him by over 200 miles of trackless forest and enemy controlled waterway. An unprepared advance and his own defeat would entail disaster to his whole strategic plan for the conquest of Canada. It has been too generally assumed that Quebec was the key to Canada: it was not, as future events were to show.

Wolfe, on 31 July had in fact been defeated in his attack at the Montmorency Falls, near Quebec. On 7 August Amherst wrote to Wolfe and sent an officer of the Rangers off with it. The next day he sent three officers with four Indians to contact the Eastern Indians to try and get them to take a letter, with a note to Wolfe to reward them. Wolfe indeed at about this time had captured some letters from the French announcing Amherst's occupation of Crown Point and the fall of Niagara.[18] It is conceivable that he did not take adequate advantage of this information to contact his superior commander.

On 14 August Amherst wrote to Gage 'to recommend the Post of la Galette as of the utmost consequence to this country'. On 16 August a deserter from the French warships on Lake Champlain arrived, bringing valuable information. The French commander, Bourlemaque, had entrenched a position on the Isle aux Noix, at the north of Lake Champlain, defended by 100 guns, and he had four warships on the lake under the command of a captain of the French Navy, manned by regular soldiers, and mounting 12-pounder, 6-pounder, and 4-pounder guns. Amherst sent for Loring and told him that a force superior to these ships would have to be prepared.

On 17 August Amherst had a discussion with Loring as to the best type of craft to build to take on the French ships. Loring said that the Ticonderoga saw mills would be functioning again in two or three days. He added that the brig he was building would be insufficient by itself and that he and Ord were of the opinion that the quickest and best way of solving the problem was to build a sort of *radeau*, or raft, to carry six 24-pounder guns, and that this could be done in about ten days.

During this period of waiting Amherst put regiments on to building a road from Ticonderoga to Crown Point, the construction of a fort at Crown Point, and the stocking there of provisions. Scouting parties were out constantly and detachments were engaged in tracking and engaging marauding parties of enemy Indians. Reconnaissance patrols were despatched to report on other possible water routes between the Hudson and Lake Champlain. It would be important to watch any such routes for possible enemy counter-movement, but none were found. He had some trouble with desertions; on 29 August he ordered out on duty a provincial company from one of the posts, but sixty-four men deserted out of a total strength of eighty, and on 31 August three Rangers deserted.

On 8 September Amherst had news of Wolfe in a letter from Thomas Pownall, the Governor of Massachusetts. The master of a ship had arrived from the Isle of Orleans near Quebec on 16 August with defeatist rumours of a garrison being left for the winter, with the fleet stationed off the Gaspe peninsula at the mouth of the St Lawrence. The ship must have left the Isle of Orleans shortly after Wolfe's defeat at the Montmorency. Amherst wrote: 'This will frighten and throw into despair all New England, but I flatter myself, notwithstanding the Masters news Mr Wolfe will take Quebec.' Indeed, as Amherst made this entry in his journal, Wolfe was planning to do just that thing.[19]

On 12 September Amherst had a letter from Brigadier-General Stanwix which caused him to comment in exasperation,

'Very great backwardness in everything that should be going on there'. The next day he sent off an officer to try and quicken up Loring because his ten days were long since past and there was no sign of the *radeau* being finished. The officer came back with the information that the saw mill was often out of repair. On 18 September he had a letter from Gage, who said he had given up the idea of taking La Galette. Amherst was furious. Three days later he entered in his journal: 'I answered Br Gages Letter I received the 18th, with great concern that he had given up La Gallette which the Enemy could not have hindered him from taking and which he had my positive orders for doing; he may not have such an opportunity as long as he lives. I ordered it because I knew the situation of the Enemy was such that it could not fail. They have found difficulties where there are none, and must have given them more difficulty than the taking of la Gallette would have done; it is now too late to remedy this. He could have gone the 6th of this month.'[20]

On 19 September Amherst received a letter from Brigadier-General Whitmore, commanding at Louisburg, enclosing a letter he had from Wolfe, dated 11 August. In this Wolfe said that he was in some doubt of being able to take Quebec, but would destroy everything and take post on the Isle of Coudres. He had heard nothing of Amherst. However, when Amherst got this letter it was already six days since Quebec had fallen and Wolfe had been killed.

Three regiments were at this time employed in repairing Fort Ticonderoga and in building Loring's two vessels. On the afternoon of 29 September the *radeau* was launched and named *Ligonier*. On 9 October the officer whom Amherst had sent to Wolfe on 7 August returned. Wolfe had sent him off down the St Lawrence on 7 September with another officer. Off Halifax the vessel had been boarded by a pirate and the latter officer had thrown all the despatches overboard, 'so', wrote Amherst, 'I am not the whit the wiser, except that he says Gen Wolfe had got with allmost his whole Army above the Town & he thinks he will not take it.'

At last everything was ready and on 11 October the force embarked and set off on the seventy-mile passage to the Isle aux Noix. Progress was held up by stormy weather; the flotilla had to seek the shelter of a bay on 12 October, and they were forced to remain there by gale force winds. On 14 October Amherst received a report from Loring that he had put all the French ships out of action so that command of Lake Champlain was now assured. On 18 October he received letters with the news of the capture of Quebec and the death of Wolfe. The wind being northerly, it would take him another ten days to get to the Isle aux Noix, and as the whole French army would now, he reckoned, be concentrating at Montreal, there would be no chance of his plan of sending a detachment to surprise Montreal succeeding. Amherst therefore decided to return to Crown Point to finish the works there before the army went into winter quarters.

This was the end of the campaign of 1759. On 21 October Amherst was back at Crown Point and sent off orders to Gage about quartering the troops for the winter. There was still much to be done at Crown Point to put it into a state of defence for the winter. It was getting cold and the provincial troops wanted to go home. On 1 November the Massachusetts and New Jersey troops mutinied and started marching off, but Amherst took the picquet out and stopped them. On 3 November news arrived that a battalion of the Massachusetts Regiment on Lake George had run away but that General Lyman had gone after them with his Connecticut Regiment to bring them back. On 10 November it was the King's Birthday; Amherst, after a special parade and a Royal Salute, distributed rum and beer to each regiment so that every man could drink the King's health. But the next day he noted, 'The Provincials have got home in their heads and will now do very little good.' And so on 12 November he allowed the provincial regiments to start marching off, after handing in tents, arms, and cartridge boxes. The last of them, Fitch's Connecticut Regiment, left on 25 November. Two days later Amherst himself followed Fitch's with the Regular regiments, leaving the 27th Foot and 200 Rangers to garrison Crown Point. On 27 November they reached Fort George; but freezing of the rivers now held up the boat flotillas, and on 5 December Amherst ordered the troops to leave the boats and march. As he was in a hurry, he set off ahead of them, and writes: 'On foot, crossed the river and walked 22 miles to Esqr Quaggenbush's at Kinderhook, a sandy poor soil the whole way.' On 6 December he covered 28 miles, on the 7th 22, on the 8th 30 miles, and on the 9th he 'went 28 miles through the Highlands . . . a very up and down hill road all the way'. On 10 and 11 December he covered 26 miles and a final 14 miles into New York. His journal is full of comments on the countryside, its state of development, and its future prospects. He might, in fact, have been going for a country stroll; but perhaps few general officers of today would have cared to undertake this formidable walk, particularly in a phenomenally hard winter.[21]

It had been a remarkably successful campaign. Once Louisburg had been captured, thereby denying access to the St Lawrence to the French fleet, the key to Canada lay, not in Quebec, but in Ticonderoga and Crown Point. These two places constituted a pivot of manoeuvre, aimed at the heart of the French defence, and a bulwark against any French counter-offensive against the American Colonies.

Amherst's plan for 1760 was a continuation of that of 1759—an attack up the St Lawrence from Quebec, and advance from Crown Point northwards, and a descent from Lake Ontario via the St Lawrence: all three movements being directed on Montreal. That town had indeed been designated as the political objective for the coming campaign, and it coincided closely enough with the military objective. Montreal could doubtless have been captured by a thrust from the newly established base at Crown Point, supported by an advance up the St Lawrence from Quebec. But, as already pointed out, the French army, the military objective, could have escaped up the St Lawrence to the Great Lakes.

As in the previous year, Amherst ordered the concentration at Albany to start at the beginning of May, and again, as he no doubt expected, the provincial regiments were slow in assembling. He wrote to the Governors concerned to hurry them on and ordered provisions for the campaign to be got ready as fast as possible so that the troops could take with them all that they could carry. On 12 May he noted that the preparation of batteaus and whale boats was going on well at

Albany, and the next day he started the artillery moving along the 200-mile line of communication between Albany and Fort Oswego. Six 24-pounder guns were by his orders sent to Shenectady, and a company of New York troops there were to take them on to Fort Stanwix. These guns were followed by some 9-pounders and 6-pounders, escorted by sailors and New York troops.

On 19 May Amherst received a letter from Pownall, the Governor of Massachusetts enclosing one from Brigadier-General the Hon. James Murray, commanding at Quebec. Murray reported that on 28 April he had marched out to attack the enemy who were advancing on Quebec. He had been defeated at Sainte Foy by the Chevalier de Lévis and had retreated into the city with the loss of all his guns. He added that he had been forced to go out and fight, because the enemy could have taken possession of the heights which command the town, and Quebec had not yet been re-fortified. He hoped he would not be reduced to extremity, but that the fleet would arrive, in which case he would retreat to the Island of Orleans to await reinforcements, unless he could do better. Amherst immediately sent orders to Louisburg for the despatch of the 8th and 22nd Foot to reinforce Murray, and detailed an officer to go to Boston and arrange the ships for their transport.

Amherst does not seem to have been seriously disturbed by the news of Murray's reverse. Operating on such a wide front, beyond reach of mutual support, there was always the risk of defeat in detail by an enemy operating on interior lines. But even if Quebec fell, and as long as Murray's army was not destroyed, pressure from the three directions should eventually force the French to withdraw from Quebec and concentrate on the approaches to Montreal.

The propaganda in England over the fall of Quebec the previous year had been such that the prospect of its loss shook public opinion. The effect of the news of Sainte Foy is well shown by the following comment by Horace Walpole: 'Who the deuce was thinking of Quebec? America was like a book one has read and done with; but here we are on a sudden reading our book backwards'.[22]

On 9 May Quebec was relieved by the arrival of a frigate,

heralding the approach of a British squadron. It had been a near thing; for had Lévis assaulted Quebec after the battle of Sainte Foy he would probably have captured it. The advantage of the interior lines had enabled him to mass over 7,000 men against the 3,266 rank and file that Murray had fit for duty in or near Quebec.

On 16 May the weak French naval squadron which carried Lévis's stores of food and ammunition was destroyed by ships of the British squadron. The next day Lévis retreated. The Navy had already saved Quebec, therefore, when Amherst received Murray's letter. As late as 28 May he received a report from Oswego that the French had captured Quebec, but on the same day he had a letter from Colonel Haviland, commanding at Crown Point, saying that two British prisoners who had escaped from Montreal on 18 May reported that the French had given up the siege and retired from Quebec. It was not till 11 June, however, that Amherst had complete and accurate intelligence of affairs at Quebec from an Indian party.

Build up of troops and stores continued along the line of the Mohawk to Oswego and at Ticonderoga and Crown Point. Provincial regiments and detachments were still arriving at Albany during the first part of June. On 12 June Amherst wrote in his journal: 'Col Worcester of the Connecticut Troops arrived, said their quota which ought to be 5000 would want 2000 of being compleat. The notions of peace have made all the provincials neglect raising their men & trouble themselves very little whether they were compleat. The fears they had of the French are now over & nothing but being in danger will induce them to assert themselves, tho' it must be of as much consequence this Campaign as ever it was that they should do it.'[23]

On 13 June Amherst sent Colonel Haviland 'his Instructions with orders to command the Troops to assemble at Crown Point'. For this campaign Amherst had decided to command personally the force assembling at Oswego, and on 19 June he left Albany on his way there. Along the route he exerted himself, pushing on provincial regiments, and then was taken ill with a pain in his breast which held him up for two

days. On moving on again he was much annoyed at finding the
1st Battalion 42nd Royal Highlanders much farther back than
he expected them, and wrote: 'Lt Col Hunt has greatly re-
tarded the whole by not advancing in front as expeditiously as
he should have done'. On 3 July Amherst reached Fort Stanwix,
about 120 miles from Albany. Beyond this post was the 'Great
Carrying Place' where boats, provisions, etc. were carried
over the eight miles from the Mohawk over the watershed
to Canada Creek, leading into Lake Oneida. Twelve miles
beyond the west end of the lake were the Oswego Falls,
where the boats were moved unloaded over rollers for sixty
yards to avoid the falls. They were then launched again and,
Amherst says, 'go down a very rapid & bad Stream where they
seldom miss being much damaged'. He thought that this showed
that building the boats at Albany was very extravagant, and
that it would have been much cheaper to have built them at
Lake Ontario.

On 11 July Amherst entered in his journal: 'I wrote to
Col Haviland, sent him a plan I had received from Quebec of
the Isle au Noix, & a letter from thence wrote by the Engineer
giving a description of it.' This was no doubt captured from
the French.[24]

Before Amherst could cross Lake Ontario he had to wrest
command of it from the French. Two French warships were
off Oswego on 12 July observing as much as they could of
Amherst's preparations. On 14 July, however, Loring arrived
from Niagara with his two new 'snows'. (A snow resembled a
brig, but carrying in addition to a main and foremast, a supplementary trysail mast close behind the mainmast.) The vessels
had sailed from Niagara before the 100 seamen, guns and
ammunition, despatched there by Amherst had arrived. However, Loring only wanted another forty seamen and three 6-
pounder guns and Amherst was able to supply these. One ship
now had sixteen 6-pounders and the other four 9-pounders.
Three whale boats manned by thirty picked soldiers were
added to Loring's command, and with this flotilla he departed
to look for the French. However, on 24 July Loring reported
that the French vessels had escaped into the St Lawrence, and
Amherst commented: 'So he will see them no more and a fine

opportunity is lost.' Nevertheless Amherst now had command
of Lake Ontario, and on 29 July he wrote to Haviland and
fixed 10 August as the date when the latter should start his
advance down Lake Champlain. Murray was too far away to
communicate with, but he, in accordance with a general
directive from Amherst, had started his movement up the St
Lawrence on 15 July. He had 2,450 men in thirty-two vessels
and a number of boats, and this force was followed by another
1,300 from Louisburg. That fortress, having no further value,
had been dismantled to free its garrison. The force advanced
slowly, landing occasionally to deal with enemy detachments
who were following the fleet on shore. On the evening of
4 August Murray's army reached the village of Sorel, about
fifty miles from Montreal, where there was a large force of the
enemy on each shore under command of Bourlamaque and
Dumas. Lévis was with the main French force at Montreal,
and the commanders at Sorel had orders to keep abreast of the
fleet as it advanced to Montreal. Murray sent off a patrol to
try and get news of Haviland. He then moved slowly on and,
by threatening to burn any houses from which men were absent,
secured the desertion of large numbers of the Canadian militia.
On 24 August he encamped on the Isle Sainte-Thérèse to await
the arrival of Amherst and Haviland.[25]

On 7 August, his concentration at last complete, Amherst
sent off an advanced detachment under command of Colonel
Haldimand, consisting of the light and grenadier companies of
the force, the 1st Bn. 42nd, and a company of Rangers, escorted
by the two snows. On 10 August the main body moved off,
with the 80th Light Infantry as advanced guard, followed at
10 a.m. by Amherst with the regulars and the artillery, whilst
Gage left in the evening with the provincials. The total strength
of the force was 10,142, together with about 700 Indians. The
regular element consisted of eight weak battalions.[26]

About thirty miles from the start the expedition was forced
to take shelter in a river, owing to a strong wind arising. The
provincials had to return to Oswego and Haldimand was held
up about six miles ahead of the main body. It was not till the
afternoon of the following day that the wind abated sufficiently
for the advance to be resumed. During the ensuing four days

the main body, pursuing a tortuous course close to the shore and disembarking at night, covered nearly 100 miles, and on 15 August it joined Haldimand's party on an island well down the St Lawrence. The next day the force moved seventeen miles farther on to Oswegatchie, about 120 miles from Montreal, where one of the French warships was encountered. Loring was still some way behind because he had not as yet been able to find a channel for his ships through the numerous islands. However, on 17 August the French ship was attacked by a flotilla under the command of Colonel Williamson consisting of five row galleys, of which four were each armed with one 12-pounder gun and the fifth with a howitzer. Amherst says that the galleys behaved very well and fired 118 shot against the Frenchman's 72, after which the latter struck. In this remarkable action the galleys were out-gunned, for the French ship mounted one 18-pounder, seven 12-pounders, two 8-pounders, and four swivels. This must be one of the few naval actions in history in which vessels under army command and manned by soldiers have defeated a regular warship! One imagines that Loring must have been the victim of some ribald comments when he eventually turned up two days later!

On 18 August Amherst began his movement against Fort Lévis on the Isle Royale, the only military obstacle between him and Montreal. The fort was strong and gallantly defended, and it was not till 25 August that it surrendered. The day before this event an officer arrived from Crown Point with a letter from Haviland, dated 7 August, in which he said that he would set off from Crown Point on 11 August, 'which', wrote Amherst, 'will very well answer'. That this letter took seventeen days to reach him, again underlines the great distances and consequent difficulties of intercommunication. On 28 August some Indians came in with the information that Murray had arrived at Montreal, and Amherst commented: 'So that I don't think it unlikely but that Mons Vaudreuil may capitulate for the Country'.[27]

Haviland had embarked at Crown Point with 3,400 regulars, provincials, and Indians, and on 15 August had arrived at Isle aux Noix. This post was defended by Bougainville with 1,700 men, whilst twelve miles away at St John was Roquemaure with another 1,200–1,500 and all the Indians. Haviland operated against Bougainville's communications with such success, that on 27 August the latter abandoned Isle aux Noix and fell back on St John. Haviland followed up and the united French forces retreated from St John to join Bourlemagne on the banks of the St Lawrence. Haviland was now outnumbered, so he halted, opened communications with Murray on the Isle Saint Thérèse, and consolidated his position to await Amherst's advance.[28]

Amherst was busy repairing his boats and the fort and was not ready for further movement till 30 August. Ahead lay the hazardous passage of the rapids, and Amherst decided to move the army in two halves; one half in boats while the other half was concentrated and ready to support if necessary. On 31 August the first half passed through the Galops rapids without difficulty and encamped on the Isle au Chat, about twenty-four miles from Fort Lévis (now renamed Fort William Augustus). On 1 September Amherst sent scouts forward along each side of the Long Sault rapids to make sure there was no enemy ambush, and he wrote to Gage to tell him that he was going forward to the Point de Maline and that he could move on himself or not as he thought fit. As the scouts had found no trace of the enemy, Amherst went on through the Long Sault rapids, which he says were 'frightful in appearance but not dangerous', and camped at Point de Maline, about fourteen miles from the Isle au Chat. He then sent parties forward to reconnoitre both shores of Lake St Francis. At 9 a.m. the next day Gage arrived, and at 11.30 the army started to row the 24 miles through Lake St Francis to La Pointe à Boudet. On 3 September it rained and blew hard all mornng so that no further progress was possible that day. Indians brought in a French prisoner, who said that a force of about 400 men had been at the Cedars rapids, but on news of Amherst's advance, they had retreated to Montreal. He also said that the Isle aux Noix had been captured, but that Murray was some distance from Montreal. (The last bit of information was of course untrue.)

On 4 September the boats moved off in one column as the next rapids would only take one boat abreast. Amherst made most of the men march on foot to make the boats lighter, for these rapids, the Cedars, the Buisson, and the Cascades, were the worst of the lot. Nevertheless, eighty-four men were drowned and fifty-six boats, together with artillery stores and some guns, were lost. The army camped at Isle Perrot, about thirty miles from La Pointe à Boudet. The next day was spent in closing the force up. An officer arrived from St John with a letter from Haviland, and Amherst wrote to Murray to notify him of his position.

On 6 September the army rowed in four columns to the Island of Montreal, and landed against only slight opposition. Amherst then marched his troops to within view of Montreal, and here they lay on their arms all night.

The following morning, as Amherst was riding round his force, he had a report from the advanced guard that two officers had arrived from de Vaudreuil, the Governor of Canada, to speak to him. They brought a request for a cessation of arms till de Vaudreuil, who was expecting a courier, knew whether or not peace had been declared. Amherst writes: 'This of course I refused & said I was come to take Canada and I did not intend to take anything else.' At daybreak on 8 September de Vaudreuil signed Amherst's terms, and the latter ordered Haldimand to take possession of the town with the light infantry and grenadiers. Murray and Haviland arrived to report.

It was doubtless with justifiable pride that Amherst wrote the following comment on the campaign: 'I believe never three Armys, setting out from different & very distant Parts from each other joyned in the Center, as was intended, better than we did, and it could not fail of having the effect of which I have just now seen the consequence.[29]

It had indeed been a remarkable achievement. Other than the battles of Quebec and Sainte Foy (both of which were probably unnecessary and were beyond his control), Amherst had conquered Canada without any major action and with astonishingly few casualties. The thoroughness of his administrative planning and the careful consolidation of every step made the whole affair appear so simple in retrospect and the final result so inevitable, that Amherst has been criticised for being too slow and cautious. But the reader will remember

Clausewitz's comment, recorded in the previous chapter, that 'Everything is very simple in war, but the simplest thing is difficult'.

One of the greatest difficulties with which Amherst had to contend was his lack of information both of the enemy and of the movements of his own subordinate commanders. More than most commanders, he had to contend with the fog of war. To quote Clausewitz again:

'The great uncertainty of all data in War is a peculiar difficulty, because all action must, to a certain extent, be planned in a mere twilight, which in addition not unfrequently—like the effect of a fog or moonshine—gives to things exaggerated dimensions and an unnatural appearance. . . .

'A great part of the information obtained in War is contradictory, a still greater part is false, and by far the greatest part is of doubtful character. What is required of an officer is a certain power of discrimination, which only knowledge of men and things and good judgment can give. The law of probability must be his guide.'[30]

Surely no commander in British history has used the law of probability to greater effect!

Chapter 10

GENERAL SIR WILLIAM HOWE
IN AMERICA

The rebellion of the American Colonies presented Great Britain with a strategical problem of a nature which she had never had to face before. In the Seven Years War, and in all previous conflicts, the political aim had been limited to objectives which did not include the subjugation of France, or any other foreign country, to British rule. Yet the suppression of a rebellion did entail such a conquest, and, furthermore, one carried out in such a way that the population would be reconciled to British rule, because its continued imposition by force was out of the question.

There was no reason to suppose that the majority of the population in North America were implacably hostile to the British connection, but equally there was no reason to suppose that they were particularly attached to it. Most experience shows that, whilst there are devoted and even fanatical adherents of both sides in a dispute, the larger proportion of the inhabitants of a country only want the fighting to stop, and will tend to support the side which looks like winning. Our own Wars of the Roses and the struggle between King and Parliament are examples.

If the political aim was clear, the strategy to achieve it was not so readily apparent. There were no great centres of population, the occupation of which would necessarily cause the collapse of the rebellion, and though a rebel field army would be an obvious target, its destruction could still be followed by irregular armed resistance. The strategical centre of gravity lay clearly in the will to resist of a sizeable proportion of the

American people, and reports differed widely as to the relative numbers of those opposed to and loyal to the British Crown, respectively. A conceivable strategy would have been to occupy, as a first step, the most important towns as quickly as possible to demonstrate the continued reality of the King's government and to control the resources of the country. But this was quite impracticable because, as shown in Chapter 1, the British Army of the time was a very small affair. Nor could a British Army attempt to bring the rebels to heel by a policy of ruthless devastation of the countryside, as was pursued by Sherman in his March to the Sea during the American Civil War, because this would cause bitter resentment; for the British had to win the hearts as well as the minds of the people and had not, as had the Federals, the strength to dispense with the former.

In fact when hostilities opened with the few thousand British troops in America almost besieged in the hostile city of Boston, many thought that the revolt could not be quelled by military means. The more pessimistic pointed out that, of the American population of nearly three million, about 450,000 must be considered as fit to bear arms.[1] On 30 June 1775 General Harvey, the adjutant-general in Great Britain, wrote to General Irwin: 'Taking America as it present stands, it is impossible to conquer it with the British Army . . . To attempt to conquer it internally by our land force is as wild an idea as ever contraverted common sense.'[2] On the same day he wrote to Major-General Sir William Howe: 'Unless a settled plan of operations be agreed upon for next spring, our army will be destroyed by damned driblets . . . America is an ugly job . . . a damned affair indeed'.[3] Harvey's opinion was endorsed by the Secretary at War, Lord Barrington, who said that the Americans 'may be reduced by the fleet, but never can be by the army'.[4] Indeed, most military opinion took the same standpoint, and considered that the principal American ports should be occupied as naval bases and that the external and coastal trade should be cut off.[5] The disadvantage of this solution was that, even if successful, it would take a long time to be effective.

In spite of these opinions, the Government decided that troops should be used against the rebels, but the problem remained as to how they could best be used. A rapid onslaught against those centres where insurgent forces were now gathering might succeed, but if not, there was a danger that the British units might become too depleted for further action owing to the inability of the Government to provide immediate reinforcements. Another possibility suggested was the methodical reconquest of the country, area by area, using regiments raised from loyalists to garrison the territory regained to avoid tying down units of the field army. The disadvantage of this procedure was the length of time it would take, and by the end of 1775 there was news that France and Spain were arming and intended to supply the rebels with arms, whilst the Dutch in the West Indies were prepared to send them ammunition.[6] This enhanced the need for a rapid end to the contest, but it also showed the danger of depleting the troops in Great Britain below the minimum required for home defence.

Optimistic reports (subsequently proved wrong) suggested that the majority of the people in the southern Colonies were actively loyal to the Crown. As a result, it was believed by many that if the New England Colonies could be isolated from the others, the reconquest of the former would suffice to end the rebellion. General Gage, commanding the troops in Boston, shared this view, and from it there arose the idea of seizing control of the River Hudson and of opening communication with Canada via Ticonderoga and Crown Point, so severing contact between New England and the Middle Colonies. In fact the possibility of such a move had already occurred to the rebel Congress, who were then in possession of both Crown Point and Ticonderoga.

For the post of Commander-in-Chief in America, the Government made the obvious choice—Amherst. However, Amherst refused, giving as his reason his inability to command against Americans. This was understandable because so many of the officers who had served under him in the provincial regiments held posts in the rebel army. In view of Amherst's refusal, the Government took the extraordinary decision to send out to America three major-generals to assist Gage: Sir William Howe, Henry Clinton, and John Burgoyne. These officers sailed with the reinforcements which reached Boston before the battle of Bunker Hill on 17 June 1775. On 2 August 1775 the Government decided that Howe should succeed Gage in command and recalled the latter, nominally for consultation. In October 1775 Gage handed over his command and sailed for England. The following April he was formally relieved of the command of the troops in North America, and was replaced by Howe in the Colonies and by Sir Guy Carleton, the Governor of Quebec, in Canada. Howe was given the local rank of general. Apart from Amherst, General Sir William Howe was probably the most distinguished of British officers at this time. In 1758 he commanded the 58th Foot at the capture of Louisburg, and under his command it was acknowledged to be 'the best trained battalion in all America'; during the attack on Quebec he had led the forlorn hope up the heights of Abraham, a most gallant feat; and in 1774, owing to his reputation as a trainer of light infantry, he had been selected to train the light companies of all the regiments in England.[7] He was also one of the best-loved commanders in all British military history. Officers and men were devoted to him and would follow him anywhere.

Some weeks before he took over command, Howe made his own appreciation of the military situation in a letter to his brother, Admiral Lord Howe, who sent it to Lord Germain. He considered 5,000 troops necessary for the defence of Boston and proposed that an attack should be launched from the sea against New York by an army of 15,000 men, whilst 4,000 regulars accompanied by Canadian militia and Indians advanced from Canada. He recommended the appointment of a viceroy to co-ordinate these operations.[8] Howe added that he regarded these forces as the minimum necessary, and that if the Government could not provide them it should withdraw altogether from the Colonies.

On 9 October 1775, after he had taken over command, Sir William Howe submitted an official appreciation to Lord Dartmouth, Secretary of State for the American Colonies, which showed some modification of his previous views, and which embodied those of Gage, Clinton, and Burgoyne. He stated that the strength of the army would not be sufficient to hold both Boston and New York, and his estimate of the force required to capture the latter city was now 12,000 men. After New York had been won, five battalions would suffice to hold it whilst the rest of this force was used to open communications with Canada in conjunction with an army of 3,000 operating from that province. Once established, these communications should be secured by proper posts and the rebels in New York province reduced. After this had been accomplished, the two forces might advance into the province of Massachusetts by separate routes 'as circumstances may arise'.[9] At this stage, then, Howe seems to have agreed with the prevailing view that in New England lay the seat of the rebellion, and that if it could be conquered the revolt would collapse.

Now, using the River Hudson and the river and lake chain north to Canada as a base of operations and as a line of communications for an attack on New England, and also as a barrier against rebel reinforcements from the west, was a defensible strategy—particularly whilst the main American forces were concentrated in New England. But to hold the Hudson as a barrier to isolate the New England Colonies from the others was not a practical strategy at all, as Howe realised. Yet it was the fascination of such an idea (which may have seemed feasible to politicians poring over a small-scale map) that led to the disaster of Saratoga and France's entry into the war. To hold a river line with reasonable success demands large forces. Clausewitz calculated that if an enemy could pass 20,000 men across a river in twenty-four hours, and if the defender could appear at any point of the river within twelve hours with 20,000 men, then the passage could not be forced. He continued: 'Now as in twelve hours, the time for intelligence included, we can march twenty miles, therefore every forty miles 20,000 men would be required, which would make 60,000 for the defence of a length of one hundred and twenty miles of river.'[10] This is about the length of the Hudson which would have to be defended. Even if the maximum American force which might attempt to pass the river was 10,000, then 30,000 British troops would have been required for its defence on Clausewitz's calculations. In fact, however, there is no example in military history of a river line being held successfully for a long period against determined efforts to cross it.

It does not appear that Burgoyne, who commanded the army which operated from Canada and surrendered at Saratoga, ever considered this idea of isolating New England as a practicable proposition. In a paper submitted to Germain on 28 February, 1777, he discussed the problems of the proposed operation and added: 'These ideas are formed upon the supposition that it be the sole purpose of the Canada army to effect a junction with General Howe, or after co-operating so far as to get possession of Albany and open the communication to New York, to remain upon the Hudson River and thereby enable that general to act with his whole force to the southward.'[11] Nothing here about isolating New England, and either of Burgoyne's alternative objectives would have been more easily achieved by moving his army by sea to New York. In fact Burgoyne himself suggested this, if his force was primarily intended to reinforce Howe.

Meanwhile to Howe, when he took over command, it was apparent that his small army was in an impossible position and he recommended that Boston should be evacuated. Lord Dartmouth had come to the same conclusion and on 9 November Howe received an order from him to carry out the evacuation. Shortly after issuing this order Dartmouth handed over the office of Secretary of State for the American Colonies to Lord George Germain (the former Lord George Sackville who had been court-martialled for his conduct at the battle of Minden and declared unfit to serve the King in any capacity). Shortage of transport and the advent of the winter gales stopped Howe from embarking his troops for the time being, and it was not till March 1776 that the ships carrying the army and its dependents sailed from Boston to Halifax.

Before he left Boston, Howe's later thoughts on the strategy which should be pursued are hinted in a letter he wrote to Dartmouth (not knowing that Germain had taken over) in January 1776. He said:

'With a proper army of 20,000 men, having 12,000 at New York, 6,000 at Rhode Island, and 2,000 at Halifax, the present unfavourable appearance of things would probably wear a different aspect before the end of the ensuing campaign. With fewer troops the success of any offensive operations will be very doubtful, the enemy possessing advantages that will not be readily overcome by a small force; neither is their army to be despised, having in it many European soldiers, and all or most of the young men of spirit in the country, who are exceedingly diligent and attentive to their military profession.'[12]

From this assessment it would appear that Howe was no longer interested in the project of an advance from Canada to the Hudson. His comment on the worth of the American army was timely, because there was an all too prevalent opinion in England that the Colonials could only muster a half-trained mob of militia who could be easily brushed aside.

Howe was very annoyed at the despatch of an expedition to Charleston in South Carolina, which Dartmouth had been persuaded would rally the loyalists in the Carolinas and Virginia. He wrote in another letter to Dartmouth of January 1776: 'But I am free to own my opinion to your Lordship which has been to leave the southern provinces in the fullest persuasion of their security, until the rebels should have been defeated on the side of New York, which event appears to me more clearly than ever of so much consequence that our utmost strength should be exerted to accomplish it before designs of less importance are taken up inconsistent with the general plan of operations for the ensuing campaign.'[13] Howe then went on to explain the serious effect which diversions could have on the main campaign. It was a well-merited rebuke on the evils of departing from the principle of concentration.

On 1 May 1776 Admiral Lord Howe, who had been appointed to the naval command in American waters, and Sir William Howe were appointed joint civil commissioners, in addition to their military functions, with rather restricted powers for negotiating peace with the rebels. The consequent task of combining military force and civil persuasion affected, of course, the way the brothers carried out their operations.

On 12 May Howe wrote to Germain from Halifax, saying that he proposed to occupy Rhode Island as soon as the situation at New York was in hand. He emphasised that the British Army must not get involved again in the occupation of a defensive position as at Boston. He hoped that the army from Canada would be able to reach the Hudson and join him. This crossed a letter from Germain of 3 May agreeing Howe's plan for attacking New York but directing him to await the arrival of the reinforcements from England before doing so. On 11 June 1776 the army sailed from Halifax on its way to New York.

The reinforcement which Howe might expect had been notified to him by Germain at the end of March. These included 12,000 Hessian mercenaries, over 3,000 Highlanders, and the 2,000 troops who had been sent to Charleston.

The American Army with which Howe had to deal was a curious affair. Each colony, or province, had its militia from which came the provincial regiments that had fought under Amherst some fifteen years previously. In addition to the militia, however, a 'Continental', i.e. regular, army had been created in June 1775, which was intended to consist of 20,370 men. Initial enlistments had been slower than expected and the strength at the end of the year had only reached about 6,000 men. All the original battalions had been raised in New England, which in that year alone did indeed constitute the core of the rebellion; but in 1776 Continental regiments were being raised in all the Colonies, and during the year there served a total of 46,900 regulars and 42,700 militia. But the militia strength grew or dropped according to whether or not their own colony was being menaced. During the whole war about 250,000 men passed through the ranks of the Continental army and the militia.[14]

Howe's army landed on Staten Island on 2 July and awaited the reinforcements from England and Charleston. By 22 August all these troops had arrived and Howe had completed the organisation and equipment of his army. A landing was then effected on Long Island to attack Washington's army, defending the approaches to New York. Five days later Howe won an easy victory at the battle of Long Island, and the Americans retreated across the East River to Manhattan Island. It was some time before Howe followed, and he was criticised both for this delay and for his failure to storm the redoubts held by the American rearguard on Long Island. But as he says himself:[15] 'I knew well that any considerable loss sustained by the army could not speedily nor easily be repaired. I also knew that one great point towards gaining the confidence of an army (and a general without it is upon dangerous ground) is never to expose the troops when, as I said before, the object is inadequate.' One ponders these wise words of Sir William Howe, when one contemplates the expensive assaults on the Western Front during the First World War.

Before the East River could be crossed, small boats had to be moved by the Navy and positioned opposite the point selected for attack. Owing to difficult tides and the necessary restriction of the movement to the hours of darkness, this took time, and it was not till 15 September that Howe was able to mount his attack and occupy New York. He now consolidated his hold on the city so that the troops could be sure of spending the winter in safety and comfort. During this period he amassed information about the surrounding country for the campaign of the following year, because he considered it too late in the season to attempt a decision in the remaining period of suitable weather. Of this information, he says:[16] 'With regard to the knowledge of the country, so necessary to be obtained previous to the movement from New York, I beg leave to mention the difficulties we laboured under in that respect throughout the war. The country is so covered with wood, swamps, and creeks, that it is not open in the least degree to be known, but from post to post, or from accounts to be collected from the inhabitants, entirely ignorant of military description.'

Washington's troops, in the meantime, remained in their fortified positions at the northern end of Manhattan Island, including the strong posts of Fort Washington and Fort Lee, opposite each other on the left and right banks of the Hudson respectively.

On 11 October Howe was ready and moved troops by boat up the East River with the object of landing and marching against Washington's communications to force him to abandon his Manhattan Island positions. Washington retreated immediately, leaving 3,000 men to garrison Fort Washington, and took up a defensive position at White Plains, about fourteen miles north of Manhattan Island.

On 28 October Howe carried out a preliminary attack to seize an American advanced position on the west of the Bronx River. After a tough struggle this was successful, and Howe was now poised for the main attack. This, however, was never launched because of what Howe called 'political reasons'.[17] But he had no regrets over a lost opportunity, for he writes:

'If, however, the assault had been made and the lines carried, the enemy could have got off without much loss, and no way had we, that I could ever learn, of cutting off their retreat by the Croton Bridge . . . By forcing the lines we should undoubtedly have gained a more brilliant advantage, some baggage, and some provisions; but we had no reason to suppose that the rebel army could have been destroyed. The ground in their rear was such as they could wish for securing their retreat, which seemed to be their principal object.'[18]

Howe would have had Clausewitz's support for this statement, for the latter lists three possible aims of battle: the destruction of the enemy's force, the conquest or defence of a place, and the conquest or defence of an object.[19] Howe says that he could not have achieved the first, he did not covet the position of White Plains, and Washington's baggage and provisions did not constitute an adequate object.

If the British force had included a strong body of cavalry then it might have been possible to destroy Washington's army, which had practically no cavalry of its own at that time. It is true that the country was difficult, but several regiments of light dragoons (instead of only two), with their ability to fight on foot, would have given Howe a mounted arm, with the speed to counter the rapidity of withdrawal by the lightly equipped Americans. Indeed, if he had had, say, six regiments of cavalry, Howe might have destroyed Washington's army in 1777. However, the difficulty lay in the provision of horses. There were not many available in America, and a high proportion of those sent by sea died during the passage. Of 950 horses embarked in one convoy, for instance, more than 400 never reached New York;[20] and in January 1780 the ships carrying Clinton's expedition to Savannah ran into a storm and all the cavalry horses perished.

After this latter disaster Lieutenant-Colonel Banastre Tarleton managed to requisition local horses to remount the small force of dragoons, but these were very inferior to the horses that had been lost, and the men were determined to capture better horses from the enemy.[21]

The 'political reason' which caused Howe to call off his attack at White Plains was probably the arrival of an American officer deserter from Fort Washington who brought plans of the fort and the consequent promise of an easy victory. As the war was still in progress when Howe was addressing the House of Commons Committee, it would obviously have been undesirable to reveal this information. Fort Washington was a far better prize than the baggage and provisions of Washington's army, and on 16 November 1776 Howe attacked and captured it, together with its garrison and valuable stores and equipment. It was a major disaster for the Americans, particularly as it had been tying down a large British garrison for the defence of New York. Fort Lee, on the opposite bank, was captured by Lord Cornwallis, the garrison abandoning it on his approach.

Washington's army, joined by the garrison of Fort Lee, retired through Newark to New Brunswick and beyond, pursued by Cornwallis, who halted for six days at New Brunswick. Washington withdrew his troops across the River Delaware. Cornwallis, addressing the Parliamentary Committee, explained why his prolonged halt at New Brunswick was necessary. 'We arrived,' he said, 'at Brunswick the night of the first of December. We had marched that day twenty miles through exceeding bad roads. We subsisted only on the flour we found in the country; and as the troops had been constantly marching ever since their first entrance into the Jerseys, they had no time to bake their flour; the artillery horses and baggage horses were quite tired.'[22]

By the time that Cornwallis had renewed his pursuit and reached the Delaware, the Americans had crossed the river and, of course, removed all the boats. The defence of Trenton on the Delaware was allotted by Howe to the Hessians, because they were traditionally on the left of the British line. He despatched Clinton with 6,000 men to take possession of Rhode Island. The harbour there was of importance to the Navy because the New York rivers were ice-bound in winter.

Early on Christmas Day Washington crossed the Delaware and surprised the Hessian brigade at Trenton. Colonel Rahl, who had failed to obey orders to construct defensive works and had been slack in his duty, was killed, and his brigade of 1,300 men surrendered. The worst effect of this incident was the boost it gave to the morale of Washington's army, which had sunk very low. Washington advanced to Morristown, which was some forty miles north-east of Trenton and twenty-five miles west of New York.

On 30 November 1776 Howe wrote to Germain giving his plans for the next campaign and the number of troops he would require to execute them. He planned two offensive operations, each requiring 10,000 men; one from Rhode Island towards Boston and the other from New York towards Albany. Rhode Island itself would be garrisoned by 2,000 men and New York by 5,000; while another 8,000 would be needed in New Jersey to hold Washington there by threatening Philadelphia. In the autumn he proposed to attack Philadelphia, the leading city of America and the capital of the revolutionary government, and then Virginia. He would follow this up by a winter campaign against South Carolina and Georgia. To enable him to carry out this programme, he needed another 15,000 infantry, an additional battalion of artillery, and ten ships of the line. This would give him an army of 35,000 men to oppose the 50,000 voted by Congress for the next campaign, exclusive of large bodies of militia.

It will be seen from this that Howe intended first to clear up New England and New York Province, and then move gradually southwards, using the winter for campaigning in the southern Colonies.

Germain received Howe's letter on 30 December, and on 9 March Howe received his reply, dated 14 January, which was hardly satisfactory. Germain could not provide the battalion of artillery and he proposed sending 7,800 reinforcements which he reckoned should bring Howe's strength up to the required 35,000. Meanwhile he postponed a decision on the plan till the arrival of Howe's next letter. Howe could only conclude that Germain, in his calculations as to the army's strength, must have included wounded, sick, and prisoners of war. However, after writing his letter of 30 November, Howe had begun to doubt whether the comparatively large reinforcements he had asked for would reach him in time to start the extensive campaign that he had proposed. Knowledge of Germain must also have played some part in these doubts. Information, which he considered reliable, led him to believe that he could reduce Pennsylvania, even if he started the campaigning season with no more than 19,000 fit men. Accordingly he wrote a second letter to Germain on 20 December 1776 proposing a modified plan in which he would act offensively only in Pennsylvania, leaving the operation against Boston until the necessary reinforcements could arrive from Europe. At the same time he asked for information as to any other general plans which might be thought advisable, both with the army under his command at its existing strength and after it had been reinforced. Howe says that this letter was received in England on 23 February 1777, which was so long before Burgoyne's departure that Germain had ample opportunity to tell him the contents. Howe followed this up with a private letter to Germain on 20 January, urging the supply of more troops. He needed 20,000, but would be satisfied with the 15,000 he had asked for. The extra 5,000 would enable him to send a detachment by sea towards Philadelphia, whilst the main body advanced overland through New Jersey. The private letter was sent, of course, after the reverse at Trenton. It also reached England before Burgoyne sailed.

When on 9 March Howe received Germain's letter of 14 January, he assumed that his modified plan would be approved, and on 2 April he wrote to Germain saying that as the reinforcements he had asked for could not be expected, he had relinquished the idea of any operations except to the southward, and a possible diversion to the Hudson. Owing to the difficulties of crossing the Delaware by a march through Jersey, he proposed to invade Pennsylvania by sea, and would probably have to abandon the Jerseys. The army would thus be out of touch with New York and the Hudson until Philadelphia had been taken. In the previous campaign, he added, his force had been equal to the task of an advance overland, but the posts he would now have to leave to protect his long line of communications (nearly 100 miles) would leave the army too weak. His numbers fit for duty amounted to 18,100 (exclusive of 3,000 provincials), which he would distribute as follows: 11,000 for the invasion of Pennsylvania, 4,700 for the defence of New York, and 2,400 to garrison Rhode Island.

Germain answered Howe's letters of 20 December and 20 January on 3 March 1777, and the reply reached Howe on 8 May. Germain approved Howe's modified plan, but could now only provide 2,900 men as reinforcements. At the same time, he recommended a diversion to the Massachusetts and New Hampshire coasts as far as the main plan would permit! After consulting with Admiral Lord Howe, as Germain had requested, Sir William Howe replied in June 1777 that no such diversion was practicable, without interfering with the main operations which Germain had approved.

Howe's letter of 2 April was answered by Germain on 18 May 1777, giving approval to the expedition to Pennsylvania. He added that he could not furnish the supplies requested, and was concerned that Howe's force was not as suitable for the operations proposed as it had been in the previous campaign. Seldom can a commander have been so ill supported by the responsible minister!

Howe complains that Germain did not seem to realise that the provision of garrisons for various posts must of necessity weaken the field army. And as regards an overland advance to Philadelphia he adds: 'The communications for provisions through such an extent of country could not possibly be maintained with the force at my command!' Germain assumed too, from various reports he had received, that Washington's army was weak and that the inhabitants were so loyal to the Crown that it would be easy to raise a force from them for interior defence. He preferred to believe these reports rather than those of the commander-in-chief.[23]

After the affair of Trenton, Howe had withdrawn his outpost line to New Brunswick and the Raritan River. In May 1777 Washington moved south from Morristown to Middlebrook, seven miles upstream from New Brunswick, where he would flank any British advance overland to Philadelphia.

On 5 June Howe received a copy of Germain's letter to Carleton in Canada, dated 26 March 1777, giving him the plan for Burgoyne's advance from Canada to the Hudson and saying that he would write to Sir William Howe by the first packet. There were no instructions to Howe included with the copy of the letter sent to him, nor was the letter to be written to him by the first packet ever sent.[24]

Before embarking for Pennsylvania, Howe feinted across the Raritan to make Washington think that he was advancing on Philadelphia. Washington, however, did not react. Howe then tried a rapid retreat to make his opponent think that the British were evacuating New Jersey in a hurry and in some confusion. This time Washington took the bait and followed. Howe then moved forward again, sending Cornwallis to the right to cut off Washington's retreat to the mountains. Cornwallis ran into and beat Washington's left column, but this warned him of the danger and he escaped Howe's trap. Howe then gave up his attempt to draw Washington into battle and moved to Staten Island to embark.[25]

Howe gave the following reasons for selecting Philadelphia as his principal objective:[26]

'In Pennsylvania [as compared with New England] . . . The increase of force which that country could afford to Washington was small in comparison to the other, and the defence of Philadelphia was an object which I justly concluded would engage the whole of his attention. It was incumbent upon him to risk a battle to preserve that Capital. And as my opinion has always been that the defeat of the regular army is the surest way to peace, I invariably pursued the most probable means of forcing its commander to action, under circumstances the least hazardous to the royal army; for even a victory, attended by a heavy loss of men on our part, would have given a fatal check to the progress of the war, and might have proved irreparable.'

That last phrase shows the difficulties under which Sir William Howe waged his war. With a Government unwilling, or unable, to supply him with reinforcements, heavy losses would so weaken his strength in relation to the large reserves of manpower available (potentially at any rate) to the rebel Congress, that he would eventually be unable to prosecute offensive operations.

As regards criticism that he should have gone up the River Hudson to facilitate the approach of Burgoyne's army to Albany, Howe pointed to the obstacles to be surmounted in penetrating such difficult country defended, as it would have been, by Washington's whole force. He then asks what would have been gained if he had then reached Albany after expending the whole campaign on that object alone.[27] What indeed? Howe's simple question shows how weak and pointless was the strategy which dictated Burgoyne's advance.

The importance of Philadelphia to the rebels was stated by Howe as follows:[28] 'A city from whence by means of the River Delaware, the rebels drew the greatest part of their supplies— the capital of Pennsylvania—the capital, as it were, and residence of the Congress in North America, situated in one of the most fertile provinces of that Continent.'

It is apparent how the views of the British commander-in-chief changed as more and more intelligence reached him of the strength and distribution of the American forces, the political situation, the resources available to the rebels, and the feelings of the inhabitants.

On 15 July Howe received a letter from Burgoyne informing him on his capture of Ticonderoga, which was to be garrisoned from Canada so that his whole force should be available for further operations. Howe replied that he expected Washington would follow him to Pennyslvania, but that if he went north he 'should soon be after him'.[29]

The field army which embarked for the Philadelphia campaign consisted of 14,000 men, whilst about 3,000 were left in Rhode Island and 8,500 in New York. Howe knew Washington to have about 15,000 regulars 'exclusive of almost any number he pleased of militia'.[30] The force sailed from New York on 23 July and arrived off the Delaware on 30 July. Howe had written to Germain on 16 July saying that he proposed to go up the Delaware, instead of the Chesapeake as he had originally intended, so that he would be nearer to New York in case he had to follow Washington; though he expected the latter to follow him to Pennsylvania.[31] (It is interesting that it does not seem to have occurred to Washington that his surest way of defending Philadelphia would have been to move against Burgoyne.)

The Delaware was known to be blocked by floating batteries and obstructions, but the troops could doubtless have been landed. However, after sailing into Delaware Bay, news reached Admiral Lord Howe and his brother Sir William that Washington had crossed the Delaware and was marching towards Wilmington. This completely altered the situation. Not only was a landing from the Delaware likely to be opposed, but as Washington had indeed brought his army south to defend Philadelphia, there was no further necessity to be prepared to follow him north. The expedition accordingly turned about and headed for the Chesapeake.[32] Unfavourable winds delayed the passage and it was not till 25 August that the army landed at the Head of Elk (the mouth of the Elk River). The landing was not opposed by the Americans because when the fleet left the Delaware Washington at first thought that the troops had returned to co-operate with Burgoyne and later that they had gone to Charleston.[33]

On 11 September Howe defeated Washington at the battle of Brandywine. It was unfortunately impossible to pursue the retreating Americans because the flanking column under Cornwallis was worn out after marching eighteen miles and the horses of the only cavalry regiment, the 16th Light Dragoons, were in a wretched condition after the long voyage.[34] On 25 September the British troops marched into Philadelphia.

Howe now despatched a column of 3,000 men to bring up his supply column from the Elk River and sent other detachments to capture the forts covering the Delaware and open up the channel. Knowing that Howe's army had been weakened by these detachments, Washington attempted a surprise attack on the British lines at Germantown on the western side of Philadelphia. The attack was mounted on 4 October, and though Washington did indeed achieve a surprise, his army was again defeated.

Ten days later Burgoyne's army of 3,500 men surrendered to the American General Gates, with about 20,000 regulars and militia under his command. So ended a remarkably foolish expedition.

In Philadelphia the army settled down into comfortable winter quarters. As regards the situation of Washington's army, Howe said:[35]

'The entrenched situation of the enemy at Valley-Forge, twenty-two miles from Philadelphia, did not occasion any difficulties so pressing as to justify an attack upon that strong post during the severe weather, and though everything was prepared for that intention, I judged it imprudent, until the season should afford a prospect of reaping the advantages, that ought to have resulted from success in that measure; but having good information in the spring that the enemy had strengthened the camp by additional works, and being certain of moving him from thence when the campaign should open, I dropped all thoughts of an attack.'

In other words, Howe was certain of his ability of being able to manoeuvre Washington out of his Valley Forge position without having to incur heavy casualties in attacking it.

But Howe was not going to be able to carry out his projected destruction of Washington's army in the campaign of 1778 because, disgusted at Germain's failures to give him adequate support, he had asked to be relieved of his command. He explains his reasons as follows:[36]

'I continued my remonstrance for more troops. Perhaps it was impossible for the minister to send more. Such an acknowledgement would have been no reflection upon himself, and would have relieved my mind from the uneasiness it laboured under, in conceiving that my opinions of the necessity of reinforcements were deemed nugatory: and that, of course, I had lost the confidence of those, who were in the first instance to judge of my conduct. It cannot be surprising that, finding myself in this situation, I desired his Majesty's permission to withdraw from the command. I gave the true reason for that request—the loss of confidence. The reason was tacitly acknowledged to be well founded, for it was acquiesced in; and his Majesty was pleased to appoint a successor to the command of the army ... I am to this hour confident that if sufficient reinforcements had been sent from hence, and the plan of operations which I took upon me to propose had been adopted in its proper extent, the war in North America would have now worn a very different aspect.'

Howe was given the most outstanding farewell by his army that has ever occurred in British military history. It took place on 18 May 1778 and opened with a naval regatta and a display of dressed warships and salutes. Sir William Howe, accompanied by his brother the Admiral, then traversed a long avenue between the regiments, paraded with their colours. In the evening there was a ball and a display of fireworks, the whole entertainment having been paid for by the officers and named the *Meschianza*. On 25 May Howe handed over command to Sir Henry Clinton and sailed for England. Of his departure, one of his staff, Major Andre, wrote in his diary:

'I am just returned from conducting our beloved general to the water-side, and I have seen him receive a more flattering testimony of the love and affection of his army, than all the splendour and pomp of the *Meschianza* could convey to him. I have seen the most gallant of our officers, and those whom I least suspected of giving such instances of their affection, shed tears while they paid him farewell.'[37]

Clinton had had a letter from Germain saying that the friendly disposition of the inhabitants assisted by the new peace commission about to be sent out would probably end the war without further fighting. He added that only a few thousand of the year's reinforcements could be spared for Clinton and that he was to abandon any thought of offensive operations unless an opportunity arose of a decisive battle with Washington. He was to organise attacks on various parts of the coast and was authorised to evacuate Philadelphia. In the autumn Georgia and South Carolina were to be conquered, because reports had been received of strong loyalist sentiment in that area. The northern Colonies were then to be left alone except for a blockade, which, together with the political loneliness caused by the return of the southern Colonies to their allegiance, would probably end the rebellion there.[38]

It is hard to dignify with the name of strategy a policy based solely on wishful thinking—and thinking which had only the flimsiest grounds for support. Worse was to follow. The Franco–American alliance became known, and before ever he took up his command Clinton had received orders to evacuate Philadelphia and send a large part of his army to the West Indies and Florida. Further, if New York and Rhode Island could not be held, the remaining troops were to be evacuated to Halifax.[39]

And so Germain, with the possibility of decisive victory in his grasp, threw it all away. The evacuation of Philadelphia was the turning point of the war. Howe speaks of the result of occupying Philadelphia as follows:[40]

'The inhabitants in general of the province of Pennsylvania, those of the lower counties on Delaware, and those of the lower part of Jersey, were forward to return to their allegiance, and even to assist offensively in compelling his Majesty's revolted subjects to their duty. This favourable disposition, however, did not appear immediately—An equivalent neutrality was all I first experienced; our successes and apparent ability to retain our advantages induced the inhabitants at last to be less reserved. Secret intelligence, which, until that period, had been extremely difficult to procure, was then so good, and so readily obtained, that I could not but attribute it to the possession of Philadelphia, which convinced the country of the superiority, and persuaded them of the established power, of his Majesty's arms. The difficulties of the Congress, in raising supplies, and in recruiting Mr Washington's army, then indeed became real, and had the appearance of being insurmountable. But the French treaty, and our orders to evacuate Philadelphia, by which measure the protection of his Majesty's forces was to be withdrawn from the province, made a sudden and melancholy change in our affairs. The rebels were inspired with fresh hope; the friends of government were dismayed.'

This was the point that Germain and other politicans were unable to grasp. As pointed out at the start of this chapter, un-committed public opinion is likely to swing to the side which is apparently winning, and it was quite wrong to suppose that large numbers of enthusiasts in Georgia, Carolina, and else-where were only awaiting the opportunity to rush to arms in support of the British Crown.

Victory in America obviously depended on the destruction of the rebel forces and gaining at least the tacit acquiescence of a majority of the population. Given these twin aims, and the comparatively few troops at his disposal, it is difficult to see what other strategy would have been an improvement on that of Sir William Howe.

Chapter 11

RAMILLIES

Ramillies, Marlborough's masterpiece and one of the most brilliantly fought battles in military history, is an obvious choice to illustrate the tactics of the battlefield at the start of the eighteenth century. Fontenoy, fought under similar conditions, though in the middle of the century, is an entirely different encounter, in which the fighting and tactical ability of the British infantry almost snatched victory, in spite of the brilliance of Marshal Saxe, the enemy commander, and the indifferent performance of the Duke of Cumberland. Camden and Guildford, on the other hand, show how, towards the end of the century, troops trained in the techniques of forest warfare could be led to victory by that master of colonial warfare, Lord Cornwallis, against an enemy skilled in the knowledge and use of his own terrain.

At the opening of the campaigning season of 1706, the French forces in the north were grouped into three armies. Marshal Villeroy, with 60,000 men, was in Brabant facing the Duke of Marlborough; on the Upper Rhine Marshal Villars had 40,000 men to confront the Margrave of Baden; and between the two was Marshal Marsin, about the Upper Moselle with 25,000; whilst close to the last were the Household Cavalry—the *Maison du Roi*.

Early in May Marlborough's army began to assemble near Bilsen, some ten miles west of Maastricht. The British troops marched from the winter quarters on 8 May, and on 18 May they joined the Dutch at Bilsen. The Danish contingent was still two marches away, and neither the Prussians nor the Hanoverians had yet moved. Including the Danes, Marl-

RAMILLIES 175

borough had 130 squadrons of cavalry, 75 battalions of infantry, and 90 pieces of artillery. The British contingent of cavalry and infantry amounted to 15 squadrons and 15 battalions. These consisted of the regiments which later became the 1st, 3rd, 5th, 6th, and 7th Dragoon Guards, the 2nd and 5th Dragoons, the Grenadier Guards, the 1st (Royal Scots) (two battalions), the 3rd (Buffs), 8th (Kings), 10th (Lincolns), 15th (East Yorks), 16th (Bedfordshire and Hertfordshire), 18th (Royal Irish), 21st (Royal Scots Fusiliers), 23rd (Royal Welch Fusiliers), 24th (South Wales Borderers), 26th (Cameronians), 28th (Gloucesters), 29th (Worcestershire), and 37th (Hampshire). There were also the subsequently disbanded regiments of Evans, Macartney, and Stringer, as well as four battalions of the Scots Brigade in the Dutch service.

The French King, Louis XIV, intended that both Marsin and the *Maison* should join Villeroy, who was to lure the Duke of Marlborough to action by laying siege to the small fortress of Leauwe on the Little Geete River, about twenty miles west of Bilsen. Villeroy was well aware that neither the Danes nor the Prussians had as yet joined Marlborough, and he hoped therefore to be able to muster a superior strength against his opponent. He had also heard that a prominent citizen of Namur was in touch with Marlborough with a view to assisting him in the capture of this great fortress.[1]

Marlborough was also anxious for action, but not knowing of Louis's instructions to Villeroy, he did not think that the latter would move, and hoped to force him to by threatening Namur. On 18 May, however, he received information that Villeroy was concentrating his army between Wavre and Louvain. On 19 May he learned that the French were on the move and were approaching Tirlemont on the Great Geete River. Marlborough immediately sent word to the Duke of Würtemberg, commanding the Danes, asking him to join him as soon as possible, sending his cavalry on ahead. He then marched west to Borchloen on 20 May, but bad weather forced him to halt there during the whole of the following day. On 22 May he heard that Villeroy and the Elector of Bavaria had united their forces between Tirlemont and Judoigne on the Great Geete and were marching south.[2]

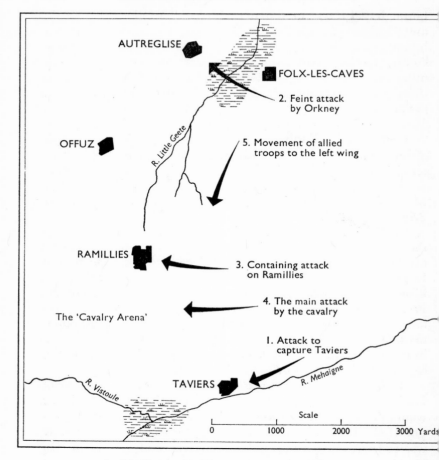

AUTREGLISE

FOLX-LES-CAVES

2. Feint attack
   by Orkney

5. Movement of allied
   troops to the left wing

OFFUZ

R. Little Geete

RAMILLIES

3. Containing attack
   on Ramillies

4. The main attack
   by the cavalry

The 'Cavalry Arena'

I. Attack to
   capture Taviers

R. Mehaigne

R. Vistoule

TAVIERS

Scale

0   1000   2000   3000 Yards

5. Marlborough's Plan at the Battle of Ramillies.

It was clear to Marlborough that Villeroy was seeking a
general action, and he decided to march round the source of the
Little Geete (which rose near Ramillies) and seize the high
ground lying between the two Geetes and the Mehaigne. The
ground bordering all these three rivers was very marshy at the
time, but they were separated by low ridges. One such ridge
runs south from Ramillies to the Mehaigne, and westwards this

opens out on to a plain on which stands the Tomb of Ottomond, the highest point in the immediate area.

About one and a half miles south of Ramillies is the village of Taviers on the Mehaigne. A mile north of Ramillies, and about half a mile west of the Little Geete, is the little village of Offuz, and a mile north again is Autreglise, also a little west of the Little Geete. Opposite Autreglise, beyond the east bank of the Little Geete, is Folx-les-Caves.

Shortly after midnight on 22/23 May Marlborough despatched Lord Cadogan with a cavalry escort, and accompanied by the regimental quartermasters, on a reconnaissance, with instructions to mark out a camp site if he did not encounter the enemy. Behind this party the army was on the march at 3 a.m. At 8 a.m. Cadogan's escort encountered French hussars just east of Ramillies. Cadogan sent back a report to Marlborough, who rode forward to join him at about 10 a.m.

Much of what was marshland at the time of the battle has since been drained and is now meadow, so that the Mehaigne and the Little Geete are not such great obstacles to movement as they were then. Apart from this, the battlefield probably looks little different today than it did in 1706. The villages have doubtless been mostly rebuilt, but they are unlikely to be very much bigger than they were then. The author arrived on the battlefield on the actual anniversary of the battle, 23 May, when the crops of this still primarily agricultural countryside were presumably at very much the same height. With these tall crops and the numerous minor ridges, it is apparent how much of the movement of his troops Marlborough was able to conceal from the enemy. The great cavalry arena between Ramillies and the Mehaigne must look much as it did at the time, and there is still some marsh about the little Vistoule stream which, running from the west, sweeps south to join the Mehaigne and create the angle between the two rivers in which Lieutenant-Colonel de La Colonie and his brigade were able to take refuge from the Allied cavalry.

There is an interesting glimpse of the French troops approaching the battlefield. De La Colonie wrote his memoirs of the period 1692 to 1717. At the battle of Ramillies he was serving as a Lieutenant-Colonel in the army of the Elector of Bavaria, which was of course allied with the French. He writes:[3]

'So vast was the plain of Ramillies that we were able to march our army on as broad a front as we desired and the result was a magnificent spectacle. The army began its march at six o'clock in the morning formed in two large columns, the front of each consisting of a battalion; the artillery formed a third which marched between the two infantry columns. The cavalry squadrons in battle formation occupied an equal extent of ground, and there being nothing to impede the view, the whole force was seen in such a fine array that it would be impossible to view a grander sight. The army had but just entered on the campaign, weather and fatigue had hardly yet had time to dim its brilliance and it was inspired with the courage born of confidence. The late Marquis de Goudrin, with whom I had the honour to ride during the march, remarked to me that France had surpassed herself in the quality of these troops; he believed the enemy had no chance whatever of breaking them in the coming conflict; if defeated now we could never again hope to withstand them.'

Soon after the French army had formed, de La Colonie could see from his position the advance of the Allied troops, who were now within range of the French artillery.

Cadogan had arrived just in time to see the French army moving into position. The greater part of the French cavalry— over 82 squadrons, including the *Maison du Roi*—took up a position on the ridge running south from Ramillies to the Mehaigne, formed in three lines and interlined with some of the best infantry. The sector from Ramillies to Offuz was covered by two lines of infantry, Ramillies itself having been hastily entrenched and garrisoned with twenty battalions. Between Offuz and Autreglise were more infantry with 50 squadrons of cavalry in immediate support.[4] In thus putting some cavalry on the left instead of placing all of it on the good cavalry ground on the right of his position, Villeroy had conformed to Marlborough's wishes, for seeing that the British general had drawn up some cavalry on his own right, Villeroy felt obliged to place cavalry to oppose them.[5]

The Allied army had advanced in eight columns parallel to the Mehaigne and had deployed over a four-mile front. It was about 1 p.m. when they came within effective artillery range of the enemy and a little after that the French guns opened fire. On the right of the Allied line were the bulk of the British infantry under the command of Lord Orkney, supported by the British cavalry commanded by Lumley. Marlborough's centre was composed mostly of Dutch infantry with Danish cavalry in support, whilst on the left were the mass of Dutch cavalry, ranged against the enemy cavalry on the Mehaigne-Ramillies ridge.

Marlborough, looking at the French position, saw that Villeroy's right rested on the swampy ground bordering the Mehaigne, just behind the village of Taviers. This village formed a potential bastion which would have to be seized because if the enemy held it they could flank with fire a cavalry attack on the Mehaigne–Ramillies ridge. Ramillies, held by the French, was a bastion on the other flank and would have to be neutralised. Towards the enemy's left the swampy borders of the Little Geete were something of an obstacle to an attack in that quarter. Marlborough noted that owing to the nature of the ground the French had had to take up a position which was concave in its general alignment. This enabled his own alignment to be convex, to conform with that of the enemy, which would give him the advantage of having a shorter distance over which to move troops from one part of the line to reinforce another part. In addition, the marshes which hindered an advance from his right would also impede any enemy counter-attack which sought to take advantage of any reduction of the number of troops facing them. Marlborough, however, was faced with no easy problem. Villeroy's position was strong and his army was about the same size as Marlborough's in cavalry and infantry, though the latter had some superiority in artillery. Furthermore, the French troops were good and, according to de La Colonie, their morale was high. In these circumstances the advantage lay with the defence, and any commander would have been justified in not risking an offensive battle. Nevertheless, this is what Marlborough decided to do.

Marlborough's plan in brief was that his main attack would

be a cavalry onslaught over the open country between Ramillies
and the Mehaigne, and to support this there would be a strong
feint from his right to prevent the enemy withdrawing troops
from their left to reinforce their right and centre. To protect
the flanks of the cavalry attack, Taviers would be taken and
Ramillies would be masked by a strong infantry attack. Finally,
he would use his shorter line and the folds in the ground to
move troops under cover from enemy view from his right and
centre to reinforce his main attack.[6]

The above plan was assisted by Louis XIV's instructions to
Villeroy, for the French King had written to Villeroy a fort-
night before the battle took place, telling him that it would be
very important to pay particular attention to that part of his
line which would have to withstand attack by the English
troops. When, therefore, Villeroy saw the red coats of the
British regiments deploying opposite his left, he reacted beyond
Marlborough's expectations by withdrawing troops from other
sectors to reinforce this area, because, relying on the difficulties
which would face an attack over the Little Geete swamps, he
had allotted his least trustworthy battalions to the line Offuz–
Autreglise.[7]

The action opened with the advance on Taviers, and the
French commanders suddenly realised the importance of this
village, which was in front of their right, when they saw the
heavy columns of Dutch infantry advancing towards it. De La
Colonie says that Taviers lay beyond the marsh which protected their left flank. He writes:[8] 'The cavalry were formed on
the extreme flanks of both armies on the edge of the marsh,
which was but a pistol-shot in breadth and only practicable for
infantry; hence, whichever infantry occupied the village could
line its edge, open a destructive fire, and destroy the cavalry
without any risk whatever. The enemy, who were the first to
appreciate this fact, sent fourteen battalions across the marsh to
seize it, and then our generals realised the result this would
have on the course of the battle and resolved to drive them out
before the action began. This village was the scene of the opening engagement, and the fighting there was almost as murderous
as the rest of the battle put together.' The French force sent to
occupy Taviers consisted of five regiments of dragoons (who

were dismounted for the purpose), a Swiss infantry regiment of
three battalions, and the Bavarian brigade in which was the
regiment commanded by de La Colonie. Presumably owing to
the hurry, the orders given to the French counter-attack force
were poor. The various elements were widely separated and
were ignorant of each others routes of advance. De La Colonie's
brigade was on the right wing, forming part of the first infantry
line, that is, behind the first line of cavalry. During the bombardment he had, he says, 'ordered flourishes to be played
upon our hautboys to entertain us the while, but the booming
of the guns that went on all round so startled our musicians that
they disappeared like a flash before anyone noticed it, and
transported the melodious sounds of their instruments to some
quarter where the harmonies were not quite so discordant.'
From his position, and before he set off towards Taviers, de La
Colonie saw that the Allies were 'moving troops from their right
to their left; but it was impossible to divine their intentions'.
Marlborough therefore must have started this move at a very
early stage of the battle, though it could probably not be seen
by Villeroy, who was now somewhere between Offuz and
Autreglise in what he believed to be the decisive sector.

De La Colonie marched off with his regiment without knowing whether or not any other troops had been ordered to take
part in the Taviers attack. As he moved to the right he suffered
some casualties from artillery fire amongst his troops as they
came within view of the enemy's gunners. He adds: 'I noticed,
when passing the *Maison du Roi*, that there were large intervals
between the squadrons, and that their formation was dispro-
portionately extended. This made me think that the principal
attack was not to be made here; that there was some other and
more dangerous point that had to be provided for; and that
reliance had been placed upon the *Maison du Roi*, all picked
men, at this point.' These gaps were due, of course, to Villeroy
having massed fifty squadrons on his left wing.

The Bavarian brigade was commanded by a Bavarian colonel
and included de La Colonie's regiment and his own. This
colonel rode at the head of the brigade, and when they reached
the marsh, he went on ahead to see if a horse could traverse it.
However, he got bogged down in the middle and was rescued

and taken prisoner by the enemy. De La Colonie now took over command of the brigade. He had hardly got the brigade across the marsh when the dragoons and Swiss, who had preceded them, came he says, 'tumbling down upon my battalions in full flight, just at the time when I was reforming my men after their crossing; they brought such alarm and confusion in their train, that my own fellows turned about and fled along with them'. De La Colonie's brigade, caught in the process of reforming, was infected by the panic. With great difficulty de La Colonie and his officers rallied his own regiment (of specially enlisted French grenadiers in the service of Bavaria) and some companies of the other regiment, reorganising the whole into four small battalions. The Swiss and dragoons had attacked Taviers without waiting for the Bavarian brigade and had been repulsed with much loss by the fourteen Dutch battalions who outnumbered them by more than two to one. The Swiss regiment was practically destroyed. De La Colonie took post in the angle formed by the junction of the Mehaigne and the Vistoule, and by showing a bold front stopped the Dutch infantry from advancing to attack the right flank of the Maison du Roi.

Meanwhile on the Allied right, Orkney with his British regiments crossed the Little Geete and pushed forward against the French line between Autreglise and Offuz. He had been told that the passage of the Little Geete was not practicable, but, 'after some difficulty', he got ten or twelve battalions across the river.[9] Soon they were fighting their way into Autreglise and Lumley had some squadrons out on their right flank. A series of orders at last called the reluctant Orkney off, and the victorious and disgruntled British infantry waded back across the Little Geete. Orkney wrote: 'I think I never had more shot about my ears and I confess it vexed me to retire. However we did it very well and in good order and whenever the French pressed upon us, with the battalion of the Guards and my own [The Royal Scots] I was always able to make them stand and retire.'[10] After regaining their old position, the first line then turned about and faced the enemy, but the second line carried on its withdrawal until it dropped below the crest line, when it reformed and marched off towards the centre of Marlborough's

line, to reinforce the reserve of infantry behind the Ramillies–
Offuz sector.[11]

The containing attack against Ramillies had been carried out
by twelve battalions (including two British—the later 3rd and
21st Foot) under General Schultz, with heavy artillery support.
Under cover of this, at about 2.30 p.m., General Overkirk led
the attack by the Dutch cavalry against the French position on
the ridge south of Ramillies. The cavalry charge routed the first
line of Franco-Bavarian cavalry, but the Allied squadrons were
then checked by the infantry line in support. The regiments of
the *Maison du Roi* then counter-charged and swept back the
Dutch horse. Marlborough had ordered all the cavalry of the
right wing, except the British (who were on the extreme right)
to move to the support of the left wing, but at this juncture
they were still on their way. Marlborough himself plunged into
the fight, rallied some of the Dutch squadrons, and led them
back in another charge. In the ensuing struggle he was un-
horsed and was lucky to escape with his life. The reinforcing
cavalry from the right wing, thirty-nine squadrons, now turned
the scale. The Danish horse swung wide on the Allied left,
almost to the Tomb of Ottomond, outflanking the French
cavalry, who began to give way.

De La Colonie, from his position behind the marsh, had been
watching this epic fight. He writes:[12]

'We had not been here very long before we saw the general
action begin, and from the place where I was situated the lines
of both armies were presented to my view almost in their
entirety so that hardly any of their movements escaped my
notice. Following on the cannonading and bombarding, which
was maintained during the completion of the final dispositions,
I saw the cavalry of the enemy's left wing march to attack the
Maison du Roi, followed by their infantry in slow time, and I
was able to distinguish to perfection the great number of
squadrons they had detailed for this assault. The enemy
advanced in four dense lines like solid walls, while we had but
three lines, the third of which was composed of several squadrons of dragoons with plenty of gaps between them . . . I now
saw the enemy's cavalry advance upon our people, at first at

rather a slow pace, and then, when they had gained the proper distance, they broke into a trot to gain impetus for their charge. At the same moment the *Maison du Roi* decided to meet them, for at such a moment those who await the shock find themselves at a disadvantage. But what a contrast was shown in the *melée* that resulted! The enemy, profiting by their superiority in numbers, surged through the gaps between our squadrons and fell upon their rear, whilst their four lines attacked in front. Naturally our right was soon crushed. I noticed numbers of riderless horses make their escape, and in a short time the rout became general. The enemy took our lines in flank, rode them down, and completely routed them.'

De La Colonie's account is somewhat telescoped, and he probably had to exercise too much vigilance over his own command to see all that happened; but his is an excellent eye-witness account of a cavalry action of the period.

At about 5 p.m. the Allied cavalry were halted and reformed, so that they faced north on a line between the Tomb of Otto-mond and Ramillies. Villeroy also formed a line of cavalry to oppose them, mostly from the fifty squadrons of the left wing, for his right wing cavalry no longer existed as a fighting formation. French infantry still clung on to parts of Ramillies, at which point the French line was now bent back at a right angle from the original alignment.

At 6 p.m. the Allied cavalry advanced, but the French cavalry, their morale apparently shattered by the fate which had befallen the *Maison du Roi* and much outnumbered, wavered and then left the field. The infantry line between Ramillies and Autreglise was now untenable. The Allied infantry facing it advanced, while Schultz's regiments captured Ramillies and moved on to take Offuz in the flank. The Elector of Bavaria's Bavarian and Spanish Horse Guards counter-attacked, but were charged and routed by two British cavalry regiments, the Fourth Horse (later 3rd Dragoon Guards) and the Carabiniers. On the extreme right Lumley's British squadrons swept across the line of the French retreat and two battalions of the *Regiment du Roi* were charged at the gallop by the Greys and destroyed. The pursuit went on all through the night and Villeroy's army dissolved into a disorganised mass of refugees, hounded by the freshest cavalry, the British, along the roads towards Brussels and Louvain.[13] De La Colonie's brigade carried out its duty to the end of thwarting the fourteen Dutch battalions in Taviers from attacking the French cavalry in the flank, but after the defeat of the latter the Dutch moved off to join the main part of the Allied army in the pursuit, and about 6 p.m. de La Colonei, the battlefield about him deserted, marched off unmolested to Namur.

Marlborough's generalship in this his most brilliant victory was outstanding. His appreciation of the disadvantages of Villeroy's position and how he could profit by it to have superiority of numbers at the decisive point was masterly. The nature of the terrain convinced him that the place for that stroke was the open country south of Ramillies; and because ground favoured it and because he aimed at nothing less than the envelopment and destruction of Villeroy's army, this stroke would be delivered by his cavalry, used in the same manner as were armoured formations in the Second World War. In preparation for his grand plan he would threaten Villeroy's left with his picked British troops to make the French commander think this was the main point of attack, and then use his shorter routes to weaken his right and strengthen his centre and left. Finally, to secure the flanks of his cavalry attack he would neutralise the potential bastions of Taviers and Ramillies. The whole thing was a masterpiece which can have few rivals in the history of war.

Clausewitz, inquiring into the circumstances that give victory in battle cites, 'Surprise, advantage of ground, and the attack from several quarters'. He adds: 'The surprise produces an effect by opposing to the enemy a great many more troops than he expected at some particular point. The superiority of numbers in this case is very different to a general superiority of numbers; it is the most powerful agent in the Art of War.'[14] There is no battle in which these circumstances and that 'most powerful agent' are more successfully displayed than Ramillies.

Chapter 12

FONTENOY

In June 1743 the Allied army, under the command of King George II, defeated the French, commanded by the Duc de Noailles, at the battle of Dettingen. It was a lucky victory, due entirely to the tough fighting discipline of the British troops, for little generalship was displayed on either side. The French ought to have won, because Noailles had the British and Austrians in a strategical trap. A strange feature of this battle was that Great Britain and France were not technically at war. The British were acting as auxiliaries of Austria, whilst the French had a similar relationship with Bavaria—Austria and Bavaria being at war with each other. However, the direct clash between French and British troops led to this convenient fiction being abandoned before the end of the year. Because of his poor handling of the battle, Noailles was removed from the command of the French western armies and replaced by a much more eminent soldier, whom we have met before in these pages—Marshal Maurice de Saxe. The victory at Dettingen was to cost Great Britain dear!

The French intention for the campaign of 1744 was to attack in Flanders and also attempt an invasion of Great Britain, using the Jacobite appeal of Prince Charles Stuart. Saxe was to command the forces designated for both operations, even though, suffering from dropsy, he was far from fit. In February Saxe assembled the invasion force at Dunkirk, but two successive gales destroyed any prospect of success. Switching his attention towards his more natural environment, Saxe had some 80,000 troops concentrated along the frontier between the Rivers Sambre and Scheldt at the beginning of April. Against this strong force, the Allies (British, Dutch, and Austrian) only had 55,000, located still in their winter cantonments.

On the Allies' side the approaching campaign in Flanders was hampered by the refusal of the Dutch and Austrians to support the offensive operations proposed by Lieutenant-General Sir John Ligonier, (temporarily in command of the British forces owing to Wade's sickness). Seizing the initiative Saxe captured the important fortresses of Menin, Ypres, and Furnes from their Dutch garrisons. The Dutch army, which had fought so well under Marlborough, was now inefficient and weak in numbers. Its discipline was so bad that Ligonier complained to Lord Carteret, Minister for Foreign Affairs, that the Dutch troops in the Allied force were intolerably insubordinate and disorderly.[1]

For the campaign of 1745 the British troops in Flanders were raised to a strength of 25,000 men, but to do this, the garrison of Great Britain was reduced to 15,000 men. There was considerable argument about the selection of an Allied commander; it was settled by the appointment of a Royal Duke, and in the London Gazette of 12 March 1745 there was the announcement that William Augustus, Duke of Cumberland, was to be Captain-General of all British forces in Great Britain, and of those operating in conjunction with the forces of the Allies. As commander of the Allied army he was assisted by the seventy-five-year-old Austrian Marshal Count Königsegg, and the Dutch commander Prince Waldeck. Cumberland arrived at the Hague on 17 April 1745, and then went on to Brussels, where he attended a Council of War on 21 April. He had then yet a month to go till his 25th birthday.

The British contingent of the army for the coming campaign consisted of the following units (some of the later designations of which have been added in brackets):

Cavalry: 3rd and 4th Troops, Horse Guards; 2nd Troop Horse Grenadier Guards; Royal Horse Guards; King's Horse (1st Dragoon Guards); Ligonier's, or Black, Horse (7th Dragoon Guards); Royal Dragoons; King's Own Dragoons (3rd Hussars); Queen's Dragoons (7th Hussars); Molesworth's Dragoons (5th Lancers); Stair's Dragoons (Inniskilling).

Infantry: 1st Guards; Coldstream; 3rd Guards; Royal Scots; 'Buff' Howards (3rd Buffs); Onslow's (8th Kings'); Sowle's (11th Devon); Duroure's (12th Suffolk); Pulteney's (13th Somerset Light Infantry); 'Green' Howard's; Bligh's (20th Lancashire Fusiliers); Campbell's (21st Royal Scots Fusiliers); Royal Welsh Fusiliers; Earl of Rothes' (25th King's Own Scottish Borderers); Bragg's (28th Gloucester); 'late' Handasyde's (31st East Surrey); Skelton's (32nd Duke of Cornwall's Light Infantry); Johnson's (33rd Duke of Wellington's); Cholmondeley's (34th Border); Lord Semphill's (Black Watch). Of these Onslow's, Rothes', and Sempill's had new colonels appointed shortly before the battle but were still known by their old colonel's name. A new colonel had also been appointed to 'late' Handasyde's.

Artillery: One heavy 6-pounder serving as flag gun and drawn by nine horses; nine 6-pounders, each drawn by seven horses; four 8-inch howitzers, each drawn by five horses; twenty-seven 3-pounders and six 1½-pounders, all on 'galloping' carriages.

The Guards constituted one brigade; the seventeen line regiments were organised into four brigades named after the senior regiment in each, which, with their commanders, were Royal (George Churchill), 'Buff' Howard (H. Skelton), Onslow (J. Ingoldsby), and Sowle (Thomas Bligh).

The artillery was to march in the rear, escorted by one battalion.

The senior commanders in the force were as follows:

Inspector of Cavalry, Lieutenant-General the Hon. Sir James Campbell.

Commanders of the first line of cavalry, Major-Generals the Earl of Rothes and Humphrey Bland.

Commanders of the second line of cavalry, Major-Generals Sir John Hawley and Richard Onslow.

Commander of the Household Cavalry, Lieutenant-General the Earl of Crawford.

Inspector of Infantry, Lieutenant-General Sir John Ligonier.

Inspector of the Guards, Colonel the Earl of Albemarle.

Commanders of the first line of infantry, Major-Generals the
Hon. W. Ponsonby and W. Pulteney.

Commanders of the second line of infantry, Major-Generals
C. Howard, the Hon. J. St Claire, and John Campbell.[2]

In preparation for a French offensive, the most important
frontier fortresses had been provisioned to withstand a long
siege; these were Namur, Charleroi, Mons, Ath, and Tournai.
The Allied field force concentrated at Anderlech, a suburb on
the south-west side of Brussels, and was reviewed here by the
Duke of Cumberland. Its fighting strength amounted to 30,550
bayonets and 12,000 sabres, and it was divided into two wings
of approximately equal strength—the right wing being British
and Hanoverian and the left wing Dutch. Six squadrons of
Austrian cavalry were included in the right wing—a token
force to represent Maria Theresa's interests as Countess of
Flanders.[3]

Saxe had arrived at his base of operations at Maubeuge on
20th April, where he had immediately placed himself under the
care of a canon of the chapter of Cambrai, who was a doctor.
His treatment restored Saxe to comparative health, and he then
reviewed his field army. This consisted of 90 regular and 10
militia battalions and 160 squadrons, a total of 69,000 infantry
and 25,600 cavalry,[4] or double the number of men reviewed
by Cumberland.

Saxe was aware that the Allies intended to take the offensive.
As he also intended to take it himself, he was determined to
anticipate them in the field and to strike at Tournai, which
from its position was the key to Western Flanders. In order to
gain time in which to complete the siege works and investment,
he planned a feint to make the Allies believe that his objective
was Mons. On 26 April, therefore, he despatched a strong
detachment via St Ghislain towards that fortress, and marched
rapidly with most of his army to Tournai. He arrived outside
the city on 28 April and immediately began his siege works.
The Dutch garrison of Tournai consisted of twelve battalions
and three squadrons, which was quite a considerable force to
man strong defences. But the Dutch commanders of the town
and the citadel, respectively, had been so deceived by information that the enemy were marching against Mons, that they

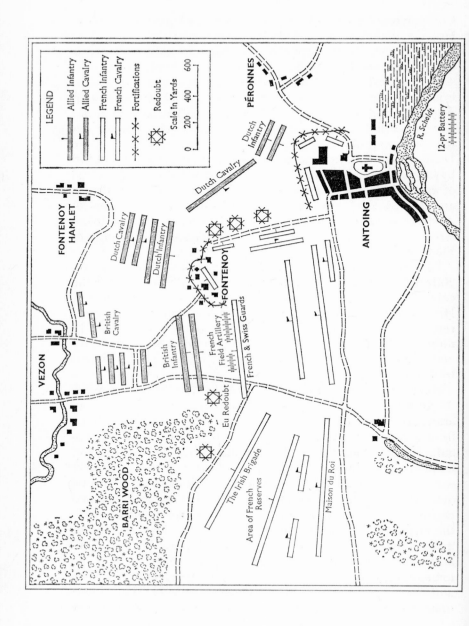

LEGEND

Allied Infantry
Allied Cavalry
French Infantry
French Cavalry
Fortifications
Redoubt

Scale In Yards
0   200   400   600

PÉRONNES

FONTENOY HAMLET

VEZON

BARRI WOOD

Dutch Cavalry

Dutch Infantry

British Cavalry

British Infantry

Dutch Cavalry

Dutch Infantry

FONTENOY

French Field Artillery

French & Swiss Guards

Eu Redoubt

The Irish Brigade

Area of French Reserves

Maison du Roi

ANTOING

R. Schelde

12-pr Battery

had neglected to put the fortress into a proper state to resist attack and were taken completely by surprise at the sudden appearance of the French army. In addition, unknown to them, their chief engineer had succumbed to French bribes and turned traitor. By 4 May the French had constructed their trenches right round Tournai and had started a bombardment of the fortifications.[5]

Meanwhile the Dutch commanders at Mons had reported, to the Allied headquarters in Brussels, the appearance on the heights commanding the town of forty squadrons of enemy cavalry supported by infantry. They were certain that this force heralded the arrival of Saxe's whole army and that Mons was his objective. This information had hardly been received in Brussels before a courier arrived from Tournai on the evening of 28 May with the news that the main French army was preparing to invest it. Faced with these conflicting reports, the Allied commanders were disposed to believe that Tournai was Saxe's true objective, but in case it was after all Mons, they decided that the march route for the relief of Tournai should follow the main road from Brussels to Mons as far as Soignies, by which time they should have firm information. This would make the distance to Tournai fifty miles instead of the forty-five by the direct route.

On 29 April the quartermaster-general issued orders for the force to march the following morning in two columns to Hal, eight miles south of Brussels on the Mons road.

Before evaluating the speed of eighteenth-century marches, it is necessary to consider the conditions. Including the troops who joined it during the march, the Allied army numbered some 46,000 men and 80 guns, and to cut down the distance from front to rear it was moving in two columns on roughly parallel routes. Clausewitz, writing of the march problems of his time—that is, at the end of the Napoleonic wars—says:[6] 'A division of 8,000 men, with its artillery and other carriages, takes up, as we know by experience in ordinary cases, a space of about three miles . . . Further, within three miles right or left of the road on which we march, in the cultivated countries of central Europe, there are generally lateral roads which can be used for a march, so that there is no necessity to go across country, as was so often done in the Seven Years War.' The space occupied on the march was probably much the same in 1745 as it was in 1815, though the eighteenth-century baggage train may have been longer. Each column of 23,000 men with their horses and vehicles would therefore have covered at least nine miles of road. Clausewitz gives the marching rate on a road as fifteen miles in eight hours, so that the tail of each of these columns would not reach camp until about four and a half hours after the head. So that if the two wings of the army had been marching on a single road it would probably have been necessary for them to be separated by a day's interval. It is conceivable that on parts of the march to Tournai there was no parallel road available, and then the infantry and cavalry of one column would have had to march across country, at a considerably slower pace, whilst artillery and vehicles followed the other column on the road. Another problem was that movement was only possible on metalled roads in all weather. Rain soon dissolved the unmetalled roads into mud and made them quite impassable for guns and wagons.

The force halted at Hal for two days, which suggests some administrative muddle. It then marched the fourteen miles to Soignies. By this time it was clear that Tournai was indeed the French objective and the field army was joined by six Dutch battalions and two Austrian squadrons from the Mons garrison, and also by two 'Free Companies' of irregular troops who had been watching the frontier.

It now started to rain, and as Soignies was the end of the metalled road on the line of advance, the force was detained there until 5 May. The army then struggled on eight miles to Cambron, but the roads were still so bad that there was another halt here for two days to give them time to dry out. On 7 May the march was continued to Moulbaix, seven and a half miles, where there was another reinforcement of two Hanoverian and four Dutch battalions from the garrison of Ath.

Cumberland had by this time received information that the French had transferred their baggage to the left bank of the Scheldt and, as they had not as yet opposed his advance, he concluded that they were going to withdraw across that river rather than oppose him.

The complete Allied field army was now composed as under:

	Bat-talions	Strength	Squad-rons	Strength	Total Strength
Right Wing					
British	20	13,000	26	3,900	16,900
Hanoverians	5	3,250	8	1,200	4,450
Austrians			8	1,200	1,200
Hussars			3	450	450
Two Free Companies		250			250
Total	25	16,500	45	6,750	23,250
Left Wing					
Dutch	27	17,550	45	6,000	23,550
Grand Total	52	34,050	85	12,750	46,800

Artillery—80 guns, ranging from 1½-pounders to 6-pounders.[7]

Saxe had had full information of the whole of the Allied advance, because he had sent out long distance reconnaissance patrols of hussars and mounted *Grassins* who had kept in continual visual touch and had sent back a stream of reports. It does not appear that there was any cavalry screen to conceal the movements of the Allied army and keep these intruders at bay. Saxe saw that from Moulbaix Cumberland could approach Tournai by three alternative routes. He could move to the right, crossing the Ath-Leuze-Tournai road, and approach the city from rather north of east, but Saxe thought this unlikely as the Allied left flank would be too exposed to attack. However, he decided to deploy two infantry brigades, covered by cavalry patrols, as an outpost line across this possible line of advance. A second alternative would be to move on Tournai by the direct road from Leuze, but this led through very wooded country intersected by ravines, and so obviously easy to defend that Saxe thought it sufficient to watch it with cavalry patrols. The third alternative was the route then followed by the road from Mons to Tournai, which skirted the southwest edge of the Barri Wood. Saxe thought this far the most likely, and he had already selected and started to prepare a defensive position to bar any approach to Tournai from this direction.

On 9 May the Allied army resumed its advance, and when

it turned left from Moulbaix, Saxe saw that the approach would indeed be by the Mons road.

The position selected by Saxe lay some five miles south-east of Tournai. It was mainly an open cultivated plain which he saw could be made extremely strong. He planned that the front of the position should run from the small town of Antoing on the broad River Scheldt, or Escaut, through the village of Fontenoy to the dense Barri Wood. From Antoing on the right to Fontenoy was about a mile, and between the two places stretched a ridge which sloped down to the village of Péronnes, 1,200 yards away. From Fontenoy to the edge of the Barri Wood, 700 yards away, there ran another low ridge, and from it a gentle glacis-like slope fell towards the village of Vezon, the first houses of which were about 1,000 yards from the ridge.

Today the battlefield has somewhat changed. The Barri Wood has gone, Antoing is an industrial town, and a new motorway crosses the area a little west of Vezon on an embankment. But the wide glacis-like slope up which the British infantry delivered their incredible attack is still there; an empty treeless expanse of cultivated land.

Saxe was firmly of the opinion that the French infantry of the time could not withstand a charge in line. He therefore decided to fortify Antoing and Fontenoy and to construct a chain of redoubts. There was considerable opposition to this by other French generals, who thought French troops could resist their foes in the open and that Saxe's plan was an insult to them. However Louis XV supported Saxe.

Saxe left the Marquis de Dreux-Brézé with 21,550 troops to man the lines of investment around Tournai and contain the garrison. Deducting the two brigades of infantry holding the outpost position mentioned above, he had available for the battlefield 59,000 men, organised in 60 infantry battalions and 110 cavalry squadrons.

Fontenoy was entrenched and the houses on its edges were reduced to rubble amongst which guns were sited. Five battalions were allotted to its defence. To Antoing were allotted another five battalions. On the ridge between Antoing and Fontenoy three redoubts were constructed and one battalion was split up between them. Two more redoubts were constructed in the Barri Wood; one on its western tip, on the ridge running to Fontenoy, and the other 400 yards farther east. Each of them was manned by one battalion of the Regiment of Eu, and the former became famous as the Eu Redoubt. An obvious omission in the defence was another redoubt half-way between the Barri Wood and Fontenoy. Saxe himself admitted that this omission nearly cost him the battle, but he could not believe that any troops in the world would attempt to force a passage at that point.[8] Around the Eu Redoubt the trees were cleared to give a field of fire, and an abatis was constructed with the felled trees. The edge of the Barri Wood was lined with *Grassins* (that is, men of the corps named the *Arquebusiers de Grassin*, which had been raised the previous year from the vagabonds of Paris by Lieutenant-Colonel de Grassin of the Regiment of Picardy as a regiment of both foot and mounted light troops). About 100 pieces of ordnance were allocated to the defence of Fontenoy, Antoing, and the five redoubts, and one battalion of infantry was detailed to assist in working them. In addition, six 12-pounders were mounted on the high ground above the left bank of the Scheldt, opposite Antoing, to enfilade any force attacking that place.

In order to secure his retreat across the Scheldt, should it become necessary, Saxe had two pontoon bridges thrown across the river, one at Calonne, about a mile downstream from Antoing, and the other at Vaulx, on the outskirts of Tournai. Each of them had a fortified bridge head garrisoned by three battalions.

Between Fontenoy and the Eu Redoubt were ten battalions of picked troops, including French and Swiss Guards, with twelve guns in front of them, and another three battalions were behind Fontenoy. Some four hundred yards behind this line of infantry were ranged fifty-two squadrons of cavalry in two lines. At right angles to these troops and behind the line of redoubts erected between Antoing and Fontenoy were five battalions of infantry with, behind them, twelve squadrons of cavalry.

The march of the Allied forces on 9 May brought them in to close contact with this formidable position. They encamped in the area about the villages Maubray, Baugnies, and Briffoeuil

—Cumberland's headquarters, the hospitals and the baggage being located in the last mentioned village. The march had taken eleven days, and Saxe was given another thirty-six hours to complete his defences before the Allies were ready to offer battle. Even given the bad weather and the consequent difficulty on the roads, there seems to have been little sense of urgency in the Allied command.

On the evening of 9 May the Allied commanders rode out on a personal reconnaissance, escorted by twelve squadrons of cavalry. A strong enemy cavalry screen prevented any close reconnaissance, but it was apparent that Fontenoy was strongly garrisoned. Vezon and the neighbouring copses and enclosures were held by outposts provided by the *Grassins*.

On the following day, 10 May, the Allied commanders met at Cumberland's headquarters to consider the situation. They decided as a first step to drive in the enemy outposts and locate the main French position. Accordingly at 10 a.m. a force under Lord Crawford, consisting of six battalions of infantry, twelve squadrons of cavalry, and eight guns, advanced towards Vezon and Fontenoy. The French outposts fell back, evacuating Vezon and Fontenoy Hamlet (half a mile south of Fontenoy), burning the latter. The British troops continued their advance through the woods and ravines of Vezon and deployed beyond it. Cumberland then entered the village and set up his headquarters. He did not unfortunately take Crawford's advice to move troops into the Barri Wood.[9]

Under cover of Crawford's screen, the Allied army deployed in and behind the woods around Vezon, the right and left wings taking up their respective relative positions. In the right wing the infantry were in front, the Hanoverians forming on the left of the British, and behind them were the British, Hanoverian, and Austrian cavalry. The Dutch infantry of the left wing formed in two bodies, one around the burnt Fontenoy Hamlet, whilst the other moved off to an area near the village of Péronnes. The Dutch cavalry marched into a locality between these two bodies, ready to form a link between them. It was evening before all the troops had reached their forming up positions.

At the end of the day's preparations, the Allied commanders

met in conference at Cumberland's headquarters. Cumberland
and Waldeck were in favour of attacking the French position.
It is said that Königsegg urged that Saxe should be compelled
to raise the siege by harassing his communications, which
indeed the Allies were well placed to do. If this account is true,
Königsegg was right. Any competent general, appreciating the
situation, would have seen how small was the prospect of
success and have realised that in the event of defeat Tournai
was bound to fall to the enemy in any case. Königsegg, however, was overruled by the other two. And so, an army under a
mediocre and inexperienced commander was about to attack
an enemy of superior strength commanded by the most brilliant
general of his time, occupying a position of his own choosing
which he had had time to fortify. That it came so near to success
was due solely to the magnificent fighting powers of the British
infantry; and that it ultimately failed was due to the poor
quality of the Dutch troops.

The plan decided on was that the infantry of the right wing
should move straight ahead up the slope between Fontenoy and
the Barri Wood, whilst the left wing infantry assaulted Fontenoy and Antoing. It was at first intended to cover the right
flank by cavalry moving through the Barri Wood, but this was
cancelled when a reconnaissance patrol was fired on from the
edge of the wood. The deployment of the right wing infantry
beyond Vezon was to be protected from interference from the
French cavalry by a screen of fifteen squadrons under Sir
James Campbell.[10]

There was a curious incident during the night before the
battle: two Scottish officers in the French service came into the
British lines to meet and talk to their friends among the officers
of the Black Watch.[11]

The infantry of the right wing had been ordered to start
moving forward to their positions in the lines of attack at
2 a.m. on 11 May. The march along narrow lanes in the dark,
followed by the defile through Vezon, was necessarily a very
lengthy affair for a mass of twenty-five battalions. At 4 a.m.
Cumberland rode out to see how matters were progressing.
Here the discovery of the Eu Redoubt by a cavalry patrol
was reported to him. It was apparent that from this work heavy

enfilade fire could be brought to bear on the British line as it advanced up the slope from Vezon. Cumberland immediately directed the formation of a special brigade of three British and one Hanoverian battalion and selected Colonel Ingoldsby of the 1st Guards to command it. He could hardly have made a more unfortunate choice. Ingoldsby's orders were to capture the redoubt undamaged, if possible, so that its guns could be turned against the French. The attack by the British infantry was now to be held up until the Eu Redoubt, Fontenoy, and Antoing had all been carried.

Ingoldsby marched off through Vezon with his brigade at 6 a.m. He then halted, sent off an officer to Cumberland to ask for some artillery, and consulted his regimental commanders as to the best plan to adopt. There now followed a series of hesitations by Ingoldsby and he seized every excuse for not doing anything. It was all very suggestive of Sackville's behaviour later at Minden.

The cavalry screen had been delayed trying to get up to Vezon in the dark, and it was not till 6.30 a.m. that Campbell led his fifteen squadrons on to the open ground beyond the village. He sent an officer to find out how Ingoldsby was progressing, as he was concerned about the vulnerability of his cavalry to enfilade fire from the wood. The officer returned with the information that Ingoldsby's brigade had not moved. As the squadrons deployed they came under fire from the French artillery. Campbell was mortally wounded, and the seventy-eight-year-old veteran was carried from the field cursing his luck in not being able to play any further part in the coming battle.

Behind Campbell's cavalry the British and Hanoverian infantry were now forming in two long lines as they emerged from Vezon, under the direction of their commander Sir John Ligonier. At 9 a.m. the infantry stood ready in order of battle, the covering cavalry trotted off to the rear, and Ligonier reported that he was ready to advance as soon as the Dutch had captured their objectives. The Dutch attack seems to have been late, but they now advanced, with a cloud of cavalry connecting the two bodies of infantry. However, the Prince of Waldeck had not arranged any proper reconnaissance of the enemy's positions and the commanders of the assaulting troops had consequently no knowledge of the strength of the positions against which they were attacking. They were therefore taken completely by surprise when they came under a devastating fire. The Fontenoy column wavered, and then sought shelter amidst the ruins of Fontenoy Hamlet. The column attacking Antoing and the connecting cavalry came under heavy fire from Antoing itself, from the three redoubts, and from the battery on the other side of the Scheldt. Both infantry and cavalry fell back in disorder, the cavalry taking post behind the left hand column of infantry. But one cavalry regiment, under its Colonel Appius, rode right off the field and did not stop till it reached the shelter of Ath, from whence Appius wrote to the States-General that the Dutch army had been cut to pieces with the sole exception of his regiment which had been saved by his prudence.[12]

It was now 11 a.m. and both of the Dutch attacks had failed. Cumberland had either to withdraw from the battle or prepare a new plan. It appears that he consulted Königsegg,[13] though if so, there is no record as to whether he took the veteran's opinion. It was decided that the Dutch should make a second attack. Ingoldsby was obviously useless, so his operation was called off and the Black Watch and Duroure's Regiment (12th) were removed from his brigade to stiffen the Dutch attack on Fontenoy. The two frustrated British regiments rushed at Fontenoy without waiting for the Dutch, and were eventually driven back by superior numbers after a hand to hand struggle. When the Dutch infantry were at last ready, the British regiments advanced again with them; but this effort also failed, and the Dutch retirement was hastened by a charge against their left flank by dragoons of the regiments stationed between Fontenoy and Antoing.

For a commander-in-chief, Cumberland now did an extraordinary thing. He took over Ligonier's job by moving to the centre of the front line of infantry and ordering the advance. It was of course a gallant action, but he lost all control of the battle, the issue of which now depended entirely on the officers and men of the British infantry regiments. It is worth listing these regiments, which were in the following order from right to left (giving later designations):

First Line—1st Guards, Coldstream, 3rd Guards, Royal Scots, 21st, 31st, 8th, 25th, 33rd, 19th.

Second Line—Buffs, 23rd, 32nd, 11th, 28th, 34th, 20th, Hanoverians.[14]

Each battalion pulled forward, with it its two light field guns.

As the lines advanced the front narrowed slightly and the Hanoverians, to avoid being cramped, had to drop back into a third line. Casualties increased with the rapidly shortening range from the French guns in front, and when the regiments drew level with Fontenoy and the Eu Redoubt, there was a tremendously heavy flanking fire which swept whole ranks away. On the far side of a sunken road, the British troops suddenly caught sight of the defending French infantry and instinctively halted. On the left of the French line were two battalions of the Swiss Guards, and next to them were four battalions of the French Guards, immediately opposite to the British Guards Brigade. Lord Charles Hay of the 1st Guards stepped forward with a flask in his hand and, raising his hat, drank to the health of his enemies. 'We are the English Guards,' he called out, 'and we hope you will stand till we come up to you and not swim the Scheldt as you did the Main at Dettingen!' He then turned round, saying, 'Men of the King's Company, these are the French Guards and I hope you are going to beat them to-day.' The men cheered. The French officers hurried to the front to return the salute, but the answering cheer was rather weak. Then the French muskets were levelled and a British guardsman said: 'For what we are about to receive may the Lord make us truly thankful!'[15] The answering British volley broke the French ranks in disorder, and the advance continued till the steady red-coated ranks stood triumphant in the centre of the enemy position. Each battalion now formed square, to meet all round attack and the inevitable cavalry charges. This caused a momentary confusion, and Saxe seized the opportunity to attack the British right flank with the eight battalions forming the second line of his reserve infantry. The attack was repulsed, but, caught in a heavy cross fire, the troops were withdrawn as far as the Fontenoy–Barri Wood ridge, where they were reformed into a single hollow square with the guns in the centre and the front. The advance was then resumed.

Saxe now launched his cavalry into an attack on the square. In charge after charge the horsemen surged round the square in their efforts to break it, suffering very heavy casualties in the process. Now was the time when a counter-charge by the British cavalry might have finally shattered the French army; but Cumberland, in the centre of the square, was no longer in command of the Allied army and had apparently forgotten everything except the fight in his immediate vicinity.

Long afterwards Saxe explained why he had continued with these expensive and unsuccessful cavalry attacks. He said that while Fontenoy remained untaken his enemy had no pivot of manoeuvre. The British success, therefore, was actually proving a disadvantage to them, because the further they penetrated the more they were exposed to the fire of the French infantry and batteries in their rear. But it was essential to distract their attention by these repeated cavalry charges to give him time to organise the counter-attack upon which all depended.[16] Nevertheless, Voltaire, in his *Siècle de Louis XV*, says that if the Dutch had now advanced to join hands with the English there would have been no retreat for the French army or for the King. Alas, there was no commander at the Allied head-quarters to order them to do so.

Cumberland at last thought of the British cavalry and sent an officer with orders to Lord Crawford to charge. By the time the officer reached Lord Crawford it was too late, for the path of the cavalry was impeded by fleeing Dutchmen. A mass of fugitive Dutch dragoons overwhelmed many of the British cavalry, including the Life Guards. Lord Crawford said that he and his charger were almost knocked over by them, and that had not his horse been of prodigious strength he would have been trampled to death. Crawford rallied the brigade of Life Guards and started moving forward again, when, as he says, 'another body of runaways came upon us and broke us anew'.[17]

It was 1.30 p.m., and the hollow square was being rapidly thinned of men. Four French guns, loaded with grape and deployed at close range, caused immense casualties. Saxe now threw in his last infantry reserve, the regiments of the Irish Brigade, against the British right flank, whilst the left flank was attacked by the regiments posted between Fontenoy and Antoing and some broken infantry who had been rallied. He followed this with furious charges by his very last reserve, the proud cavalry of the *Maison du Roy*.

Cumberland ordered a retreat and Ligonier rode off to see it properly executed. The retirement was carried out in as good order as the advance. Two squadrons of the Blues, who had managed to get through the Dutch, charged gallantly to assist the withdrawal. Lord Crawford, seeing them 'returning in the best order', got them to align themselves on his brigade.

Skelton's (32nd) and Cholmondeley's (34th) had been sent back to secure the roads through Vezon. The infantry, says Crawford, retired by succession of battalions, facing about and firing at every hundred yards by word of command as steadily as if they had been on parade. The *Maison du Roy* charged the retreating troops furiously, but were repulsed with heavy loss by the Foot Guards and the Hanoverians, who were at that time at the rear. One of the attacking cavalry regiments was almost wiped out.

Crawford, meanwhile, was waiting his moment. Addressing his brigade, he said: 'Gentlemen, mind the word of command, and you shall gain immortal honour.' He then ordered them to rein back their horses on either flank and then close in to form a screen for the retiring infantry. The brigade then held the enemy in check till the last of the retiring infantry had passed. When the cavalry at last withdrew in their turn, Crawford told the Life Guards and the Blues that they had gained as much honour in covering so great a retreat as if they had won the battle.[18] There was no pursuit.

A contemporary account of the battle from the French side is contained in the following letter from the Comte de Loss to King Augustus III of Poland, to whom Saxe, an illegitimate son of Augustus II, was a half-brother:[19]

'Sire, Although I suppose that Marshal Comte de Saxe has already sent Your Majesty a full account of the action at Fontenoy, nevertheless I do not wish to abrogate the honour of myself sending you that which the Court has published in the public gazettes, and which is the same as that carried by a courier despatched by the Most Christian King to the Queen at Versailles.

'I would add the following particulars which I have gathered from various letters I have seen from several officers who were present at the battle.

'All agree that the first line of both the French infantry and cavalry yielded to the first onset of the English and Hanoverians, who fought with incredible valour, and one could in fact say that for a period of one and a half hours the former had lost the battle. The Regiment of Guards, especially, were driven in flight by the first shots of the Allied artillery [i.e. the battalion guns], without it ever being possible to lead them into a charge. In a word, things had got to the stage that Marshal de Noailles, believing all lost, had counselled the King to think of his own safety and leave the battlefield. It appears that this advice would have been followed except for the firmness of Marshal de Saxe who opposed it and who represented, almost light heartedly, to His Majesty, that one must conquer or die, and that the situation was not yet so desperate that he could not remedy it, provided that he was left to tackle it himself without being hampered.

'The Marshal now, and just at the right time, organised a charge against the English force, which had already penetrated the centre of the position, by Count de Loewandal at the head of the Irish regiments and some other brigades (the Marshal himself leading the Carabiniers and the remains of some brigades of infantry that he had been able to rally). This forced the English to draw back, and gave time for the Maison du Roy to advance, and these charged with such violence on the English that regiments which had been formed into a square were nearly destroyed within a quarter of an hour; and from that moment victory turned in favour of the French. The Irish were marvellous. The right wing of the Allies, composed of the Dutch, did not do much, having had too much respect for the French artillery fire, from which they had suffered heavy casualties without ever daring to advance.

'All the letters, even of unbiased men, praise the Most Christian King and the Dauphin, mentioning with admiration the firmness and presence of mind which the former displayed in critical circumstances. But at the same time all are convinced that the victory was due to the wise dispositions by Marshal de Saxe, who, in spite of the bad state of his health, found the strength to overcome the fatigue that he had had to endure during the battle and to take him everywhere to restore order among the troops.'

Although a defeat, there is no battle in history that throws more lustre on British infantry than that of Fontenoy.

Chapter 13

CAMDEN AND GUILDFORD

In complete contrast to the great contests which took place on the battlefields of Ramillies and Fontenoy are two actions between comparatively small forces during the latter stages of the American War of Independence. Their particular interest lies in the demonstration they provide of the developments that had occurred in British infantry tactics to adjust the linear formations of the day to meet the conditions of the forest country in which the troops had so often to fight.

By the late spring of 1780 General Sir Henry Clinton had captured Charleston and its large garrison, and Lieutenant-Colonel Banastre Tarleton, at the head of his British Legion, had, after a long and rapid march, destroyed the last regiment of Continental infantry left in South Carolina. On 5 June 1780 Clinton sailed for New York, leaving General Earl Cornwallis with only 4,000 men to undertake the almost impossible task of first completing the subjugation of South Carolina and then subduing North Carolina. Roads throughout the area were few and poor, and for communications much use was made of the numerous rivers which, following roughly parallel courses, flowed south-easterly into the Atlantic, connecting the towns that had developed from the early settlements founded on their banks. A few of these communities were Royalist in sympathy, but most were either apathetically prepared to rally to the winning side or else were in active sympathy with the rebellion.

Although the Colony was clear of Continental (i.e. regular American) troops for the time being, it was obviously only a matter of time before Congress attempted to reconquer the territory, and in the meantime the activity of guerrilla bands entailed providing garrisons of some strength at all important posts. There were about twelve of these, comprising the bases on the coast and places of strategic importance on the upper waters of the great rivers, spread over an area nearly 150 miles square. There were not many troops available, therefore, to provide a field force.

By September the completion of the harvest and the cooler weather would favour the start of active operations, and Cornwallis hoped that until that time arrived, conditions would remain sufficiently peaceful for him to settle the civil administration and organise loyalist militia units to release his regular garrisons for field service. He was soon disappointed, for as early as 20 June news arrived of an American army assembling in North Carolina. The nucleus of this was a force which had been on the way to reinforce the garrison of Charleston, but which had halted on hearing of the town's surrender. To take command of this army Congress selected General Horatio Gates, the victor of Saratoga, whose prestige naturally stood high in American opinion. Gates arrived on 25 July and took over from the previous commander, General Baron de Kalbe. News of American preparations led to increased rebel activity in South Carolina. On 12 July Thomas Sumter, a guerrilla leader known as the 'Carolina Gamecock', surprised and destroyed a British force consisting of a small detachment of the British Legion and a body of loyalist militia. As a result of this success one complete regiment of loyalist militia deserted and joined Sumter. In the face of this threat, Colonel Lord Rawdon, commanding in this sector, ordered the evacuation of the post at Cheraw on the Peedee river, and detailed a militia unit to escort the sick men of the garrison down the river. This regiment also deserted to Sumter, taking the sick men with it as prisoners of war. Thus reinforced, Sumter made two unsuccessful attacks against posts at Rocky Mount and Hanging Rock on 1 August and 6 August respectively.

Sumter had early noted the scattered British posts as potential prizes and had drawn Kalbe's attention to their vulnerability. It was probably in the light of this report that Gates, as soon as he arrived, decided to attack the important British post at Camden on the Wateree River.¹ On 27 July, only two days after he had taken over command, Gates started off on his 120-mile march with a force of about 1,500 Continental troops on 5 August he was joined by some 2,100 North Carolina militia, and the combined force then advanced towards Lynch's Creek, about fifteen miles north-east of Camden, where there was a British outpost.²

Rawdon, in the meantime, had sent a despatch to Cornwallis at Charleston, nearly 150 miles away, that American forces in some considerable strength were approaching him. Cornwallis was in something of a dilemma. He was not yet ready to start offensive operations; yet he was certain that if he did nothing insurrection would spread rapidly and he would have to withdraw all British troops to Charleston.³ However, he set off for Camden and arrived there on 13 August.

Learning that Gates was making for Camden, Rawdon directed the garrisons of Hanging Rock and Rocky Mountain to march to that place and then hurried forward to Lynch's Creek with the few hundred troops he could spare to delay the American advance. Gates encountered him there on 11 August, holding a position behind the creek. The American general deployed his army and started a slow turning movement, and when this began to threaten his position, Rawdon fell back to Camden. Sumter had seized the two evacuated posts and then, by-passing Camden, had occupied the crossings of the Wateree south of the town. He informed Gates of his action and the latter sent him a reinforcement of 400 men and two guns with orders to interrupt Camden's communications. On 13 August the cautious Gates had got no farther than Rugeley's Mill, ten miles north of Camden. Here he was reinforced by 700 Virginian Militia, bringing his total strength to 4,100.⁴

As soon as Cornwallis reached Camden he took steps to release as many men as possible for the field force. All the reasonably fit men amongst the convalescent sick were ordered to report for duty and, together with a small body of provincials and militia, they took over guard duties at the various installations and manned the town's defences. At the request of Tarleton, Cornwallis ordered all the horses of the army to be assembled, in order that the best of them should be selected for the British Legion cavalry.[5]

The field force eventually at Cornwallis's disposal consisted of three companies of the 23rd Fusiliers, three companies of the 33rd Foot, five companies of the 71st Highlanders (which came from both battalions of the regiment and were organised as two weak battalions), four companies of light infantry from various regiments of the line, the British Legion, the Volunteers of Ireland, Hamilton's Corps, Bryan's Refugees, a detachment of the Royal Artillery with two 6-pounder and two 3-pounder guns, and a detachment of pioneers. These amounted to about 1,500 regular troops (British and Provincial) and 500 militia. The most famous of the Provincial units was the British Legion, commanded by Tarleton, who was a regular British officer seconded from the 1st Dragoon Guards. The Legion, as it was commonly known, was part cavalry and part infantry. The volunteers of Ireland had been raised by Rawdon from Irish deserters from Washington's army. Hamilton's and Bryan's units were North Carolina loyalist militia.[6]

In the afternoon of 15 August Cornwallis directed Tarleton to capture some American soldiers in order to obtain information about the enemy. Tarleton set off with a detachment of the Legion cavalry and caught three convalescents from Lynch's Creek on their way to rejoin the army. They said that Gates had ordered an advance that night as a preparation for an attack on Camden the following morning. Armed with this information, Cornwallis ordered the force to stand to arms, and at 10 p.m. the troops formed up in order of march. The advanced guard consisted of twenty dragoons of the Legion, twenty mounted infantry, and the four companies of light infantry. The main body was divided into three 'divisions': the first commanded by Lieutenant-Colonel Webster, consisting of the 23rd and 33rd; the centre division, of the Legion infantry, the Volunteers of Ireland, and the two militia units, all under Rawdon's command; and the reserve division composed of the 71st Highlanders. The remainder of the Legion cavalry supplied the rear guard. The four guns were divided between the leading and centre divisions.

The route of advance was the road running northward from

7. Plan of the Battle of Camden, from 'A History of the Campaigns of 1780 and 1781' by Lieutenant-Colonel Tarleton.

Camden to Rugeley's Mill. At about midnight the head of the force reached a ford where the road crossed Saunders Creek, a stream running westward to the Wateree River three miles away. There was a short halt beyond the stream so that the column, which had been somewhat strung out during the passage, could close up. Shortly after 2 a.m. the advanced guard cavalry encountered the head of the enemy column and promptly charged. They were driven back by the volume of the enemy fire, but under cover of this little action, Webster's infantry were deploying rapidly across the road.[7]

Gates too had marched at 10 p.m., and he had given Saunders Creek as the objective for the night's march. There was some firing now from the infantry of both sides, but this soon died down while the commanders on both sides took stock of the situation.

A rapid reconnaissance and reports from his subordinate commanders showed Cornwallis that he was already in a favourable position to meet the enemy's superior numbers, because on either flank there was a swamp, which restricted his frontage to about a mile and prevented him from being out-flanked. His scouts, however, had discovered a by-road which left the Rugeley–Camden road about four miles behind the position which Gates now occupied and ran eastwards round the swamp on Cornwallis's left flank to rejoin the main road about three miles behind his position. A small party was detailed to block this road. Gates had the advantage of slightly higher ground, but he had a wider frontage between the swamps, and, if he had to withdraw, his flanks would be wide open to attack. Between the swamps the ground was sandy and covered thickly with pine trees.[8]

Before dawn Cornwallis had completed his dispositions. Webster's division was on the right of the road and Rawdon's on the left. In Webster's command the light infantry were on the extreme right, the 23rd in the centre, and the 33rd on the left next to the road. From the left of the road Rawdon's division was in the order; Volunteers of Ireland, Legion infantry, and Hamilton's regiment, with Bryan's regiment echeloned to its left rear. Immediately on the left of the road, and in the front line were the four guns. The 71st formed a second line, with one battalion in rear of each of the forward divisions. The Legion cavalry, 'on account of the thickness of the woods', remained in column to the right of the main road and close to the right battalion of the 71st 'with orders to act offensively against the enemy, or in defence of the British troops as opportunity offered, or necessity required'.[9]

Gates had also been forming his troops before daybreak. His right wing, to the west of the road, consisted of Gists's 2nd Maryland Brigade of Continental troops, in the order from right to left of 2nd, 4th, and 6th Maryland Regiments and, immediately next to the road, the Delaware Regiment. On the east of the road were, next to it, Caswell's North Carolina Militia, and on their left Steven's Virginia Militia. Behind the Virginia militia were Porterfield's and Armstrong's Light Infantry militia units, and supporting the left flank were the mounted Legion of Colonel Armand (the Marquis de la Rouerie Tuffin). The 1st Maryland Brigade, commanded by Smallwood and consisting of the 1st, 3rd, and 7th Maryland Regiments, was in reserve, astride the main road. Most of the American artillery was in front of their centre, near the road.[10]

When dawn broke and Gates could see the dispositions of his troops, he was not satisfied with those taken up by the militia and sent orders for their alteration. The consequent movements of the two militia brigades were spotted by Webster who immediately notified Cornwallis. The Commander-in-Chief grasped the opportunity to profit by the enemy's momentary confusion and, ordering Webster to advance, he sent an A.D.C. to Rawdon directing him to do likewise.

The action became general along the whole front, and there was some stubborn fighting on the left and centre of the British line, where the 2nd Maryland Brigade and the Delaware Regiment presented a firm front. All Rawdon's troops, as well as the 33rd Regiment, came under heavy fire. As it was a hazy morning and the smoke from both armies hung in a low cloud in the still air, it was difficult to see what was going on, but the British infantry moved steadily forward. The 23rd and the light infantry companies were opposed only by militia, and as the skilled forest fighters of the light infantry advanced towards them, cheering and stopping to fire at intervals from behind the cover of the trees, the Virginians panicked, threw down their arms, and fled. Almost immediately, the North Carolinians on their right followed their example, and without most of them having fired a shot, the militiamen ran in a disorganised mass from the battlefield, throwing the reserve brigade into confusion. Instead of letting them follow the fugitives, Cornwallis directed Webster to wheel his division left and attack the left flank of the Continental troops. Kalbe, commanding the American right wing, called for support from the reserve. The 1st Maryland Brigade, which had been reformed after the disorder caused by the passage of the fleeing militia through its ranks, attempted to join with the left flank of the 2nd Brigade. Cornwallis now threw his own reserve, the 71st, into the battle, and the 1st Maryland, after twice being driven back and twice rallying, were finally defeated; as they streamed back in confusion from the battlefield, Cornwallis launched his cavalry into the attack. Part of the Legion dragoons, under Major Hanger, charged the right flank of the 2nd Maryland Brigade, whilst the remainder, under Tarleton, swung wide round the American left and charged the rear. Kalbe had led a regiment of Continental infantry in a counter-attack, but he was mortally wounded and captured, and the cavalry charges completed the disintegration of the remainder of the American army.[11] Tarleton writes:

'Brigadier-General Gist moved off with about one hundred continentals in a body by wading through the swamp on the right of the American position, where the British cavalry could not follow; this was the only party that retreated in a compact state from the field of battle. The continentals, the state troops, and the militia, abandoned their arms, their colours, and their cannon to seek protection in flight, or to obtain it from the clemency of their conquerors. As soon as the rout of the Americans became general, the legion dragoons advanced with great rapidity towards Rugeley's mills: On the road, General Rutherford, with many other officers and men, were made prisoners. The charge and pursuit having greatly dispersed the British, a halt was ordered on the south side of the creek, in order to collect a sufficient body to dislodge Colonel Armand and his corps, who, together with several officers, were employed in rallying the militia at that pass, and in sending off the American baggage. The quick junction of the scattered cavalry counteracted the designs of the enemy: Colonel Armand's dragoons and the militia displayed a good countenance, but were soon borne down by the rapid charge of the legion: The chase again commenced, and did not terminate till the Americans were dispersed, and fatigue overpowered the exertions of the British. In a pursuit of twenty-two miles many prisoners of all ranks, twenty ammunition wagons, one hundred and fifty carriages, containing the baggage, stores, and camp equipage of the American army fell into the hands of the victors.'[12]

Cornwallis's losses in killed and wounded were 324 all ranks. The Americans lost 70 officers and about 2,000 men in killed, wounded, and prisoners, eight pieces of ordnance, several colours, and all the carriages and wagons with the stores, ammunition and baggage of the whole army.[13] Seldom in military history has such a complete disaster been inflicted on an army by a force less than half its strength. As late as 1900 it was still cited as the 'most disastrous defeat ever inflicted on an American army'.[14]

Cornwallis could hardly have fought the battle better. He chose an excellent position, manoeuvred his troops with skill, and had displayed, in Saxe's words, 'the genius to seize those favourable opportunities which occur in battle and which open the way to victory'. He had followed Saxe's advice to a commander: 'When at last he sees his fair lady of opportunity, he should kiss her hand and go at once to the critical spot, striking hard with the first troops on which he can lay hands.'[15] The pursuit, in which so many commanders fail, had been a classic. But the victory had only been made possible by the superb fighting powers of the British regular infantry.

Sumter, as soon as he knew of Gates's defeat, retreated rapidly. Tarleton was sent after him, surprised him in bivouac, and destroyed his force at the cost of one officer killed and fifteen men wounded.

Cornwallis had saved the situation temporarily in South Carolina, but with his small army, now badly weakened by sickness, his position was far from secure. Many guerrilla leaders were still in the field and several of his militia units were quite untrustworthy. In addition, it was more than likely that another regular force would be sent into the area under a commander more competent than Gates. In these circumstances Cornwallis decided that his best hope of securing his position was to take the offensive himself and advance into North Carolina. On 7 September, therefore, he started from Camden, marching north in two columns, one on each bank of the Wateree. There was a shortage of forage and harassing attacks by guerrillas, and it was not till 22 September that Cornwallis reached the town of Charlottesville, about seventy miles north of Camden. Here he halted to await the progress of a column under the command of Major Patrick Ferguson which was advancing from the west. Ferguson, the inventor of a remarkable rifle, had raised a provincial unit, the American Volunteers, which was equipped with this weapon, and the column consisted of 100 of his own unit and 800 militia. At King's Mountain, thirty-five miles west of Charlottesville, disaster overtook Ferguson; he was surrounded by a large force of backwoodsmen irregulars armed with rifles, and after he himself was killed the remnants of his column surrendered.

This reverse, and its heartening effect on the rebels, ruined Cornwallis's plans and he retired southward to Winnsborough, some thirty miles north-west of Camden. Sumter now appeared on the scene, raising a partisan band about forty miles to the north. About 100 men of the 63rd Foot had been temporarily converted into mounted infantry and placed under the command of Major James Wemyss of the regiment, who had been another noted leader of provincial troops. James obtained leave from Cornwallis to go after Sumter with his mounted infantry. On 9 November he surprised Sumter in a well-planned and executed attack, but unfortunately he was wounded and captured, and the young officer who was next in command did not know what to do and abandoned the operation.[16]

On 20 November Tarleton, with 190 of his dragoons and 80 men of the 63rd's mounted infantry, caught up with Sumter, but Tarleton failed to achieve surprise, and the result was an indecisive action, though Sumter was severely wounded. During this little battle, Sumter led 400 men in an attack against the detachment of the 63rd, who had dismounted. But the 63rd not only repulsed their attackers, but counter-attacked and routed them.[17]

To succeed the incompetent Gates, Washington selected a very much more able general, Nathaniel Greene. On 2 December 1780 Greene arrived in Charlottesville, where the remnants of Gates's army had moved, and relieved Gates in command on the following day. He found that he had 2,457 men under his command, but discipline and morale were poor after the defeat of Camden, and only about 800 of them had as yet received their full clothing and equipment. However, he immediately adopted an aggressive strategy and sent off General Daniel Morgan with 600 men to link up with militia units and harry the British posts in western South Carolina.[18]

On 14 December Cornwallis was reinforced by a detachment under Major-General Alexander Leslie which landed at Charleston on that day. It consisted of the Brigade of Guards (two battalions drawn from all three regiments), six companies of the 82nd Foot (Maclean's), the Hessian Regiment of Bose (one battalion), and two provincial regiments. (Cornwallis does not seem to have thought much of these last and probably employed them on garrison duties.)

Having fixed his garrisons, Cornwallis concentrated his field army at Winnsborough. On 1 January he learned of Morgan's activities and despatched Tarleton with a mixed force of about 1,000 men to deal with him. This force included 50 troopers of the 17th Light Dragoons, 300 men of the Legion dragoons, 200 men from the 7th Fusiliers, 200 from the 71st Highlanders, 200 from the Legion infantry, 100 militia, and a detachment of artillery. Of these, the detachment from the 7th was composed almost entirely of newly enlisted recruits. With his men tired and out of breath with the rapidity of the march, Tarleton attacked with his usual impetuosity, and was beaten. The Legion, ill-disciplined and used to easy victory, disintegrated, the 7th threw down their arms and surrendered, the 71st fought gallantly until overrun, the men of the Royal Artillery died at their guns, the troopers of the 17th charged under Tarleton to try and save the guns, and were the only formed body still following their leader when he left the battlefield.[19] Morgan now hurried off to the east in case Cornwallis should cut him off. The British commander was indeed trying to do this, marching north on both banks of the Catawba River; but Morgan was too quick for him.

Greene, with his main army, had reached Cheraw on 26 December. On 23 January he learned of Morgan's success and, leaving most of his troops at Cheraw, rode 125 miles to join him on his line of retreat, and take over command. Cornwallis decided to destroy all his superfluous baggage, including tents, to lighten his army for a rapid march to destroy both Greene and Morgan. He had indeed very little choice, because to remain on the defensive while Greene was reinforced and guerrillas attacked his posts would surrender the initiative and lead ultimately to the loss of South Carolina.

By 30 January Cornwallis was on the western bank of the Catawba, eighteen miles below Greene's camp on the opposite bank. Greene had no intention of facing Cornwallis, but started a rapid retreat to draw the British farther away from their bases until he was strong enough to turn and attack them. He left 800 militia as a rear guard to contest the crossing of the Catawba, but these indifferent troops were soon dealt with by Cornwallis. After a pursuit lasting 200 miles, Greene's army escaped narrowly, and crossed the broad Dan River into Virginia. Cornwallis was foiled because Greene had removed all the boats and could block any movement towards the upstream fords. Cornwallis, 150 miles from Wilmington on the coast and his supplies, had no option but to withdraw. On 17 February 1781 he marched to Hillsborough in North Carolina. Greene, heavily reinforced, promptly moved back into North Carolina to press the British retreat and to discourage any action by loyalists.

The main American army now numbered 4,449 all ranks. Six weeks earlier Greene had reconnoitred a position at Guildford Courthouse, where he had contemplated standing and fighting towards the end of his long retreat. He now moved his army into that area and took up a defensive position.[20] Cornwallis, with only 1,900 men, had the alternative of attacking Greene or retreating. If he retreated, Greene, with his much greater strength, would obviously follow him up hard, for the American general had already showed his capacity for swift movement, and the retreat of the British force would encourage the guerrillas to harry its flanks and obstruct its line of march. They were in very hostile country, and Tarleton writes: 'The power and position of the enemy rendered all the country beyond the pickets hostile to the British cause, which had no friends or partizans at this period, except those included within the extent of the royal camp.'[21] It might be difficult, in fact, to extricate his small army at all. If he fought, the army might still be destroyed, but, on the other hand, if he managed to inflict a sharp reverse on Greene, he would be able to withdraw at leisure and with dignity. It is unlikely that he rated high his chance of inflicting the same crushing defeat on the able Greene as he had on the incompetent Gates; but he probably knew enough of Greene's character by now to reckon that he would fight a purely defensive battle. Cornwallis therefore decided to fight, even though reports which reached him exaggerated the American strength to 8,000 men.

On 14 March 1781 Cornwallis issued his orders. The wagons with the baggage, the wounded, and the sick, were to move before dawn to an area on the Deep River under an escort commanded by Lieutenant-Colonel Hamilton, consisting of his own regiment, 100 infantry of the line, and 20 dragoons of the Legion. The army was then to march from its camp at New Garden Meeting House along the main road from Salisbury to Guildford Courthouse, twelve miles away. Tarleton was to command the advanced guard, comprising the cavalry, the light infantry company of the Guards, and the jäger company of Bose's Regiment. The main body was to follow in the order: Webster's Brigade (23rd Fusiliers, 33rd Foot, and 71st Highlanders), Bose's Regiment, and the Guards Brigade. The detachments of artillery were to march with the formations to which they were allotted.

After marching for seven miles the advanced guard encountered the American outposts, and a sharp action developed. Tarleton writes:[22] 'In the onset, the fire of the Americans was heavy, and the charge of their cavalry was spirited: Notwithstanding their number and opposition, the gallantry of the light

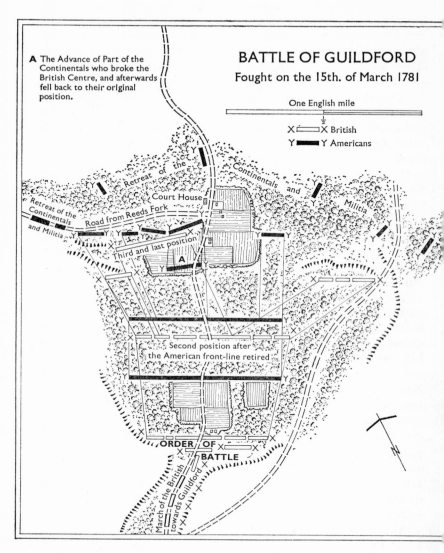

BATTLE OF GUILDFORD
Fought on the 15th. of March 1781

A The Advance of Part of the Continentals who broke the British Centre, and afterwards fell back to their original position.

One English mile

X ⊏══⊐ X British
Y ▬▬▬ Y Americans

Retreat of the Continentals and Militia

Retreat of the Continentals and Militia

Road from Reeds Fork

Court House

Third and last position

A

Second position after the American front-line retired

ORDER OF BATTLE

March of the British towards Guildford

N

8. Plan of the Battle of Guildford, from 'A History of the Campaigns of 1780 and 1781' by Lieutenant-Colonel Tarleton.

infantry of the guards, assisted by the legion, made impression upon their center, before the 23rd regiment arrived to give support to the advanced troops. Colonel Lee's dragoons retreated with precipitation along the main road, and Colonel Campbell's mountaineers were dispersed with considerable loss.'

Most of the battle area was thickly wooded. The courthouse itself stood on the western edge of a boot-shaped clearing with its toe facing west. The breadth across 'ankle' and 'foot' was about 400 yards, and the length both from north to south and from east to west was about half a mile. About 1,000 yards south of this clearing there was another one, roughly square with sides 500 yards in length, through the middle of which ran the main road from Salisbury. About 150 yards east of this there was a smaller clearing, with sides 150 yards from east to west and 200 yards from north to south. Whereas Greene had reconnoitred the area thoroughly, Cornwallis did not know what sort of country he was advancing into, and was dependent for information about it on local guides.

Greene had organised his defence in three lines. Holding the foremost line were two brigades of North Carolina Militia, each about 500 strong, and commanded respectively by Generals Butler and Easton. They were posted on the northern edge of the southern clearings and held a front about three-quarters of a mile in extent. There was a rail fence immediately in front of most of the line, which served as a convenient musket rest, and there was a clear field of fire across the clearings. In the centre of the two brigades were four 6-pounder guns, and on each flank were detachments of good infantry, so sited as to bring enfilade fire to bear across the front. On the right these consisted of 110 Delaware Continentals and 200 Virginian riflemen, whilst on the left there were 82 infantrymen of Lee's Legion and 200 more of the Virginians. Behind each flank was a squadron of cavalry, on the right 86 dragoons of Washington's Legion and on the left 75 troopers of Lee's Legion.

Some 300 yards behind the first line was a second line of the same length but completely in the woods, without any clear field of fire. Manning it were two Virginian militia brigades, each about 600 strong, and commanded respectively by General Stevens on the west and General Lawson on the east.

The third line, about 1,000 yards long, was 700 yards in rear of the second and posted on higher ground, with its left flank just south of the courthouse on the western edge of the 'ankle' and with a clear field of fire across the 'foot' of the clearing for the left half of the line. The troops manning this position were two Continental brigades: on the right a Virginian brigade under General Huger and on the left a Maryland brigade commanded by Colonel Williams, with respective strengths of 778 and 630. Two 6-pounders were posted between the brigades.

The weakness of Greene's position was that none of his troops had been given a counter-attack role. That is to say, each line was intended to defend its own position and there was no reserve to counter-attack enemy penetration of either of the first two lines. Units in the third line did indeed counter-attack, but only to restore their own local situation. Clausewitz, referring to the defensive arrangements made by a competent commander, says:[23]

'His position is *deep*, for each part in the scale of gradation in the order of battle, from the Division down to the battalion, has its reserve for unforeseen events, and for a renewal of the fight; and at the same time an important mass, one fifth to a quarter of the whole, is kept quite in the rear out of the battle ... With this body he intends to cover his flanks from wider and greater turning movements, secure himself against unforeseen events, and in the later stages of the battle, when the assailant's plan is fully developed, when the most of his troops have been brought into action, he will throw this mass on a part of the enemy's Army ...'

This is just what Greene did not do, and he lost control of the battle at an early stage.

As the British column approached the first clearing, the 6-pounders in the American first line opened fire. British artillery came rapidly into action and returned the fire. Cornwallis had a consultation with the local guides as to the nature of the country in his immediate front, and carried out a personal reconnaissance. He then made his plan. The army was to attack with the 23rd and 33rd astride the road, under command of Colonel Webster, the 23rd being on the left and the 33rd on the right. To the right of Webster, was Major-General Leslie with the 71st on the left and Bose's on the right. General O'Hara, commanding the Guards Brigade, was to detail the 1st battalion to support Leslie and the 2nd battalion and the grenadier company to support Webster. The light infantry company of the Guards and Bose's jäger company were to move in echelon behind Webster's left as soon as he advanced. The artillery, under Lieutenant Macleod, were to move along the road. (The guides had told Cornwallis that the woods on both sides of the clearing were impassable for guns.) Tarleton was to keep his regiment in reserve until the infantry reached the ground near the courthouse, where the guides said that the country was more suitable for cavalry.[24]

Whilst the troops were forming up for the attack, the British artillery was firing with considerable effect on the enemy's centre. Lieutenant O'Hara, the gallant son of the commander of the Guards Brigade, was killed while directing the fire of the 3-pounders. Tarleton was watching Webster's regiments as they advanced, and writes:

'The order and coolness of that part of Webster's brigade which advanced across the open ground exposed to the enemy's fire, cannot be sufficiently extolled: The extremities were not less gallant, but were more protected by the woods in which they moved. The militia allowed the front line to approach within one hundred and fifty yards before they gave their fire: The front line continued to move on: The Americans sent back their cannon and part of them repeated their fire: The King's troops threw in their fire and charged rapidly with their bayonets. The shock was not waited for by the militia, who retreated behind their second line.'[25]

The North Carolina Militia did not, in fact, even stop to reinforce the second line, but fled from the field. However, the flanking units held firm, and the British front had to be extended to deal with them. Bose's Regiment swerving right to deal with those at that end of the line, while the 23rd attacked the detachments on the left. To fill the consequent gaps, the grenadier company and 2nd battalion of the Guards moved into line on the right of the 33rd, and the 1st battalion of the Guards came up between the 71st and Bose's.[26]

The British advance continued towards the enemy's second line, through woods so thick, according to Cornwallis, as to render bayonets useless. There was a fierce battle along this line because the Virginian militia brigades were much better units than those of North Carolina. Cornwallis threw in his last infantry reserves, the light infantry Company of the Guards and the jäger Company of Bose's, against Stevens's Virginian brigade, and with the reinforcement of these excellent forest fighters, Stevens's command was forced back and its left bent back almost at right angles.

The British line was now getting somewhat confused, because it was difficult to keep touch and alignment in the dense woods. Leslie was pushing Lawson's brigade of the second line and the flanking detachments of the first line in a north-easterly direction. On the other flank Stevens's brigade had been broken and Webster was attacking Huger's Virginian Continental Brigade, on the right of Greene's third line, with the 33rd, the light infantry, and the jägers. (The 23rd was still dealing with the enemy flank units of their first line.) Webster found the opposition too strong for him. Tarleton says that 'after two severe struggles', the 'enemy's superiority of numbers and weight of fire obliged him to recross a ravine and take ground upon the opposite bank. This manoeuvre was planned with great judgement, and being executed with coolness and precision, gave Webster an excellent position till he could hear of the progress of the King's troops upon his right.'[27]

On Webster's right the 2nd battalion of the Guards, supported by the grenadier Company of the Guards, attacked and captured the 6-pounders in the centre of the Continental line. The 5th Maryland Regiment of Williams's brigade, a new regiment, turned and ran without firing a shot. However, the excellent 1st Maryland Regiment counter-attacked the Guards, and the cavalry of Washington's Legion charged their left flank. The exhausted and somewhat disorganised Guards were driven back. At this juncture Macleod arrived along the road with two of his little 3-pounders, and brought them into action on a rise at the edge of the clearing. Cornwallis ordered him to fire grape-shot into the enemy cavalry, even at the risk of inflicting casualties on the Guards. General O'Hara, though wounded, rallied the 2nd battalion of the Guards on to the 23rd and 71st, which Cornwallis had now directed into this sector. The 23rd had cleared up the enemy units with which it had been dealing. The 71st should have arrived earlier, but had been delayed in crossing some deep ravines. The grenadier Company of the Guards, which had lost all its officers, was led by its senior sergeant to join the artillery on the main road.

O'Hara, having reformed the Guards, 23rd, and 71st into a composite brigade, led them into a new attack which was supported by Tarleton with part of his cavalry. The Maryland Brigade was routed, and the two 6-pounders were recaptured, together with two more and two ammunition wagons. About the same time Webster's command returned to the attack and drove the Virginian Continental Brigade off the field. Cornwallis ordered the 23rd and 71st with part of the cavalry to follow up the beaten Continental troops, while Tarleton rode with a squadron of dragoons to assist Leslie, for heavy firing in that quarter showed that the fight was still going on.[28]

Of the remainder of the battle, Tarleton writes:

'The right wing, from the thickness of the woods and a jealousy for its flank, had imperceptibly inclined to the right, by which movement it had a kind of separate action after the first line the Americans gave way, and was now engaged with several bodies of militia and riflemen above a mile distant from the centre of the British army. The 1st battalion of the guards, commanded by Lieutenant-Colonel Norton, and the regiment of Bose, under Major De Buy, had their share of the difficulties of the day, and, owing to the nature of the light troops opposed to them, could never make any decisive impression: As they advanced the Americans gave ground in front, and inclined to their flanks: This sort of conflict had continued some time, when the British cavalry, on their way to join them, found officers and men of both corps wounded, and in possession of the enemy: The prisoners were quickly rescued from the hands of their captors, and the dragoons reached General Leslie without delay. As soon as the cavalry arrived, the guards and the Hessians were directed to fire a volley upon the largest party of the militia, and, under cover of the smoke, Lieutenant-Colonel Tarleton doubled round the right flank of the guards, and charged the Americans with considerable effect. The enemy gave way on all sides, and were routed with confusion and loss. This ended a general, and, in the main, a well-contested action, which had lasted upwards of two hours. General Leslie soon afterwards joined Earl Cornwallis, who had advanced a short distance on the Reedy-fork road, with the 23rd and 71st regiments to support the other squadron of the British legion, who followed the rear of the continentals.'[29]

The British losses amounted to 3 officers, 13 sergeants, and 75 rank and file killed; 24 officers, 15 sergeants, and 369 rank and file wounded; and 25 rank and file missing. The American losses amongst their Continental troops were 18 officers, 14 sergeants, and 290 rank and file killed, wounded, and missing; the Virginian militia had 27 officers, 15 sergeants, and 361 rank and file killed, wounded and missing; and the North Carolina militia had 2 officers and 3 rank and file wounded, and 4 officers and 552 rank and file missing. The British casualties and missing were therefore about 500 and those of the Americans about 1,300. Greene's army had been hit very hard and was incapable of taking offensive action for the time being. Most of the North Carolina militia dispersed to their homes instead of going to the designated rendezvous.[30] It was not possible to pursue the retreating Americans because, as Cornwallis said, his own troops were excessively fatigued and the enemy's cavalry had suffered little. Further, there were wounded scattered over a very large area who required immediate attention.

This battle, more than any other, shows the skill in forest warfare which had been attained by the British regulars. It was a skill which undoubtedly demanded considerable individual initiative, as compared with the rigid lines of the European battlefield; and it was a skill which, if they had possessed it at Fontenoy, would have enabled the British infantry to sweep through the Barri Wood, to capture the Eu Redoubt, and to win the battle. It is no wonder that Lord Cornwallis, as recorded in Chapter 5, wrote scathingly of the Prussian manoeuvres of 1785.

Cornwallis's handling of his troops in the battle was masterly. He made the very best use of his limited resources, and at the critical moment of the battle, the concentration of artillery and infantry which he brought to bear to knock the enemy's counter-attack off balance was decisive.

But of course, without his confidence in the magnificent fighting ability of his soldiers, Cornwallis would never have dared to attack Greene's position.

With the battle of Guildford Courthouse, we can leave the British Army of the eighteenth century, with the assurance that, at their best, its regiments were unmatched by those of any other army in the world.

Epilogue

In this book we have examined the organisation, administration, composition, and leadership of the British Army over a period of a hundred years; and in spite of all that has been said, one is still perhaps left wondering how such a small army, recruited as it was, achieved what it did. Generals, regimental officers, non-commissioned officers, and men share alike in its remarkable record; but perhaps it is the stocky red-coated and gallant figure of the last that grips the imagination, as he trudges stolidly through the mud of Flanders, grapples with the unfamiliar surroundings of river and forest in North America, or fights, wasted with yellow fever, in the tropical islands of the West Indies.

General Sir Henry Bunbury gives us a farewell glimpse of him in the last year of the eighteenth century.[1] In 1799 Bunbury, then a junior officer, was on the staff of the Duke of York commanding the British forces in Holland. The army of their Russian allies had been completely routed by the French and the British were accordingly withdrawing. Bunbury writes:

'I cannot help recounting here an anecdote which serves to illustrate the unyielding spirit of the British soldier. As the shots of the French who were following our rear-guard came thicker and closer, the Duke of York grew uneasy about the post of Krabbendam, and he sent me off to find any of our troops which might have entered our lines near that point, and to direct them to return and occupy the village. Krabbendam touched the lines on the outer side; and through it ran the high road from Alkmaar to the Helder. The holding of this little place was essential to the security of our position; and nine days before the enemy had exposed himself to a great loss of men in desperate attempts to take it from Sir Ralph Abercromby. But such was the discomfiture and such the want of good handling of the troops during this retreat of the 19th September, that battalion after battalion passed through the village and entered the lines without finding any general officer to give an order or a thought to the important object of keeping hold of Krabbendam. I rode till, at a short distance within the lines, I found one of the battalions of the 1st Guards, under the command of Colonel Maitland, resting on their arms in column on the muddy road. I delivered the Duke's orders to the Colonel, and begged he would not lose a moment in returning with me to Krabbendam, for the French were close at hand. He told me that his battalion was tired out; that they had been hotly engaged many hours, and had lost a large proportion of officers and men, and that their ammunition was nearly spent. I insisted; and urged the danger, and the fatal consequences which might ensue. Maitland (a brave officer, who was mortally wounded afterwards in the battle of the 6th October) still demurred. He assured me that his men were quite worn out; and he appeared to have lost the powers of his mind under fatigue of body and anxiety. At this moment a grenadier, lifting his chin from the muzzle of the musket on which he was leaning, said in a loud and steady voice, "Give us some more cartridges, and we will see what can be done." The officers who were anxiously clustering about us at the head of the column caught up the prompter's word. Maitland cried "Shoulder arms!" They marched for Krabbendam; and I galloped to find and bring to them a supply of ammunition.'

Appendix

A list of the regular infantry regiments of the British Army, showing their original numbers, and the short titles following the principal amalgamations, firstly of 1882 and secondly after the Second World War, and also the present divisional organisation of regiments. The dates in brackets after the numbers are those of the first formation of regiments, and those following regiments which have been disbanded are the dates of disbandment.

Scottish Division

1st	(1626)	Royal Scots		
21st	(1677)	Royal Scots Fusiliers	} Royal Highland Fusiliers	
71st	(1686)	} Highland Light Infantry		
74th	(1787)			
25th	(1689)	King's Own Scottish Borderers		
42nd	(1725)	} Black Watch		
73rd	(1780)			
72nd	(1778)	} Seaforth Highlanders	} Queen's Own Highlanders	
78th	(1793)			
79th	(1793)	Cameron Highlanders		
75th	(1787)	} Gordon Highlanders		
92nd	(1794)			
91st	(1794)	} Argyll & Sutherland Highlanders		
93rd	(1800)			

Queen's Division

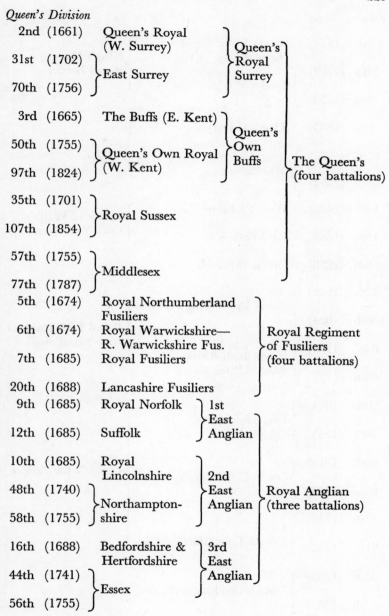

2nd (1661)	Queen's Royal (W. Surrey)	Queen's Royal Surrey	The Queen's (four battalions)	
31st (1702)	East Surrey			
70th (1756)				
3rd (1665)	The Buffs (E. Kent)	Queen's Own Buffs		
50th (1755)	Queen's Own Royal (W. Kent)			
97th (1824)				
35th (1701)	Royal Sussex			
107th (1854)				
57th (1755)	Middlesex			
77th (1787)				
5th (1674)	Royal Northumberland Fusiliers		Royal Regiment of Fusiliers (four battalions)	
6th (1674)	Royal Warwickshire— R. Warwickshire Fus.			
7th (1685)	Royal Fusiliers			
20th (1688)	Lancashire Fusiliers			
9th (1685)	Royal Norfolk	1st East Anglian	Royal Anglian (three battalions)	
12th (1685)	Suffolk			
10th (1685)	Royal Lincolnshire	2nd East Anglian		
48th (1740)	Northamptonshire			
58th (1755)				
16th (1688)	Bedfordshire & Hertfordshire	3rd East Anglian		
44th (1741)	Essex			
56th (1755)				

King's Division

4th	(1674)	King's Own Royal (Lancaster)	}	King's Own Royal Border
34th	(1702)	} Border		
55th	(1755)			

8th	(1685)	King's (Liverpool)	}	King's
63rd	(1757)	} Manchester		
96th	(1824)			

14th	(1685)	West Yorkshire	}	Prince of Wales's Own Yorkshire
15th	(1685)	East Yorkshire		

19th (1688)   Green Howards

27th	(1689)	} Royal Inniskilling Fusiliers	}	Royal Irish Rangers (two battalions)
108th	(1854)			
83rd	(1793)	Royal Irish Rifles/		
86th	(1793)	Royal Ulster Rifles		

30th	(1694)	} East Lancashire	}	Queen's Lancashire
59th	(1755)			
40th	(1717)	} South Lancashire		
82nd	(1793)			
47th	(1740)	} Loyal (North Lancashire)		
81st	(1793)			

33rd	(1702)	} Duke of Wellington's		
76th	(1787)			

Prince of Wales's Division

11th	(1685)	Devonshire	
39th	(1702)	⎫	
		⎬ Dorset	⎫ Devonshire & Dorset
54th	(1755)	⎭	

22nd (1689) Cheshire

23rd (1689) Royal Welch Fusiliers

24th (1689) South Wales Borderers ⎫

41st (1719) ⎫   ⎬ Royal Regiment of Wales

             ⎬ Welch

69th (1756) ⎭

28th (1694) ⎫

             ⎬ Gloucestershire

61st (1755) ⎭

29th (1694) ⎫

             ⎬ Worcestershire

36th (1701) ⎭   ⎫ Worcestershire & Sherwood Foresters

45th (1741) ⎫

             ⎬ Sherwood Foresters

95th (1824) ⎭

37th (1702) ⎫

             ⎬ Royal Hampshire

67th (1756) ⎭

38th (1702) ⎫

             ⎬ South Staffordshire

80th (1793) ⎭   ⎫ Staffordshire

64th (1756) ⎫

             ⎬ North Staffordshire

98th (1824) ⎭

49th   (1714) ⎫
        } Royal Berkshire   ⎫
66th   (1755) ⎭   } Duke of Edinburgh's
                                   { Royal
62nd (1756) ⎫   ⎭
        } Wiltshire
99th   (1824) ⎭

Light Division

13th   (1685)   Somerset Light Infantry ⎫ Somerset
                                        } &
32nd (1702) ⎫   } Cornwall   ⎫
        } Duke of Cornwall's   } Light   }
46th   (1741) ⎭ Light Infantry   ⎭ Infantry   }
                                                        } The
51st   (1755) ⎫   } Light
        } King's Own Yorkshire   } Infantry
105th (1839) ⎭ Light Infantry   { (three
                                                        } batta-
53rd   (1755) ⎫   } lions)
        } King's Shropshire   }
85th   (1794) ⎭ Light Infantry   ⎭

43rd   (1741) ⎫ Oxfordshire &   ⎫
        } Buckinghamshire   }
52nd   (1755) ⎭ Light Infantry   }
                                       } Royal Green Jackets
60th   (1755)   King's Royal Rifle Corps { (two battalions)
                                       }
        (1800)   The Rifle Brigade   ⎭

Disbanded

17th   (1688)   Royal Leicestershire (1970)

18th   (1683)   Royal Irish (1922)

26th   (1689) ⎫
        } Cameronians (1968)
90th   (1794) ⎭

65th   (1756) ⎫
        } York & Lancaster (1968)
84th   (1793) ⎭

68th	(1756)	
106th	(1860)	Durham Light Infantry (1969)
87th	(1793)	
89th	(1793)	Royal Irish Fusiliers (1968)
88th	(1793)	
94th	(1793)	Connaught Rangers (1922)
100th	(1858)	
109th	(1853)	Leinster (1922)
101st	(1756)	
104th	(1839)	Royal Munster Fusiliers (1922)
102nd	(1645)	
103rd	(1661)	Royal Dublin Fusiliers (1922)

Notes and References

Chapter 1

1 Charles M. Clode, *The Military Forces of the Crown* (London, John Murray, 1869), vol. I, pp. 52–3.
2 *Ibid.*, pp. 84–7.
3 Major D. H. Cole and Major E. C. Priestley, *An Outline of British Military History*, 2nd edn (London, Sifton Praed, 1937), p. 19.
    Clode, *op. cit.*, vol. I, pp. 142, 146, 181.
4 *Ibid.*, pp. 8–9.
5 J. R. Western, *The English Militia in the Eighteenth Century* (London, Routledge & Kegan Paul, 1965), p. 85.
6 C. T. Atkinson, 'Queen Anne's Army', *Journal of the Society for Army Historical Research*, vol. XXXVI (1958), pp. 25f.
7 Major R. E. Scouller, *The Armies of Queen Anne* (Oxford, Clarendon Press, 1966), pp. 81f.
8 The Hon. J. W. Fortescue, *A History of the British Army* (London, Macmillan, 1899), vol. II, pp. 3–4.
9 *Ibid.*, pp. 5–8.
    Charles Dalton, *George the First's Army 1714–1727* (1910).
10 H. M. Chichester and G. Burges-Short, *The Records and Badges of the British Army*, 2nd edn (London, Gale & Polden, 1900), p. 145.
11 Fortescue. *op. cit.*, pp. 16–18.
12 *Ibid.*, pp. 24–6.
13 *Ibid.*, pp. 56–7.
14 *Ibid.*, pp. 82–3.
15 Rex Whitworth, *Field Marshal Lord Ligonier* (Oxford, Clarendon Press, 1958), p. 84.
16 Lieutenant-General Sir Reginald Savory, *His Britannic Majesty's Army in Germany during the Seven Years War* (Oxford, Clarendon Press, 1966), pp. 5, 450–2.
17 Western, *op. cit.*, pp. 129–140.
18 Whitworth, *op. cit.*, p. 245.
    Fortescue, *op. cit.*, p. 314.
19 Savory, *op. cit.*, p. 461.
20 Whitworth, *op. cit.*, pp. 281–2.
21 *Ibid.*, pp. 289, 295.
    Western, *op. cit.*, pp. 154f.
22 Savory, *op. cit.*, pp. 477–8.

23 Whitworth, *op. cit.*, p. 317.
24 *Ibid.*, p. 329.
25 Western, *op. cit.*, pp. 171, 184.
26 Fortescue, *op. cit.*, vol. III (1902), p. 10.
   Whitworth, *op. cit.*, pp. 375–6.
27 Western, *op. cit.*, pp. 193–9, 209.
28 *Ibid.*, pp. 303–4.
29 Clode, *op. cit.*, pp. 36f.
30 Fortescue, *op. cit.*, vol. III, p. 41.
31 *Ibid.*, pp. 48, 149.
   Piers Mackesy, *The War for America* (London, Longman, 1964),
   pp. 39, 524–5.
32 Fortescue, *op. cit.*, vol. III, p. 154.
33 Mackesy, *op. cit.*, pp. 524–5.
34 Fortescue, *op. cit.*, vol. III, p. 289.
35 *Ibid.*, pp. 499, 516, 620–2.
36 Colonel L. I. Cowper, *The King's Own* (Oxford, 1939), vol. I, p. 292.
37 Sir Henry Bunbury, *The Great War with France (1799–1810)* (London,
   Richard Bentley, 1854, edn Peter Davies, 1927), pp. xvi–xvii.

Chapter 2
 1 Major R. E. Scouller, *The Armies of Queen Anne* (Oxford, Clarendon
   Press, 1966), pp. 1–4.
   Piers Mackesy, *The War for America* (London, Longman, 1964),
   pp. 12–13.
 2 Rex Whitworth, *Field Marshal Lord Ligonier* (Oxford, Clarendon
   Press, 1958), p. 215.
 3 Mackesy, *op. cit.*, pp. 14–15.
 4 Whitworth, *op. cit.*, pp. 227–8.
 5 *Ibid.*, p. 294.
 6 *Ibid.*, p. 231.
   Charles M. Clode, *The Military Forces of the Crown* (London, John
   Murray, 1869), vol. II, pp. 254–264, 335–342.
 7 H. M. Chichester and G. Burgess-Short, *The Records and Badges of the
   British Army*, 2nd edn (London, Gale & Polden, 1900), p. 152.
 8 Scouller, *op. cit.*, pp. 44f.
   Whitworth, *op. cit.*, pp. 183–4.
 9 Clode, *op. cit.*, vol. I, pp. 221f.
10 *Ibid.*
11 C. T. Atkinson, 'Queen Anne's Army', *Journal of the Society for Army
   Historical Research*, vol. XXXVI (1958), pp. 25f.
12 Whitworth, *op. cit.*, pp. 43–5.
13 Clode, *op. cit.*, vol. I, pp. 221f.
14 *Ibid.*, pp. 142, 146, 181.
   Major D. H. Cole and Major E. C. Priestley, *An Outline of British
   Military History*, 2nd edn (London, Sifton Praed, 1937), p. 19.

15 *Rules and Articles for the better Government of His Majesty's Horse and Foot Guards and all His other Forces etc.*, for the Year 1748. (Published by His Majesty's Command, London, Printed by Thomas Baskett.)

16 C. Sebag-Montefiore, *A History of the Volunteer Forces* (London, Archibald Constable & Co., 1908), pp. 68–9 (quoting 'State Papers, Domestic (George II)', Bundle 80, No. 146 and Bundle 70, No. 57).

Chapter 3

1 Colonel L. I. Cowper, *The King's Own* (Oxford, 1939), vol. I, pp. 194–5.

2 *Ibid.*, p. 195.

3 *Ibid.*, pp. 222–3.

4 Colonel H. C. B. Rogers, *The Mounted Troops of the British Army* (London, Seeley, Service, 2nd edn, 1967), p. 112.

5 *Ibid.*, pp. 121, 123.

6 Captain Hinde, *The Discipline of the Light Horse* (London, W. Owen, 1778), pp. 316–17.

7 *Ibid.*, pp. 530–1.

8 J. D. Turner, 'Army Agency', *The Journal of the Society for Army Historical Research*, vol. XIII (1934).

9 *Ibid.*

10 Cowper, *op. cit.*, pp. 130–1.

11 F. St C. Vivian, 'John Andre as a Young Officer', *Journal of the Society for Army Historical Research*, vol. XL (1962).

12 Hinde, *op. cit.*, pp. 109–10, 201–7, 555.

   A Collection of Orders etc. for the Army (published by order of the Secretary at War, 1807), 'Report on Cavalry Forage', pp. 541–3.
   Major-General G. G. Lewis and others, *Aide Memoire for the Military Sciences* (London, John Weale, 1850), vol. II, p. 276.

13 Hinde, *op. cit.*, pp. 204–7.

14 *Ibid.*, pp. 349–357.

15 Charles M. Clode, *The Military Forces of the Crown* (London, John Murray, 1869), vol. II, pp. 1f.

16 Turner, *op. cit.*

17 Thomas Simes, *A Military Course for the Government and Conduct of a Battalion* (London, 2nd edn 1777), p. 18.

18 Hinde, *op. cit.*, pp. 204–7, 416–440.

19 *Ibid.*, p. 491.

20 *Ibid.*, pp. 102–3, 416–440.

21 Bennett Cuthbertson, *Cuthbertson's System for the complete interior management and economy of a battalion of infantry etc.* (Bristol, 2nd edn, 1776), pp. 46, 107–9, 118 (quoted by Vivian, *op. cit.*).

22 Hinde, *op. cit.*, pp. 105–10, 416–440.

23 *Ibid.*, pp. 335, 416–440.

24 Vivian, *op. cit.*

25 Simes, *op, cit.*, pp. 163, 256.
   Cuthbertson, *op. cit.*, pp. 25–6.

26 *Ibid.*, pp. 36, 109.
    Simes, *op. cit.*, p. 235.
27 Cuthbertson, *op. cit.*, pp. 35, 87.
28 *Ibid.*, p. 42.
29 Hinde, *op. cit.*, p. 298.
30 Vivian, *op. cit.*

Chapter 4
1 Charles M. Clode, *The Military Forces of the Crown* (London, John Murray, 1869), vol. II, p. 62.
2 F. St C. Vivian, 'John Andre as a Young Officer', *Journal of the Society for Army Historical Research*, vol. XL (1962), pp. 24f.
3 Charles Dalton, *George the First's Army 1714–1727* (1910).
4 'The Letters of Captain Nicholas Delacherois', ed. S. G. P. Ward, *Journal of the Society for Army Historical Research*, vol. LI (1973), pp. 5f.
5 James Hayes, 'Two Soldier Brothers of the Eighteenth Century', *Journal of the Society for Army Historical Research*, vol. XL (1962), pp. 150f.
6 '"To Mr. Davenport": Letters of Major Richard Davenport to his Brother' ed. W. O. II C. W. Frearson, *Society for Army Historical Research, Special Publication No. 9* (1968).
7 Vivian, *op. cit.*
    Bennett Cuthbertson, *Cuthbertson's System for the complete interior management and economy of a battalion of infantry, etc.* (Bristol 2nd edn. 1776), pp. 14, 17, 32 (quoted Vivian, *op. cit.*).
8 Cuthbertson, *op. cit.*, pp. 30, 31.
9 Vivian, *op. cit.*
10 Colonel L. I. Cowper, *The King's Own* (Oxford, 1939), vol. I, p. 187.
11 Captain Hinde, *The Discipline of the Light Horse* (London, W. Owen, 1778), pp. 404–5.
12 *Ibid.*, pp. 473–5.
13 'Delacherois', *op. cit.*
14 Clode, *op. cit.*, vol. II, pp. 1f.
15 *Ibid.*
16 *Ibid.*
17 *The Life and Adventures of Matthew Bishop, written by Himself* (London, J. Brindley, G. Hawkins, R. Dodsley, & J. Millan, 1744).
18 *Ibid.*, pp. 160–1.
19 *Ibid.*, pp. 169–70.
20 *Ibid.*, p. 196.
21 *Ibid.*, p. 189.
22 'A Soldier's Diary of the Seven Years War: Journal of William Todd', ed. C. T. Atkinson *Journal of the Society for Army Historical Research*, vol. XXIX, pp. 118f.
23 Vivian, *op. cit.*
24 Hinde, *op. cit.*, pp. 98–100.
25 T. H. McGuffie, 'The Life of a Light Cavalry Regiment: Papers of

Henry William Paget, First Marquess of Anglesey', *Journal of the Society for Army Historical Research*, vols. XXXVIII and XXXIX (1960–61).

26 Major G. Tylden, 'The Accoutrements of the British Infantryman', *Journal of the Society for Army Historical Research*, vol. XLVII (1969).

27 E. von dem Knesebeck, *Herzog Ferdinand zu Braunschweig und Luneberg, während des Siebenjahrigen Krieges* (1857). tr. Lieutenant-General Sir Reginald Savory.

Chapter 5

1 C. T. Atkinson, *Marlborough and the Rise of the British Army* (London, G. P. Putnam's Sons, 1921), pp. 20–1.
   Colonel L. I. Cowper, *The King's Own* (Oxford, 1939), vol. I, p. 99.

2 Robert Jackson, *The Influence of Firearms upon Tactics* (1804), p. 26, quoted Colonel J. F. C. Fuller, *British Light Infantry in the Eighteenth Century* (London, Hutchinson, 1925), pp. 43–5.

3 *Mes Rêveries, Ouvrage Posthume de Maurice, Comte de Saxe*, ed. M. L'Abbé Perau (Amsterdam, Arkstée et Merkus, 1757), vol. I, p. 40.

4 Cowper, *op. cit.*, pp. 144–5.

5 Beccles Wilson, *The Life and Letters of James Wolfe* (London, William Heinemann, 1909), pp. 254–5.

6 Christopher Duffy, *The Army of Frederick the Great* (Newton Abbot, David & Charles, 1974), p. 69.

7 *Ibid.*, p. 210.

8 *Correspondence of Charles, First Marquis Cornwallis*, vol. I, p. 212, quoted Fuller, *op. cit.*, p. 190.

9 Fuller, *op. cit.*, p. 86.

10 *Ibid.*, pp. 102–4.

11 Robert Jackson, *A Systematic View of the Formation, Discipline and Economy of Armies*, pp. 176f.

12 The Hon. J. W. Fortescue, *A History of the British Army*, (London, Macmillan, 1899), vol. II, p. 323.

13 *Ibid.*, p. 324.

14 H. M. Chichester and G. Burges-Short, *The Records and Badges of the British Army*, 2nd edn (London, Gale & Polden, 1900).

15 *Ibid.*

16 Fuller, *op. cit.*, p. 92.

17 'The Letters of Captain Nicholas Delacherois', ed. S. G. P. Ward, *Journal of the Society for Army Historical Research*, vol. LI (1973), pp. 5f.

18 Fuller, *op. cit.*, pp. 124–5.

19 Fortescue, *op. cit.*, vol. III, pp. 539–30.

20 Colonel H. C. Wylly, *A Life of General Sir Eyre Coote, K.B.* (Oxford, Clarendon Press, 1922), p. 198.

21 Fuller, *op. cit.*, quoted pp. 193–4.

22 Rev. P. Sumner, 'Standing Orders for Dragoons', *Journal of the Society for Army Historical Research*, vol. XXIII (1945).

23 *Ibid.*
24 Captain Sir George Arthur, Bart., *The Story of the Household Cavalry* (London, Archibald Constable, 1909), p. 453.
25 Jay Luvaas, ed. and tr., *Frederick the Great on the Art of War* (New York, The Free Press, 1966), pp. 81, 149–53.
26 Fortescue, *op. cit.*, vol. III, p. 538.
27 Captain Hinde, *The Discipline of the Light Horse* (London, W. Owen, 1778), pp. 27f.
28 Fortescue, *op. cit.*, vol. II, pp. 87–8.
   Colonel H. C. B. Rogers, *Artillery through the Ages* (London, Seeley Service, 1971), pp. 59–60.
29 *Ibid.*, pp. 65–70.
   John Muller, *A Treatise of Artillery* (London, John Millan, 1780), pp. 180, 192.

Chapter 6
1 C. T. Atkinson, *Marlborough and the Rise of the British Standing Army* (London, G. P. Putnam's Sons, 1921), pp. 10–11.
2 Major R. E. Scouller, *The Armies of Queen Anne* (Oxford, Clarendon Press, 1966), pp. 217–220.
3 'Gleanings from the Cathcart MSS', ed. C. T. Atkinson, *Journal of the Society for Army Historical Research*, vol. XXIX (1951), pp. 21f.
   Hon. J. W. Fortescue, *The British Army 1783–1802*, 1905.
4 'A Soldier's Diary of the Seven Years War—The Journal of William Todd', ed. C. T. Atkinson, *Journal of the Society for Army Historical Research*, vol. XXIX (1951), pp. 119f.
5 Lieutenant-General Sir Reginald Savory, *His Britannic Majesty's Army in Germany during the Seven Years War* (Oxford, Clarendon Press, 1966), pp. 413–5.
6 Scouller, *op. cit.*, pp. 217–220.
   Fortescue, *The British Army 1783–1802*, *op. cit.*
7 Hon. J. W. Fortescue, *A History of the British Army* (London, Macmillan & Co., 1902), vol. III, pp. 410–3.
8 Fortescue, *The British Army 1783–1802.*
9 'A Soldier's Diary of the Seven Years War', *op. cit.*
10 *Ibid.*
11 *Ibid.*
12 Savory, *op. cit.*, p. 279.
13 'A Soldier's Diary of the Seven Years War', *op. cit.*
14 Fortescue, *The British Army 1783–1802*, *op. cit.*
15 John Fortescue, *The Royal Army Service Corps*, vol. I (Cambridge, University Press, 1930), pp. 22–3.
16 Scouller, *op. cit.*, pp. 206–7.
17 'Gleanings from the Cathcart MSS', *op. cit.*
18 'An Order Book of the Seven Years War', ed. C. T. Atkinson, *Journal of the Society for Army Historical Research*, vol. XXX (1952), pp. 2f.
19 Scouller, *op. cit.*, pp. 173–4, 203.

20 John Muller, *A Treatise of Artillery*, 3rd edn (London, John Millan, 1780), pp. 125–43.
21 *Ibid.*, pp. 109, 199.
22 *Ibid.*, pp. 192–3.
23 Major G. Tylden, *Horses and Saddlery* (London, J. A. Allen & Co., 1965), pp. 9–17.
24 Colonel H. C. B. Rogers, *The Mounted Troops of the British Army*, 2nd edn (London, Seeley, Service & Co., 1967), p. 117.
25 *Ibid.*
    Tylden, *op. cit.*, pp. 9–17.
26 *Ibid.*
27 Rogers, *op. cit.*, p. 132.
28 E. E. Curtis, *The Organisation of the British Army in the American Revolution* (New Haven, Yale University Press, 1926), p. 7.
29 Savory, *op. cit.*, p. 260.
30 Colonel H. C. B. Rogers, *Tanks in Battle* (London, Seeley, Service & Co., 1965), pp. 170–1.
31 Savory, *op. cit.*, pp. 293–4.
32 *Ibid.*, pp. 303–8.
33 M. K. and C. I. A. Ritchie, 'The Troubles of a Commissary during the Seven Years War', *Journal of the Society for Army Historical Research*, vol. XXXVI (1958), pp. 157f.
34 *Ibid.*
35 *Ibid.*
36 Savory, *op. cit.*, pp. 304–8.
37 'A Soldier's Diary of the Seven Years War', *op. cit.*
38 *The Life and Adventures of Matthew Bishop*, written by Himself (London, J. Brindley, G. Hawkins, R. Dodsley, & J. Millan, 1744), pp. 167–8.
39 E. W. Sheppard, *Coote Bahadur* (London, Werner Laurie, 1956), pp. 130–2.
40 Colonel H. C. Wylly, *A Life of General Sir Eyre Coote, K.B.* (Oxford, Clarendon Press, 1922), p. 117.
41 Curtis, *op. cit.*, pp. 81–4.
42 *Ibid.*, pp. 88–119.
43 Fortescue, *The British Army 1783–1802, op. cit.*
44 H. M. Chichester and G. Burges-Short, *The Records and Badges of the British Army*, 2nd edn (London, Gale & Polden, 1900).
45 Wylly, *op. cit.*, p. 80.
46 Savory, *op. cit.*, p. 306.
47 Fortescue, *A History of the British Army*, vol. III, pp. 226, 338.
48 Savory, *op. cit.*, pp. 462–4.
49 Curtis, *op. cit.*, pp. 10–11.

Chapter 7
1 C. T. Atkinson, *Marlborough and the Rise of the British Standing Army* (London, G. P. Putnam's Sons, 1921), pp. 186–247.

Winston S. Churchill, *Marlborough, His Life and Times* (London, George G. Harrap, 1947), Book I, pp. 740–868.

2 Lieutenant-General Sir Reginald Savory, *His Britannic Majesty's Army in Germany during the Seven Years War* (Oxford, Clarendon Press, 1966) pp. 370f., 500–3.

J. Tory, Soldier in the Third Regiment of Guards, *A Journal of the Allied Army's Marches from the first arrival of the British Troops to the Present Time* (Osnabruck, 1762), pp. 54–5, 60.

3 Atkinson, *op. cit.*, pp. 284f, 335f.

4 Churchill, *op. cit.*, pp. 465–6.

5 *Ibid.*, p. 466.

6 Savory, *op. cit.*, pp. 458–9.

7 Lieutenant-Colonel W. B. R. Neave-Hill, 'The Rank Titles of Brigadier and Brigadier General', *Journal of the Society for Army Historical Research*, vol. XLVII (1969), pp. 96f.

8 *Ibid.*

9 *Mes Rêveries, Ouvrage Posthume de Maurice, Comte de Saxe.* ed. M. L'Abbé Perau (Amsterdam, Arkstée et Markus, 1757), vol. II, pp. 142–50. (Passage tr. by Colonel H. C. B. Rogers).

Chapter 8

1 General Carl von Clausewitz, *On War,* tr. Colonel J. J. Graham, 1873, ed. Colonel F. N. Maude (London, Routledge & Kegan Paul, eighth impression, 1968), vol. I, pp. 86, 94.

2 *Ibid.*, p. 77.

3 C. T. Atkinson, *Marlborough and the Rise of the British Standing Army* (London, G. P. Putnam's Sons, 1921), pp. 163–5.

4 Winston S. Churchill, *Marlborough, His Life and Times* (London, George G. Harrap, 1947), Book I, p. 516.

5 Major R. B. Pargiter and Major H. G. Eady, *The Army & Sea Power* (London, Ernest Benn, 1927), p. 53.

6 E. H. Jenkins, *A History of the French Navy* (London, Macdonald and Jane's, 1973), p. 101.

7 Atkinson, *op. cit.*, pp. 165–71.
   Churchill, *op. cit.*, pp. 574–87.

8 Clausewitz, *op. cit.*, vol. I, pp. 172–3.

9 Atkinson, *op. cit.*, pp. 186–98.
   Churchill, *op. cit.*, pp. 727–69.

10 *Ibid.*, Book II, p. 839.

11 Atkinson, *op. cit.*, pp. 440–1.

12 Churchill, *op. cit.*, Book II, p. 842.

13 *Ibid.*, Book II, pp. 837–57.
   Atkinson, *op. cit.*, pp. 436–51.
   Major D. H. Cole and Major E. C. Priestley, *An Outline of British Military History* 2nd edn. (London, Sifton Praed, 1937), pp. 46–8.

Chapter 9

1 Rex Whitworth, *Field Marshal Lord Ligonier* (Oxford, Clarendon Press, 1958), p. 201.

2 *Ibid.*, pp. 247–8.

3 General Carl von Clausewitz, *On War*, tr. Colonel J. J. Graham, 1873, ed. Colonel F. N. Maude (London, Routledge & Kegan Paul, ninth impression, 1968), vol. III, p. 171.

4 *Ibid.*, p. 173.

5 Soame Jenyns, *A Simile*; quoted by Walter Evelyn Manners, *The Right Hon. John Manners, Marquis of Granby* (London, Macmillan & Co., 1899), p. 61.

6 Whitworth, *op. cit.*, pp. 237–42, 247–8.

     Major D. H. Cole and Major E. C. Priestley, *An Outline of British Military History* 2nd edn. (London, Sifton Praed & Co., 1937), pp. 71f.

7 Francis Parkman, *Montcalm and Wolfe* (1884, Eyre & Spottiswoode edn of 1964), p. 517.

8 Whitworth, *op. cit.*, p. 278.

9 Clausewitz, *op. cit.*, vol. III, p. 106.

10 *The Journal of Jeffery Amherst*, ed. J. Clarence Webster (Toronto, The Ryerson Press, 1931), p. 109.

11 *Ibid.*, p. 112.

12 *Ibid.*, p. 115.

13 *Ibid.*, pp. 114–17.

14 *Ibid.*, pp. 118–20.

15 *Ibid.*, pp. 118–27.

16 *Ibid.*, pp. 127–33.

17 *Ibid.*, pp. 141–51.

18 Beckles Wilson, *The Life and Letters of James Wolfe* (London, William Heinemann, 1909), p. 463.

19 Amherst, *op. cit.*, pp. 151–66.

     Wilson, *op. cit.*, pp. 472–5.

20 Amherst, *op. cit.*, pp. 170–1.

21 *Ibid.*, pp. 170–98.

22 Parkman, *op. cit.*, p. 598.

23 Amherst, *op. cit.*, p. 210.

24 *Ibid.*, pp. 217–18.

25 Parkman, *op. cit.*, pp. 602–3.

     The Hon. J. W. Fortescue, *A History of the British Army* (London, Macmillan & Co., 1899), vol. II, p. 397.

26 *Ibid.*, p. 398.

     Parkman, *op. cit.*, p. 605.

27 Amherst, *op. cit.*, pp. 225–41.

28 Parkman, *op. cit.*, p. 605.

29 Amherst, *op. cit.*, pp. 242–7.

30 Clausewitz, *op. cit.*, vol. I, pp. 105–6, 75.

Chapter 10
1 Piers Mackesy, *The War for America 1775–1783* (London, Longmans, 1964), p. 29.
2 The Hon. J. W. Fortescue, *A History of the British Army* (London, Macmillan & Co., 1902), vol. III, pp. 167.
3 *Ibid.*, p. 169.
4 Mackesy, *op. cit.*, p. 38.
5 Fortescue, *op. cit.*, p. 167.
  Lieutenant-General Sir George MacMunn, *The American War of Independence in Perspective* (London, George Bell & Sons, 1939), p. 110.
6 Mackesy, *op. cit.*, p. 70.
7 MacMunn, *op. cit.*, p. 209.
8 Troyer Steele Anderson, *The Command of the Howe Brothers during the American Revolution* (New York, Oxford University Press, 1936), pp. 110–11.
9 *Ibid.*, pp. 112–13.
10 General Carl von Clausewitz, *On War*, tr. Colonel J. J. Graham, Ninth Impression (London, Routledge & Kegan Paul, 1968), vol. II, p. 266.
11 Anderson, *op. cit.*, pp. 246–7.
12 *Ibid.*, p. 116.
13 *Ibid.*, pp. 118–19.
14 Mark M. Boatner, *Cassell's Biographical Dictionary of the American War of Independence 1763–1783* (London, Cassell, 1973), pp. 262–4.
15 *The Narrative of Lieut. Gen. Sir William Howe in a Committee of the House of Commons on the 29th of April 1779* (London, H. Baldwin, 2nd edn 1780), p. 5.
16 *Ibid.*, p. 6.
17 *Ibid.*, p. 7.
18 *Ibid.*, p. 7.
19 Clausewitz, *op. cit.*, vol. I, p. 254.
20 Mackesy, *op. cit.*, p. 67.
21 Lieutenant-Colonel Tarleton, *A History of the Campaigns of 1780 and 1781 in the Southern Provinces of North America* (London, T. Cadell, 1787), pp. 4, 7, 8.
22 Howe, *op. cit.*, p. 65.
23 *Ibid.*, pp. 9–14, 16.
   Anderson, *op. cit.*, pp. 215–27.
24 Howe, *op. cit.*, p. 15.
25 Anderson, *op. cit.*, pp. 238–9.
26 Howe, *op. cit.*, p. 19.
27 *Ibid.*, pp. 19–20.
28 *Ibid.*, p. 21.
29 *Ibid.*, pp. 22–3.
30 *Ibid.*, p. 23.
31 Anderson, *op. cit.*, p. 258.
32 *Ibid.*, pp. 281–2.

33 *Ibid.*, pp. 282–3.
34 Mackesy, *op. cit.*, p. 128.
35 Howe, *op. cit.*, p. 30.
36 Ibid., pp. 30–1.
37 MacMunn, *op. cit.*, pp. 206, 208.
38 Anderson, *op. cit.*, p. 306.
39 MacMunn, *op. cit.*, p. 214.
40 Howe, *op. cit.*, pp. 32–3.

Chapter 11
  1 Winston S. Churchill, *Marlborough, His Life and Times* (London, George G. Harrap, 1947 edn), Book II, pp. 91–2.
  2. C. T. Atkinson, *Marlborough and the rise of the British Standing Army* (London, G. P. Putnam's Sons, 1921), p. 284.
  3 M. de La Colonie, *The Chronicles of an Old Campaigner*, tr. W. C. Horsley (London, John Murray, 1904), p. 305.
  4 Atkinson, *op. cit.*, p. 287.
    Churchill, *op. cit.*, p. 98.
  5 *Ibid.*
  6 Atkinson, *op. cit.*, pp. 285–7.
  7 *Ibid.*, p. 288.
    Churchill, *op. cit.*, p. 99.
  8 De La Colonie, *op. cit.*, pp. 306–11.
  9 Atkinson, *op. cit.*, p. 289.
 10 *Ibid.*, p. 290.
 11 Churchill, *op. cit.*, p. 112.
 12 De La Colonie, *op. cit.*, pp. 311–16.
 13 Churchill, *op. cit.*, 114–16.
    Atkinson, *op. cit.*, pp. 293–5.
 14 General Carl von Clausewitz, *On War*, tr. Colonel J. J. Graham (London, Routledge & Kegan Paul, ninth impression 1968), vol. II, pp. 138–9.

Chapter 12
  1 The Hon. J. W. Fortescue, *A History of the British Army* (London, Macmillan & Co., 1899), vol. II, p. 108.
  2 F. H. Skrine, *Fontenoy* (Edinburgh, William Blackwood & Sons, 1906), pp. 131–5.
  3 *Ibid.*, p. 128.
  4 *Ibid.*, p. 137.
  5 *Ibid.*, pp. 138–9.
  6 General Carl von Clausewitz, *On War*, tr. Colonel J. J. Graham (London, Routledge & Kegan Paul, ninth impression 1968), vol. II, p. 63.
  7 Skrine, *op. cit.*, p. 142.
  8 *Ibid.*, p. 155.
  9 *Ibid.*, pp. 146–9.

10 *Ibid.*, pp. 149–50.
   Fortescue, *op. cit.*, pp. 110–11.
11 Skrine, *op. cit.*, p. 150.
12 *Ibid.*, pp. 165–6.
13 *Ibid.*, p. 167.
14 Fortescue, *op. cit.*, pp. 113–14.
15 *Ibid.*, p. 115.
   Skrine, *op. cit.*, p. 171.
16 *Ibid.*, p. 177.
17 Captain Sir George Arthur, *The Story of the Household Cavalry* (London, Archibald Constable, 1909), vol. II, pp. 416–17.
18 *Ibid.*, pp. 417–18.
19 Maurice Comte de Saxe, *Lettres et Documents*, ed. M. Le Comte C. F. Vitzthum D'Eckstaedt (Leipzig, Ludwig Denicke, 1867), pp. 484–5, tr. Colonel H. C. B. Rogers.

Chapter 13
 1 Mark M. Boatner, *Cassell's Biographical Dictionary of the American War of Independence 1763–1783* (London, Cassell, 1973), p. 159.
 2 *Ibid.*, pp. 160–1.
 3 The Hon. J. W. Fortescue, *A History of the British Army* (London, Macmillan & Co., 1902), vol. III, pp. 314–16.
 4 Boatner, *op. cit.*, p. 163.
 5 Lieutenant-Colonel Tarleton, *A History of the Campaigns of 1780 and 1781 in the Southern Provinces of North America* (London, T. Cadell, 1787), pp. 103–4.
 6 *Ibid.*, p. 104.
   Boatner, *op. cit.*, p. 163.
   Lieutenant-General Sir George MacMunn, *The American War of Independence in Perspective* (London, G. Bell & Sons, 1939), pp. 250–1.
 7 Tarleton, *op. cit.*, p. 104.
 8 *Ibid.*, p. 103.
   Boatner, *op. cit.*, p. 165.
 9 Tarleton, *op. cit.*, p. 106.
10 *Ibid.*, p. 106.
   Boatner, *op. cit.*, p. 166.
11 *Ibid.*, pp. 167–8.
   Tarleton, *op. cit.*, pp. 106–7.
12 *Ibid.*, pp. 108–9.
13 *Ibid.*
14 Boatner, *op. cit.*, p. 169.
15 See Chapter 7.
16 Fortescue, *op. cit.*, p. 356.
17 Boatner, *op. cit.*, pp. 78–9.
18 *Ibid.*, p. 1018.
19 *Ibid.*, pp. 291–300.
20 *Ibid.*, p. 460.

21 Tarleton, *op. cit.*, p. 270.
22 *Ibid.*, p. 271.
23 General Carl von Clausewitz, *On War*, tr. Colonel J. J. Graham, 1873, ed. Colonel F. N. Maude (London, Routledge & Kegan Paul, eighth impression, 1968), vol. II, p. 190.
24 Tarleton, *op. cit.*, pp. 272–3.
25 *Ibid.*, p. 273.
26 *Ibid.*
   Boatner, *op. cit.*, p. 465.
27 Tarleton, *op. cit.*, p. 274.
28 *Ibid.*, pp. 274–5.
   Boatner, *op. cit.*, pp. 466–8.
29 Tarleton, *op. cit.*, pp. 275–6.
30 *Ibid.*, pp. 276–7.

Epilogue
1 Sir Henry Bunbury, *The Great War with France* (London, Richard Bentley, 1854), pp. 12–13.

Index

Abercromby, General Sir Ralph 226
Abercromby, Major-General James 131, 132
Academy, Royal Military 79
Adjutant-General 35
Agent, Regimental 37, 45
Aix-la-Chapelle, Treaty of 23
Albemarle, Colonel the Earl of 188
American War of Independence 33, 44, 73, 91, 95–6, 102; strategical problem of 153–5; the American Army 160; 205
Amherst, Field Marshal Lord 14, 34; battle drill 72–3; orders on cavalry attack 79; 131; Ligonier's instructions to 132–3; his plan for the conquest of Canada 133–5; capture of Fort Ticonderoga and after 135–44; his plan and campaign of 1760 144–51; French surrender to him at Montreal 151; his achievement 151–2, 155
Andre, Major John 171
Anhalt, Lieutenant-General Prinz von 102
Anne, Queen 19, 20, 34–5, 43, 61
Anson, Admiral of the Fleet Lord 129
Appius, Colonel 199
Armand, Colonel Charles 211–13
Army and Air Force Annual Act 39
Arrears 47
Articles of War 39, 40, 61
Athlone, the Earl of 113
Austrian Succession, War of the 22, 69

Bakeries, field 83–4
Barracks, policy on 38–9
Barrington, Viscount William 154
Bauer, Colonel Friedrich Wilhelm von, duties of 104

Bavaria, the Elector of 117, 119–21 123, 175, 178
Beating orders 59
Belford, Major-General William 80
Billets: 38; procedure at 49–51
Bishop, Corporal Matthew: his record of service 61–2; on Oudenarde 62; on General Webb 62–3; description of a march 94–5
Bland, Major-General Humphrey 188
Blenheim, battle of 100–1, 123
Board of General Officers 37, 46
Bolingbroke, Viscount Henry 20
Boscawen, Admiral the Hon. Edward 131
Boufflers, Marshal Louis Francois, Duc de 113–16
Bouquet, Colonel Henry, his system of training 71–2
Brabant, the Lines of 111, 115, 117
Braddock, General Edward 23, 70–1
Bradstreet, Colonel John 138–9
Brandywine, battle of 102, 169
Brunswick, the Erbrinz of 102
Bunbury, General Sir Henry 31, 226
Bunker Hill, battle of 30, 156
Burgoyne, General Sir John: mess discipline 58; 155–8, 165, 167–9; surrender at Saratoga 170
Butler, General, 219

Cadogan, Brigadier-General the Earl of 100; assessment of and duties 103–4; 127–8; at Ramillies, 177–8
Camden, battle of 14, 174, 207–13
Campbell, Lieutenant-General the Hon. Sir James 188, 197
Campbell, Major-General John 189, 198
Captain-General, appointment and duties of 34